Study Guide

Christine Stamm-Griffin

Gilbert Noussitou
Camosun College

On Cooking

A Textbook of Culinary Fundamentals

Fourth Canadian Edition

Sarah R. Labensky, CCP

Alan M. Hause

Fred L. Malley
SAIT Polytechnic

Anthony Bevan
Humber College Institute of Technology and Advanced Learning

Settimio Sicoli
Vancouver Community College

PEARSON
Prentice Hall

Toronto

ISBN-13: 978-0-13-205186-6
ISBN-10: 0-13-205186-9

Acquisitions Editor: Chris Helsby
Sponsoring Editor: Carolin Sweig
Supervising Developmental Editor: Suzanne Schaan
Production Editor: Cheryl Jackson
Production Coordinator: Janis Raisen

1 2 3 4 5   12 11 10 09 08

Printed and bound in Canada.

CONTENTS

Answers

PREFACE

The finest food comes from the finest ingredients but it requires a professional cook with a solid knowledge of fundamentals to put it all together in a large scale while meeting the consumer's demands as well as management's expectations. Creativity is only limited by one's imagination and an artistic mind can create a stunning-looking platter, but without the knowledge and understanding of the science supported by a sound discipline to put it together, the result may not meet professional standards. Professional cooking is not just about applying heat, procedures and methods; it is also about developing a vast knowledge and understanding of foods, ingredients, wine, beer and other beverages.

This course is designed to help the apprentice cook learn the techniques and acquire the knowledge to develop a sense of assurance needed to face the complexities of the modern kitchen. To help you achieve this, we have supplemented your textbook with this study guide. It is designed to help you review the material through exercises that will check your knowledge, comprehension and ability to think critically. A thorough reading of your textbook followed by a careful review of all the sections and completing all of the exercises will be critical in understanding the concepts.

Each chapter begins with an outline that parallels the **Learning Outcomes** featured in the textbook. Studying this outline will help you organize the material as it highlights specific ideas, concepts and issues that you need to understand. The **Key Terms** are important words related to ingredients, equipment, techniques, or concepts; these words are bolded throughout the text and may be defined in the sidebars.

Test Your Knowledge provides a variety of study questions; an answer key is found at the back of the text.

- The **Terminology** section tests your ability to match these terms with their definitions.
- **Fill in the Blank** questions test various concepts, including labelling diagrams.
- **Short Answer** questions will help you integrate information presented throughout the chapter.
- Finally, **Multiple Choice, Matching,** and **True/False** questions will help you determine how well you have mastered the concepts and information presented in the text.

This study guide is a tool and as such, it is only as good as you make it to be. We believe that you will find it to be a valuable resource to prepare for a rewarding career in the fascinating art and science of professional cooking with its endless opportunities for new ideas and the creation of innovative dishes and recipes.

Good luck and happy cooking!

Gilbert Noussitou

PART 1 PROFESSIONALISM

Chapter 1

Professionalism

Cookery is a noble profession with a rich history and one steeped in tradition. This chapter provides an overview of the chefs that played an important role in the development of culinary arts, discusses their contributions, and then identifies the important attributes that a professional chef should possess and maintain.

At the end of this chapter the student should be able to:

1. Name key historical figures responsible for developing food service professionalism.
2. Discuss the development of the modern food service industry.
3. Explain the organization of classic and modern kitchen brigades.
4. Explain the role of the professional chef in modern food service operations.
5. Identify the attributes an apprentice or student cook needs to become a professional chef.

Key Terms

Cooking	National cuisine	Executive chef
Cookery	Regional cuisine	Sous-chef
Professional cooking	Ethnic cuisine	Executive sous-chef
Grande cuisine	Slow food	Line cooks
Carême	Carlo Petrini	Pastry chef
Cuisine classique	Massimo Mondanari	Apprentices
Escoffier	Brigade	Kitchen helpers
Nouvelle cuisine	Gastronomy	Line/short-order cook
Point	Gourmet	Institutional cook
Fusion cuisine	Gourmand	Camp cooks
Global cuisine	Gourmet foods	

Test Your Knowledge

The practice sets provided below have been designed to test your comprehension of the information found in this chapter. It is recommended that you read the chapter completely before attempting these questions.

A. Terminology

Fill in the blank spaces with the correct term.

1. _____ A cuisine for the French aristocracy and upper classes that was rich and elaborate, and emphasized strict culinary principles that distinguished this style of cooking from regional or "traditional" cooking.

2. _____ A late 19th- and early 20th-century refinement and simplification of *grande cuisine* that emphasizes thorough exploration of culinary techniques and principles.

3. _____ The master of French *grande cuisine* whose writings almost single-handedly refined and summarized 500 years of culinary evolution by analysing cooking, old and new, and emphasizing procedure and order.

4. _____ A master of simplicity and refinement in cooking whose work was carried to greater heights by a generation of chefs he trained, including Bocuse, the Troisgros brothers, Chapel, Bise, Outhier, Guérard and Verge.

5. _____ Heat energy transfer to food in order to alter a food's texture, flavour, aroma and appearance.

6. _____ The art and science of eating well.

7. _____ Believed to be the owner of the first restaurant.

8. _____ 18th-century cooks who used to cook the main cuts of meat.

9. _____ A set of recipes based upon local ingredients, traditions and practices.

10. _____ The blending or use of ingredients and/or preparation methods from various ethnic, regional and national cuisines in the same dish.

11. _____ A movement created to counteract the proliferation of fast food.

12. _____ The cuisine of a group of people having a common cultural heritage.

Fill in the blank spaces with the correct definition.

13. Gourmand _____

14. Auguste Escoffier _____

15. Brigade _____

16. Nouvelle cuisine _____

17. National cuisine _____

18. Marcel Kretz _____

19. Professional cooking _____

B. Fill in the Blank

Fill in the blank provided with the response that correctly completes the statement.

1. _____ is the founder of the slow food movement

2. _____ is terminology used in reference to the food service industry to describe the area where guests are welcome and serviced, as in the dining room.

3. _____ is terminology used in reference to the food service industry to describe the area where guests are generally not allowed, such as the kitchen.

4. In _____ service, the entrée, vegetables, and potatoes are served from a platter onto a plate by the waiter.

5. _____ is the French term that literally means "everything in its place."

6. The _____ is responsible for fish and shellfish items as well as their sauces.

7. The _____ is preparing buffets and cold food items including salads and salad dressings.

8. The _____ is responsible for all sautéed items and most sauces.

9. The _____ is also known as a swing cook or roundsman.

10. The _____ makes candies and petit fours.

11. The _____ makes show pieces and special cakes.

C. Short Answer

Provide a short response that correctly answers each of the questions below.

1. List three (3) advantages that the introduction of the cast-iron stove lent to professional, 19th-century cooking.

    a. _____

    b. _____

    c. _____

2. List three (3) examples of food preservation and storage techniques that were developed in the 19th century.

a. _____

b. _____

c. _____

3. List five (5) aspects of demographic information that food service operators use to determine customer needs or desires.

a. _____

b. _____

c. _____

d. _____

e. _____

4. List three (3) of the five ways a professional chef can show pride in performing his/her job.

a. _____

b. _____

c. _____

5. What is *nouvelle cuisine* and what is its origin?

_____

_____

_____

6. What are some of the effects of advancements in agriculture on the food industry?

_____

_____

_____

7. When and where did the slow food movement originate?

_____

_____

_____

8. What are the goals of the slow food movement?

_____

_____

_____

9. How did the demographic and social changes contribute to the diversification of the food service industry?

_____

_____

_____

D. Multiple Choice

For each question below, choose the one response that correctly answers the question.

1. The French term used to identify precisely cut thin stick shape pieces of food is
   a. batonnet
   b. sachet
   c. julienne
   d. emincé

2. A preparation made of chocolate and cram are main ingredients is known as:
   a. fondue
   b. chocolate candy
   c. ganache
   d. chocolate sauce

3. Foods that are processed into a smooth pulp are referred to as:
   a. smashed
   b. puréed
   c. pasted
   d. blended

4. A shallow and wide container with straight sides and two loop handles is known as a:
   a. sauteuse
   b. sautoir
   c. sauce pot
   d. rondeau

5. Half brown sauce and half brown stock reduced by half produces a sauce known as:
   a. reduction
   b. espagnole
   c. glace
   d. demi glace

6. The term Brunoise refers to
   a. browning
   b. chopping
   c. a small dice
   d. cutting in thin sticks

7. A Bain Marie is a
   a. trolley to move foods
   b. cooking pot used to braise foods
   c. hot water bath used to gently cook foods
   d. holding cabinet

8. A sauce made of oil, vinegar, herbs, spices and seasonings is known as
   a. basic French
   b. emulsion sauce
   c. vinaigrette
   d. salad dressing

9. Aromatic ingredients tied in cheese cloth makes a
   a. bouquet
   b. sac
   c. bag
   d. sachet

10. An appetizer composed of a small piece of bread or toast topped with savoury spread or garnish is known as:
    a. barquette
    b. canapé
    c. cromesqui
    d. toast

E. Matching

I. Defining Professionalism

A student chef should try to develop six basic attributes in readiness for his/her role as a professional chef. Fill in the blank with the term that best matches the definition given on the right. (Term choices: training, skill, taste, judgment, dedication, and pride)

Term	Definition
1. _____	The desire to continually strive for the utmost professionalism and quality in spite of the physical and psychological strains of being a chef.
2. _____	An ability developed through practical, hands-on experience that can only be perfected with extended experience.
3. _____	The understanding of a base of information that enables a chef to perform each aspect of the job.
4. _____	The ability to make sound decisions such as what items to include on the menu; what, how much, and when to order food; and approving finished items for service—all of which can be learned only through experience.
5. _____	A chef's ability to prepare flavourful and attractive foods that appeal to all senses and to the desires of the clientele.
6. _____	The desire to show pride in one's personal and professional accomplishments by means of such details as professional appearance and behaviour.

II. Brigade Members

Match each brigade member in List A with the appropriate duty/responsibility in List B. Each choice in List B can only be used once.

	List A		*List B*
____1.	Saucier	a.	French bread
____2.	Friturier	b.	Steamed asparagus with hollandaise sauce
____3.	Potager	c.	French fries
____4.	Garde-manger	d.	Ground beef
____5.	Rôtisseur	e.	Roast pork with apple chutney
____6.	Poissonier	f.	Grilled veal tenderloin with black bean sauce
____7.	Pâtissier	g.	Veal stock
____8.	Grillardin	h.	Poached sole with caper sauce
____9.	Boucher	i.	Caesar salad
____10.	Boulanger	j.	Chocolate éclairs
		k.	Sautéed items and most sauces

F. True or False

For each question below, circle either True or False to indicate the correct answer.

1. Today most well-run food service operations use the formal kitchen brigade system as the means for organizing the kitchen staff.
    True   False

2. It was not until the early 1900s that advances in transportation efficiency improved to the point where the food service industry finally began to expand.
    True   False

3. Massimo Montanari and Carlo Petrini spearheaded the creation of the University of Gastronomic Sciences in Piedmont and Emilia-Romagna, Italy.
    True   False

4. Alice Waters was the Chef-Owner of La Sapinière in Quebec.
    True   False

5. Aside from quickly preparing foods to order, a *short order cook* may serve much the same role as a tournant, having mastered many cooking stations.
    True   False

6. Most issues in the food service industry that are brought to the forefront for discussion, such as nutrition and sanitation, are brought about by the government.
    True   False

7. The biggest difference among establishments serving buffets is that restaurants charge by the dish whereas cafeterias charge by the meal.
    True   False

8. A chef that prepares effective "mise en place" is one concerned only with classic cuisine.
   True   False

9. *Cuisine bourgeoise* refers to the style of cooking used by middle-class home cooks.
   True   False

10. Escoffier is credited with developing the kitchen brigade system used in large restaurant kitchens.
    True   False

11. Although sun-drying, salting, smoking, pickling, and fermenting are effective means of preserving foods, they were passed up for newer technologies due to the labour-intensive preparation.
    True   False

12. Most consumers choose a restaurant or food service establishment because it provides quality service and food for a price they are willing to pay.
    True   False

Chapter 2

Food Safety and Sanitation

One of the most important responsibilities of food service workers is to supply food that is safe to eat. Anyone handling food or the equipment used for its preparation needs to know how food-borne illnesses are caused and how they can be prevented.

At the end of this chapter the student should be able to:

1. Identify the causes of food-borne illnesses.
2. Handle foods in a safe manner.
3. Take appropriate actions to create and maintain a safe and sanitary working environment.

Key Terms

Sanitation

Contamination

Direct contamination

Cross-contamination

Microorganisms

Putrefactives

Pathogenic

Intoxication

Toxins

Infection

Toxin-mediated infection

Potentially hazardous foods (PHF)

Temperature danger zone

Time-and-temperature principle

Lag phase

Log phase

Decline or negative growth phase

pH

Aerobic bacteria

Anaerobic bacteria

Facultative bacteria

Trichinosis

Anisakiasis

Cyclospora

Hepatitis A

Norwalk virus

Fermentation

Clean

Sanitize

Sterilize

Rotate stock

Critical control point

Test Your Knowledge

The practice sets provided below have been designed to test your comprehension of the information found in this chapter. It is recommended that you read the chapter completely before attempting these questions.

A. Terminology

Fill in the blank spaces with the correct term.

1. _____ Poisoning of the consumer can actually occur when the toxins produced by pathogenic bacteria are ingested. Such toxins cannot be seen, smelled, or tasted.

2. _____ The transfer of microorganisms to foods and food contact surfaces by humans, rodents, or insects.

3. _____ To remove visible dirt and soil

4. _____ A measurement of the acidity or alkalinity of a solution or product.

5. _____ The leading cause of food-borne illnesses in spite of only being single-cell microorganisms.

6. _____ A type of bacterial illness caused when live pathogenic bacteria are ingested and live in the consumer's intestinal tract.

7. _____ The broad range of temperature (4° to 60°C, or 40°F to 140°F) at which bacteria thrive and reproduce best.

8. _____ The smallest known form of life that invades living cells of a host, takes over those cells' genetic material, and causes the cells to produce more viruses.

9. _____ The contamination of raw foods, or the plants or animals from which they come, in their natural setting or habitat.

10. _____ To reduce the pathogenic organisms to safe levels.

11. _____ The time it takes a bacterium to divide under favourable conditions.

12. _____ Chemical substances that may cause danger to the safety of food.

13. _____ The cause for the most common food-borne bacterial infection.

14. _____ The process used by bacteria to reproduce.

15. _____ The amount of chlorine bleach needed for 4.5 L (1 gal.) of water when preparing a sanitizing solution.

16. _____ The minimum amount of time needed to wash hands properly.

17. _____ The temperature of the rinse water in manual dishwashing.

Fill in the blank spaces with the correct definition.

18. HACCP _____

19. Pathogen _____

20. Physical hazard _____

21. Biological hazard_____

22. Sterilize _____

23. Fungi _____

24. Putrefactive _____

25. Toxin _____

26. Parasites _____

27. C.F.I.A. _____

B. Fill in the Blank

This section provides a review of information regarding food-borne illnesses. Fill in the blanks provided with the response that correctly completes each portion of the statement. Below is a definition of each of the points needing answers for each question.

Organism: What type of organism causes the illness? Is it a bacteria, parasite, virus, fungi, mould, or yeast?

Form: Especially relevant to bacteria, what form does it take? Is it a cell, a toxin, or a spore?

Source: In what foods might this organism be found, or what is the source of the contaminant?

Prevention: How can an outbreak of this illness be avoided?

1. *Hepatitis A*

   Organism: _____

   Form: _____

   Source: _____

   Prevention: _____

2. *Botulism*

   Organism: _____

   Form: _____

   Source: _____

   Prevention: _____

3. *Norwalk Virus*

   Organism: _____

   Form: _____

   Source: _____

   Prevention: _____

4. *Strep*

    Organism:_____

    Form: _____

    Source: _____

    Prevention:_____

5. *Perfringens or CP*

    Organism:_____

    Form: _____

    Source: _____

    Prevention: _____

6. *Salmonella*

    Organism:_____

    Form: _____

    Source: _____

    Prevention: _____

7. *Trichinosis*

    Organism:_____

    Form: _____

    Source: _____

    Prevention: _____

8. *E. Coli or 0157*

    Organism:_____

    Form: _____

    Source: _____

    Prevention: _____

9. *Staphylococcus*

    Organism:_____

    Form: _____

    Source: _____

    Prevention:_____

10. *Anisakiasis*

    Organism:_____

    Form: _____

    Source: _____

    Prevention:_____

11. *Listeriosis*

    Organism:_____

    Form: _____

    Source: _____

    Prevention:_____

C. Short Answer

Provide a short response that correctly answers each of the questions below.

1. Name four common toxin-producing bacteria.

    a._____

    b. _____

    c._____

    d. _____

2. List six conditions that bacteria need to grow.

    a._____

    b. _____

    c._____

    d. _____

    e._____

    f._____

3. List three acceptable ways to thaw foods.

    a._____

    b._____

    c._____

4   List three main ways to reduce or prevent cross-contamination.

    a._____

    b._____

    c._____

5. List seven points to consider reducing cross-contamination through personal hygiene.

    a._____

    b._____

    c._____

    d._____

    e._____

    f._____

    g._____

D. Multiple Choice

For each question below, choose the one response that correctly answers the question.

1.   Which of the following is *not* a necessity for bacteria to survive and reproduce?
      a.   sunlight
      b.   time
      c.   moisture
      d.   food

2.   The federal government enacted legislation designed to reduce hazards in the work area and therefore reduce accidents. This legislation is called:
      a.   Occupational Health and Safety Act (OHSA)
      b.   Occupational Hazards Prevention Policy (OHPP)
      c.   Safety and Health for Working Canadians (SHWC)
      d.   Safe Jobs for Working Canadians Act (SJWCA)

3.   Which of the following accurately defines potentially hazardous foods?
      a.   Foods used to prepare less popular menu items that require longer storage and therefore may promote bacterial growth.
      b.   Foods high in protein that without careful handling may support bacterial growth.
      c.   Various food products that have been sliced with the same knife on the same cutting board without intermittent sanitizing.
      d.   The presence, generally unintentional, of harmful organisms or substances.

4.   Choose the statement that accurately describes how frozen foods should be defrosted. Pull the product from the freezer and:
      a.   microwave on high in a plastic pan deep enough to catch the moisture.
      b.   thaw at room temperature in a pan deep enough to catch the moisture.
      c.   thaw in a warming oven on a roasting rack.
      d.   thaw under refrigeration in a pan deep enough to catch the moisture.

5.   Foods that are considered acidic have a pH that is:
      a.   at 7.0
      b.   8.5–10.0
      c.   0–below 7.0
      d.   10.0–14.0

6. Which of the following would be classified as a biological contamination?
    a. smoked salmon infected with clostridium botulinum
    b. oysters that fed in toxic marine algae
    c. spinach containing pesticide residues
    d. grains contaminated by soil fumigants

7. Which of the following would be classified as cross-contamination?
    a. an infected worker touching food
    b. a cutting board used for cutting meat and vegetables
    c. properly cooked poultry placed on a cutting board
    d. a case of celery with pesticide residues

8. Washing machines clean dishes with detergent in wash water of at least:
    a. 55°C (131°F)
    b. 65°C (149°F)
    c. 60°C (140°F)
    d. 70°C (158°F)

9. Which of the following would cause a biological food-borne illness?
    a. chemicals
    b. viruses
    c. lead
    d. putrefactive bacteria

10. Which of the following microorganisms is known to provoke intoxication?
    a. Listeria monocytogens
    b. salmonella
    c. streptococcus
    d. Staphylococcus aureus

11. Which of the following bacteria can cause toxin-mediated infection?
    a. Escherichia coli 0157:H7
    b. Clostridium perfringens
    c. Clostridium botulinum
    d. a and b only

For questions 12 and 13, consider the following statement: *When bacteria are moved from one place to another, they require time to adjust to new conditions.*

12. The resting period during which very little growth occur is known as the:
    a. negative growth phase
    b. log phase
    c. lag phase
    d. decline phase

13. The period of accelerated growth that lasts until the bacteria begin to crowd others is known as the:
    a. log phase
    b. lag phase
    c. negative growth phase
    d. decline phase

14. Anisakis is a:
    a. bacteria
    b. virus
    c. protozoa
    d. parasite

15. Clostridium botulinum is:
    a. anaerobic
    b. aerobic
    c. facultative
    d. none of the above

16 Colour coded cutting boards are recommended to
    a. ensure cleanliness
    b. cut costs
    c. prevent cross-contamination
    d. a and b only

17. In manual dishwashing, the temperature of the washing water should be no less than:
    a. 35°C (95°F)
    b. 82°C (185°F)
    c. 77°C (170°F)
    d. 45°C (113°F)

18. In manual washing, dishes are rinsed by immersing them in hot water for two minutes. The temperature of the water should be:
   a. 35°C (95°F)
   b. 77°C (170°F)
   c. 45°C (113°F)
   d. 82°C (185°F)

19. Fire suppression systems are required:
   a. in institution kitchens only
   b. in large commercial kitchens
   c. only in kitchens with deep fryers
   d. all commercial kitchens

20. To extinguish a small grease flare-up in a pan or on a cooktop, douse it quickly with:
   a. baking powder
   b. baking soda
   c. flour
   d. water

E. True or False

For each question below, circle either True or False to indicate the correct answer.

1. A contaminated food will have an unusual odour.
   True   False

2. The time-temperature principle is one of the best rules to follow to control the growth of bacteria.
   True   False

3. The first thing that should be done when a pest infestation is discovered is to try to find the source.
   True   False

4. Food handlers are a major cause for the spread of bacteria.
   True   False

5. Semi-solid foods should be cooled in containers that are less then 5 cm (2 inches) deep.
   True   False

6. A dish can be clean without being sanitary.
   True   False

7.   Human immunodeficiency virus (HIV) can easily be spread by food.
     True   False

8.   Anisakis is bacteria commonly found in fish.
     True   False

9.   Escherichia coli 0157:H7 (E-coli) is only found in beef burger.
     True   False

10. Gloves are a good substitute for proper handwashing.
     True   False

11. Rotating stocks is often recommended as part of a good pest control program.
     True   False

12. Towel drying is an effective way to dry dishes.
     True   False

13. HACCP programs focus on the flow of food through the food service facility.
     True   False

14. Use of the two spoons method when tasting food is a way of preventing cross-contamination.
     True   False

15. Any type of fire extinguisher can be used on a grease fire.
     True   False

16. Grease fires in ventilation hoods are the primary cause of restaurant fires.
     True   False

17. Every food service operation should be equipped with a first-aid kit.
     True   False

18. One employee per shift should be trained in basic emergency procedures.
     True   False

Chapter 3

Nutrition

Chefs have always been expected to serve foods that are nutritionally balanced in terms of protein, carbohydrates, fat, fibre, vitamins, and minerals. This unwritten rule has been determined by the public's understanding of the correlation between good eating habits, good health, and longevity.

At the end of this chapter the student will be able to:

1. Identify categories of nutrients and explain their importance in a balanced diet.
2. Explain the evolution of Canada's Food Guide and its significance in planning nutritious menus.
3. Describe the effects storage and preparation techniques have on various foods' nutritional values.
4. Identify the use of ingredient substitutes and alternatives.
5. Understand product nutrition labels.
6. Provide diners with nutritious foods.

Key Terms

Essential nutrients	Dietary fibre
Acids	Bases
Calorie	Metabolism
Coenzymes	Flavonoids
ple carbohydrates	Ingredient substitute
Complex carbohydrates	Ingredient alternative

Test Your Knowledge

The practice sets provided below have been designed to test your comprehension of the information found in this chapter. It is recommended that you read the chapter completely before attempting these questions.

A. Terminology

Fill in the blank spaces with the correct term.

1. _____ Vital dietary substances that are not manufactured by the body, but are needed to regulate metabolism, and therefore must be supplied by food.

2. _____ The group of essential nutrients that supply energy

3. _____ A group of compounds composed of oxygen, hydrogen, and carbon atoms that supply the body with energy and can be classified as saturated, monounsaturated, or polyunsaturated.

4. _____ A group of compounds composed of oxygen, hydrogen carbon, and nitrogen that are necessary for manufacturing, maintaining, and repairing body tissue and may also be used as an alternative source of energy. Each chain is constructed of various combinations of amino acids.

5. _____ Inorganic micronutrients necessary for regulating body functions and proper bone and teeth structures. These cannot be produced by the body, but must be attained by eating certa[...] plant materials or animals that have eaten such plants.

6. _____ A carbohydrate not digestible by the human body.

7. _____ Those fats that are mainly found in animal products and in tropical oil

8. _____ Those fats primarily found in plant foods such as avocados and olives.

9. _____ Those fats primarily found in plants such as soy and corn or fish.

10. _____ Any of various small substances, many of which contains a B vitamin, that promote or assist an enzyme's activities

11. _____ Non-nutritive components of plant foods that may be important in preventing some forms of cancer, diabetes, Alzheimer's, heart disease and other degenerative diseases.

Fill in the blank spaces with the correct definition.

12. Calorie _____

13. Essential nutrients _____

14. Ingredient substitutes _____

15. Carbohydrates _____

16. Metabolism _____

17. Hydrogenation _____

18. Amino acids _____

19. R.N.I. _____

20. Micronutrients _____

21. Lactose _____

22. Maltose _____

23. Flavonoids _____

Parts of a Product Label

Identify the five (5) areas of importance on the food label format. Briefly explain the significance of each.

Part of label	**Significance**
a. _____	_____
b. _____	_____
c. _____	_____
d. _____	_____
e. _____	_____

C. Short Answer

Provide a short response that correctly answers each of the questions below.

1. List five (5) things a food service worker can do to meet the diverse nutritional needs of the consumer.

   a. _____

   b. _____

   c. _____

   d. _____

   e. _____

2. Give three (3) examples of unsaturated oils.

   a. _____

   b. _____

   c. _____

3. Give three (3) examples of saturated fats.

    a. _____

    b. _____

    c. _____

4. Briefly discuss how you feel a chef should determine what and how many healthful food items should be included on a restaurant menu without limiting or "turning off" other guests.

    _____

5. Explain how vitamin retention can be maximized during the preparation of foods.

    _____

6. Explain why it is important to control the use of terms and expressions related to nutritional and health claims.

    _____

    _____

    _____

    _____

7. Explain why carbohydrates form a very important group of nutrients.

    _____

    _____

8. Explain ingredient substitution.

    _____

    _____

List three (3) principles a cook should follow when attempting to modify a recipe to make a dish healthier.

a. _____

b. _____

c. _____

10. List nine (9) food ingredients identified by the Canadian Food Inspection Agency as being accountable for 95 percent of reactions.

a. _____

b. _____

c. _____

d. _____

e. _____

f. _____

g. _____

h. _____

i. _____

D. Multiple Choice

For each question below, choose the one response that correctly answers the question.

1. Which of the following promotes absorption of calcium?
   a. vitamin D
   b. milk
   c. vitamin C
   d. fibre

2. Which of the following nutrients does not supply energy?
   a. protein
   b. fat
   c. fibre
   d. sugar

3.   Which of the following provides the most calories?
     a.   14 g flour
     b.   7 g sugar
     c.   12 g protein
     d.   8 g fat

4.   Of the following, which one is only found in plant foods and in milk sugars?
     a.   amino acid
     b.   lactose
     c.   dietary fibre
     d.   polyunsaturated fat

5.   Which of the following is a monosaccharide?
     a.   lactose
     b.   glucose
     c.   sucrose
     d.   maltose

6.   Which of the following oils is high in monounsaturated fats?
     a.   margarine
     b.   sunflower oils
     c.   soy oils
     d.   canola oil

7.   Which of the following fats is high in polyunsaturated fats?
     a.   fish oil
     b.   butter
     c.   olive oil
     d.   rapeseed oil

8.   Which of the following nutrients produces antibodies that are necessary for combating diseases?
     a.   vitamins
     b.   proteins
     c.   fats
     d.   carbohydrates

Which of the following vitamins are water soluble?

a. A and E

b. C and K

c. B and C

d. D and B

10. Food products must have a best-before date if they have a durable life of less than:

a. 90 days

b. 60 days

c. 40 days

d. 20 days

11. An adverse reaction to foods that involves an immune response, also called food hypersensitivity reaction, is referred to as:

a. food intolerance

b. food reaction

c. food allergy

d. food poisoning

12. An adverse reaction to a food that does not involve the immune system is referred to as:

a. food intolerance

b. food reaction

c. food allergy

d. food poisoning

E. Matching

This section is designed to test your knowledge and therefore covers many different aspects of the chapter.

Match each of the items in List A with the appropriate letter in List B. Each choice in List B can only be used once.

List A		List B	
____1.	Monosaccharides	a.	Simple sugars
____2.	Water	b.	Recommended nutrient intake
____3.	Saturated fat	c.	Sucrose is one of them
____4.	RNI	d.	Transports nutrients and wastes through body
____5.	Disaccharides	f.	Prevent some forms of cancer and heart disease
____6.	Lipids	g.	An important source of energy for the body
____7.	Fibre	h.	Helps to generate energy from foods we eat
____8.	Cholesterol	i.	The body produces all it needs
____9.	Proteins	j.	Keeps digestive track running smoothly
____10.	Vitamins and minerals	k.	Provides calories, helps carry fat-soluble vitamins, and gives food a pleasant mouth feel
____11.	Carbohydrates	l.	Found mainly in animal products and tropical oils
		n.	Necessary for manufacturing, maintaining and repairing body tissue, and regulating body processes

Chapter 4

Menu Planning and Food Costing

This chapter gives an in-depth explanation of one of the most important aspects of food service—the cost. The techniques used here to control costs and set prices are the basic ingredients for either success or failure in the food service industry.

At the end of this chapter, the student should be able to:

1. Identify the different types and styles of menus.
2. Explain the purpose of standardized recipes.
3. Calculate the cost per portion for recipes.
4. Convert recipe yield amounts.
5. Determine menu prices and calculate food cost percentages.
6. Control food costs.

Key Terms

Entree	Volume	Food cost
Static menu	Count	Cost of goods sold
Cycle menu	Yield	Inventory
Market menu	Conversion factor (C.F.)	Food cost percentage
Hybrid menu	As-purchased (A.P.)	Contribution margin
À la carte	Unit cost	Prime cost
Semi à la carte	Total recipe cost	Parstock
Table d'hôte or prix fixe	Cost per portion	FIFO (First In, First Out)
Recipe	Edible portion (E.P.)	
Standardized recipe	Yield factor	
Weight	Trim loss	

Test Your Knowledge

The practice sets provided below have been designed to test your comprehension of the information found in this chapter. It is recommended that you read the chapter completely before attempting these questions.

A. Terminology

Fill in the blank spaces with the correct term.

1. _____ A menu developed for a set period of time that repeats itself at the end of that period.

2. _____ A menu that combines a static menu and a cycle menu.

3. _____ The figure used to increase or decrease ingredient quantities for recipe yields.

4. _____ The term used to describe the minimum amount of stock necessary to cover operating needs between deliveries.

5. _____ A menu that offers an entire meal at a fixed price.

6. _____ The term for food cost plus direct labour cost, which is used to determine menu price.

7. _____ The most commonly used measuring system in the world.

8. _____ A method of storage that requires older food items to be used first.

9. _____ A recipe producing a specific quality and quantity of food.

10. _____ A menu that is influenced by market availability.

11. _____ The total cost of ingredients for a recipe, excluding overhead, labour, fixed expenses, and profit.

12. _____ A measuring system that uses pounds for weight and cups for volume.

Fill in the blank spaces with the correct definition.

13. À la carte _____

14. Food cost percentage _____

15. Entrée _____

16. Inventory _____

17. Recipe _____

18. Food cost _____

19. Unit cost _____

20. Trim loss _____

21. Yield _____

23. Count _____

24. Kilo _____

25. Hecto _____

26. Milli _____

27. Centi _____

28. Deci _____

B. Fill in the Blank

I. Units of Measure

Fill in the blanks for the following conversions.

1.   1 lb   =   _____ oz

2.   1 oz   =   _____ g

3.   1 lb   =   _____ g   =   _____ kg

4.   1 kg   =   _____ g

5.   1 g   =   _____ oz

6.   1 kg   =   _____ oz   =   _____ lb

7.   1 c   =   _____ tbsp   =   _____ fl. oz

8.   2 pt   =   _____ qt   =   _____ fl. oz

9.   2 qt   =   _____ gal   =   _____ pt

10.   1 c   =   _____ tbsp   =   _____ fl. oz

II. Recipe Conversion

The following recipe yields 4 L (3 qt 21 oz). Convert the quantities in the recipe to yield 18 180-mL (6-oz) portions and 40 240-mL (8-oz) portions. (Recipe 11.5, page 245)

NOTE: Remember to convert new yields back into pounds, ounces, and quarts.

Purée of Split Pea Soup

	Old Yield	*New Yield I*	*New Yield II*
	4 L (3 qt 21 oz) 22 Portions 180 ml (6 oz) each	_____ 18 Portions 180 ml (6 oz) each	_____ 40 Portions 240 ml (8 oz) each
Split peas	800 g (1 lb 12 oz)	_____	_____
Salt pork	100 g (3 oz)	_____	_____
Mirepoix	500 g (1 lb)	_____	_____
White stock	3 L (3 qt)	_____	_____

31

| Garlic cloves | 10 g (2) | _____ | _____ |

| Ham hocks | 700 g (1 lb 9 oz) | _____ | _____ |

Sachet:

Bay leaves	2	_____	_____
Dried thyme	0.25 g (1/8 tsp)	_____	_____
Peppercorns	0.5 g (1/4 tsp)	_____	_____

| Sat & pepper | TT | _____ | _____ |

Croutons   as needed for garnish

III. Unit Costs

Calculate the unit cost in each of the following problems.

1. One case of mayonnaise costs $27.20 and there are 4 jars of 4 L in each case. How much does 1 L of mayonnaise cost?
   Answer: $_____

2. One flat of eggs costs $4.80 and there are 2.5 dozen eggs in each tray. How much does 1 egg cost?
   Answer: $_____

3. One case of cornstarch costs $20.40 and there are 12 1-kg boxes in the case. How much does 1 kg of cornstarch cost?
   Answer: $_____

4. One case of sugar costs $35.00 and there are 12 5-lb bags in each case. How much does 1 pound of sugar cost?
   Answer: $_____

5. One case of oranges costs $26.00 and the count is 113. Nine oranges had to be thrown away because they were mouldy. What is the cost of one orange?
   Answer: $_____

IV. Recipe Costs

For each of the following six problems use the two figures that are given to calculate the missing figure on each line.

	Cost per Portion	# of Portions	Total Cost
1.	$1.75	25	$_____
2.	$_____	6	$5.10
3.	$1.95	_____	$23.40

	Cost per Portion	# of Portions	Total Cost
4.	$8.50	75	$_____
5.	$_____	125	$806.25
6.	$5.50	_____	$220.00

V. Yield Factor and Percentage

Calculate the total yield weight, yield factor, and yield percentage for each of the following.

	A.P. Quantity	Trim Loss	Total Yield Wt.	Yield Factor	Percentage
1.	4500 g (10 lb)	900 g (2 lb)	_____	_____	_____
2.	240 g (8 oz)	48 g (1.5 oz)	_____	_____	_____
3.	900 g (2 lb)	144 g (5 oz)	_____	_____	_____
4.	6750 g (15 lb)	1485 g (3 lb 4 oz)	_____	_____	_____
5.	11 250 g (25 lb)	150 g (5 oz)	_____	_____	_____
6.	22 500 g (50 lb)	6810 g (15 lb 2 oz)	_____	_____	_____

VI. Applying Yield Factors

Determine the E.P. (Edible Portion) unit cost of the following problems using the same weights and yield factors that were calculated in section V.

	Weight	A.P. Cost	A.P. Unit Cost	Yield Factor	E.P. Unit Cost
1.	4.5 kg (10 lb)	$5.99	_____	_____	_____
2.	0.240 kg (8 oz)	$15.54	_____	_____	_____
3.	0.9 kg (2 lb)	$3.26	_____	_____	_____
4.	6.75 kg (15 lb)	$14.29	_____	_____	_____
5.	11.25 kg (25 lb)	$21.67	_____	_____	_____
6.	22.5 kg (50 lb)	$18.45	_____	_____	_____

VII. Food Cost

Provide answers for each of the food cost problems below.

1. If sandwiches for the month of January cost $635 to make and sales totalled $1750, what is the food cost percentage for sandwiches this month?
   Answer: _____%

2. If it costs $1.25 for 1 bowl of soup and the minimum desired food cost percentage is 30%, what would the selling price be?
   Answer: $_____

3. The food cost for sole meunière is $10.95. It takes 5 minutes to have the sole cleaned and skinned at a labour cost of $8.00 per hour.

   a. What is the prime cost?
      Answer: $_____

   b. What is the selling price if the minimum desired prime cost percentage is 40%?
      Answer: $_____

4. If 150 portions of apple pie were sold in the restaurant in the first week of January and the cost of the food to produce the pies totalled $37.50, what would the minimum selling price per portion be if the desired food cost percentage was 25%?
   Answer: $_____

VIII. Cost of Goods Sold

1. The value of food inventory at the beginning of the period is $9,246.00, the food purchases during the period amount to $26,749.00, the value of inventory at the end of the period is $10,648.00, and the staff meals and other credits amount to $6,712.00.

   a. Calculate the cost of food sold:
      Answer: $_____

   b. If the sales during the same period are $90,110.00, what is the food cost percentage during the period?
      Answer: $_____

   c. What should the cost of food sold be to achieve a 27% food cost?
      Answer: $_____

C. Short Answer

1. Explain the differences between the metric and imperial system.

   _____

   _____

   _____

   _____

2. When converting a recipe, is the cooking time converted the same way? Explain.

   _____

   _____

   _____

   _____

3. What is the formula used to calculate the cost of goods sold?

   _____

   _____

   _____

   _____

D. Multiple Choice

1. In which measuring system are cups used?
   a. US
   b. Imperial
   c. Metric
   d. British

2. Which of the following prefixes signifies 100 times larger?
   a. centi
   b. hecto
   c. deci
   d. deca

3. Which of the following prefixes signifies 10 times larger?
   a. centi
   b. hecto
   c. deci
   d. deca

4. Which of the following prefixes signifies 100 times smaller?
   a. centi
   b. hecto
   c. deci
   d. deca

5. Which of the following prefixes signifies 10 times smaller?
   a. centi
   b. hecto
   c. deci
   d. deca

6. If a recipe requires 2.4 kg of stewing beef and you only have 1.8 kg on hand, the recipe can be produced by proportionally decreasing all the other ingredients. The conversion factor will be:
   a. 1.33
   b. 1.8
   c. 0.75
   d. 0.85

7. If the AP cost of food items is $13.75 per kg and the yield percentage is 87%, the EP cost is:
   a. $15.54
   b. $15.80
   c. $11.96
   d. $15.95

8. The yield factor of carrots is 1.28 and the AP cost per kg is 0.65. What is the EP cost of one 85 g portion?
   a. $0.07
   b. $0.05
   c. $0.06
   d. $0.04

9. Using the factor pricing method and assuming the food cost is $4.85, the direct labour cost is $1.70, and the desired food cost percentage is 26%, what is the selling price of this item?

   a. $18.65

   b. $25.19

   c. $20.35

   d. $23.49

10. The pricing method that uses the total of raw food cost plus direct labour as the basic cost is known as _____ pricing method.

    a. real cost

    b. non-cost based

    c. factor

    d. prime cost

11. If the cost of the food is $9.60 per portion, the direct labour cost is $2.10 and the desired prime cost percentage is 48%, what should the selling price be?

    a. $24.36

    b. $15.63

    c. $18.60

    d. $32.50

12. If the market value of an item is $15.95, the desired profit is 6% of sales, overhead expenses are 24% of sales, and labour costs 32% of sales, what should the food cost be?

    a. $8.72

    b. $7.46

    c. $6.06

    d. $5.15

Chapter 5

Tools and Equipment

This chapter is a guide to the basic tools used in the food service industry. It emphasizes the importance of safety and use of the correct tool for the job. The following exercises will help you to understand the tools you will be working with and their many uses.

At the end of this chapter the student should be able to:

1. Recognize a variety of professional kitchen tools and equipment.
2. Select and care for knives properly.
3. Understand how a professional kitchen is organized.

Key Terms

Carbon steel	Flat top
Stainless steel	Griddles
High carbon stainless steel	Salamander
Turning knife	Rotisserie
Scimitar	Insulated carriers
Whetstone	Chafing dishes
Scale	Heat lamps
Measuring spoons	Work stations
Measuring cups	Work sections
Liquid measuring cups	
Vertical cutter/mixer	

Test Your Knowledge

The practice sets provided below have been designed to test your comprehension of the information found in this chapter. It is recommended that you read the chapter completely before attempting these questions.

A. Terminology

Fill in the blank spaces with the correct term.

1. _____ The most important item in the tool kit.

2. _____ A device used to measure temperatures in food, refrigerators, and freezers.

3. _____ An enclosed space where food is cooked, surrounded by hot dry air.

4. _____ An alloy of carbon and iron.

5. _____ The part of the blade where it meets the handle.

Fill in the blank spaces with the correct definition.

6. Turning knife _____

7. Whetstone _____

8. Aluminum _____

9. Stove top _____

10. Combitherm _____

11. Work station _____

12. Work section _____

13. Soyer _____

B. Fill in the Blanks

I. General Questions

Fill in the blank with the response that correctly completes the statement.

1. The _____ _____ _____ develops industry standards for food service equipment; its product certification mark indicates that the item has been tested and meets the set standards.

2. A _____ knife is used for general purpose cutting of fruits and vegetables.

3. Identify the different parts of a knife in the following diagram:

1. _____

2. _____

3. _____

4. _____

5. _____

6. _____

7. _____

4.	The part of the knife known as the _____ is the part of the blade that is inside the handle.

5.	_____ cooking uses a special coil placed below the stove top's surface in combination with specially designed cookware made of _____ _____ or_____ _____ _____.

6.	Short order and fast food operations often use a flat metal surface known as a _____ on which to cook food.

7.	A _____ is useful for chopping large quantities of foods to a uniform size.

8.	It is advisable to use _____ spoons when cooking with nonstick surfaces.

9.	A butcher knife is also known as a _____.

II. Equipment Identification

Identify each of the following items and give a use for each.

1.	Name of item: _____

	Major use: _____

2.	Name of item: _____

	Major use: _____

3.	Name of item: _____

	Major use: _____

4.	Name of item: _____

	Major use: _____

5.   Name of item: _____

     Major use: _____

6.   Name of item: _____

     Major use: _____

7.   Name of item: _____

     Major use: _____

8.   Name of item: _____

     Major use: _____

9.   Name of item: _____

     Major use: _____

10. Name of item: _____

    Major use: _____

11. Name of item: _____

    Major use: _____

12. Name of item: _____

    Major use: _____

13.   Name of item: _____

       Major use: _____

14.   Name of item: _____

       Major use: _____

15.   Name of item: _____

       Major use: _____

16.   Name of item: _____

       Major use: _____

17. Name of item: _____

    Major use: _____

18. Name of item: _____

    Major use: _____

19. Name of item: _____

    Major use: _____

20. Name of item: _____

    Major use: _____

C. Short Answer

Provide a short response that correctly answers each of the questions below.

1. Describe four (4) important criteria for evaluation of equipment for kitchen use.

    a. _____

    b. _____

    c. _____

    d. _____

2. List and describe the three (3) types of metals used in knife blades.

    a. _____

    b. _____

    c. _____

3. Describe a balance scale and explain its advantages.

    _____

    _____

    _____

4. Describe how a stem thermometer can be calibrated.

    _____

    _____

    _____

5. How is a candy/fat thermometer different from others?

    _____

    _____

    _____

D. Multiple Choice

1. A balance scale is also known as:
    a. two-tray scale
    b. baker's scale
    c. spring-loaded scale
    d. roman scale

2. The most precise way to measure is by:
    a. volume
    b. count
    c. weight
    d. cups

3. The number stamped on either the handle or the release mechanism of a portion scoop refers to:
    a. the number of scoops per litre (or quart)
    b. the number of millilitres or ounces it contains
    c. the diameter of the opening
    d. how high the scoop is in millimetres or inches

4. A mould with hinged sides is properly referred to as a _____ mould.
    a. French
    b. ballotine
    c. terrine
    d. pâté en croûte

5. A long-handled tool used to remove foods or impurities from liquids is a(n):
    a. lifter
    b. étamine
    c. spider
    d. strainer

6. A hotel pan is:
    a. an aluminum pan used for roasting
    b. a storage container used in hotels
    c. also known as a steam table pan
    d. none of the above

7. An étamine is
   a. a conical strainer with a very fine mesh
   b. a chinois with a coarse mesh
   c. the same as a colander
   d. the same as a sieve

8. A steamer that cooks without the use of pressure is known as a:
   a. low-pressure steamer
   b. combination steamer
   c. conventional steamer
   d. convection steamer

9. Griddles differ from flat tops in that they:
   a. don't get as hot
   b. have a thinner metal plate
   c. have a thicker metal plate
   d. get much hotter

10. A fire extinguisher designed to deal with fires involving oil, grease, or flammable chemicals is identified by a:
    a. star
    b. circle
    c. square
    d. triangle

E. Matching

Match each of the pieces of equipment in List A with the appropriate letter definition in List B. Each choice in List B can only be used once.

List A		*List B*
___1. Mandoline	a.	Can be used in food up to 204°C (400°F).
___2. Refrigerator	b.	The metal used most commonly for commercial small utensils.
___3. Candy thermometer	c.	A metal that holds and distributes heat very well but is quite heavy.
___4. Salamander	d.	Food is placed on a revolving spit.
___5. Copperware	e.	An overhead broiler used to brown the top of foods.
___6. Rotisserie	f.	A loosely woven cotton fabric used to strain sauces and stocks.

47

____7. Cast iron	g.	The metal that is the most effective conductor of heat for cookware.
____8. Cheesecloth	h.	Used for food storage, may be walk-in or reach-in.
____9. Tilting skillet	i.	A manually operated slicer used for small quantities of fruit and vegetables.
____10. Aluminum	j.	A piece of equipment that can be used for frying or braising.
	k.	A metal that changes colour when in contact with acid foods.

F. True or False

For each question below, circle either True or False to indicate the correct answer.

1. Stem-type thermometers should be thrown away when they are dropped.
    True   False

2. Ventilation hoods should be cleaned and inspected by the hotel/restaurant maintenance staff.
    True   False

3. Some handmade imported pottery may contain lead in the glaze.
    True   False

4. Class A fire extinguishers are used for fires caused by wood, paper, or cloth.
    True   False

5. High-carbon stainless steel discolours when it comes in contact with acidic foods.
    True   False

6. A steam kettle cooks more slowly than a pot sitting on a stove.
    True   False

7. When purchasing equipment, one should look for the CSA symbol.
    True   False

8. Combitherm ovens can function as a low-pressure steamer.
    True   False

9. Induction burners are not very practical on buffets as they can get really hot.
    True   False

10. Copper pots are an excellent choice to use with induction cooktops.
    True   False

Chapter 6

Knife Skills

Good knife skills are essential to maximizing efficiency and safety in the kitchen. This chapter outlines these important skills, which should be practised until they become second nature.

At the end of this chapter the student should be able to:

1. Care for knives properly.
2. Use knives safely and properly.
3. Cut foods into a variety of classic shapes.

Key Terms

Whetstone

Steel

Chiffonade

Rondelles

Rounds

Diagonals

Oblique cuts

Roll cut

Lozenges

Butterfly

Pocket

Chop

Julienne

Brunoise

Allumette

Small dice

Batonnet

Medium dice

Baton

Large dice

Paysanne

Mince

Tourner

Parisienne

Gaufrette

Test Your Knowledge

The practice sets provided below have been designed to test your comprehension of the information found in this chapter. It is recommended that you read the chapter completely before attempting these questions.

A. Terminology

Fill in the blank spaces with the correct term.

1. _____ Also known as a sharpening stone.

2. _____ An instrument used to straighten the blade of the knife between sharpenings.

3. _____ The smallest cube-shaped cut 1–2 mm × 1–2 mm × 1–2 mm (1/16 inch × 1/16 inch × 1/16 inch).

4. _____ Finely shredded leafy vegetables used as a garnish or a base for cold presentations.

5. _____ A wedge-shaped cut of vegetable.

6. _____ Round slices from a cylindrical vegetable such as a carrot.

7. _____ A stick-shaped cut, slightly larger than julienne 6 mm × 6 mm × 5 to 6 cm (1/4 inch × 1/4 inch × 2 to 2-1/2 inches).

8. _____ The recommended angle to hone a knife on the steel.

9. _____ Ridged slices usually cut with a mandoline.

10. _____ To slice horizontal.

11. _____ Grip the handle in a fist with your fingers and thumb. This allows you to cut around joints and separate flesh from bone when boning meat and poultry.

Fill in the blank spaces with the correct definition.

12. Honing _____

13. Julienne _____

14. Small dice _____

15. Tourner _____

16. Medium dice _____

17. Mincing _____

18. Paysanne _____

19. Large dice _____

20. Diagonals _____

21. Chopping _____

B. Fill in the Blank

Fill in the blank with the response that correctly completes the statement.

1. There are _____ methods of cutting, one where the _____ acts as the fulcrum and the other where the _____ acts as the fulcrum.

2. Parsley and garlic should be chopped with one hand flat on the _____ of the knife, using a _____ motion.

3. When cutting food always cut _____ from yourself and never cut on _____, _____, or _____ surfaces.

4. When using a whetstone, start by placing the _____ of the knife on the stone. Start sharpening on the _____ side of the stone and finish with the _____ side.

5. An onion is diced by cutting in half and then making incisions towards the _____ of the onion, without cutting through it.

6. A steel generally _____ sharpen a knife. Instead, it is used to _____ the blade.

7. To use a whetstone, place the _____ of the blade against the whetstone at a _____ angle.

8. Small balls or spheres cut from various vegetables or fruits are referred to as _____.

C. Short Answer

1. Is it acceptable to wash kitchen knives in the dishwasher? Explain.

    _____

    _____

    _____

2. List ten (10) rules that apply to safe knife handling procedures.

    a. _____

    b. _____

    c. _____

    d. _____

    e. _____

    f. _____

g. _____

h. _____

i. _____

j. _____

3. Briefly explain the most common method of gripping a knife.

_____

_____

_____

_____

4. Briefly explain why it is important to cut vegetables uniformly.

_____

_____

_____

D. Matching

Draw the following cuts of vegetables to scale and describe their dimensions. Point out any similarities between the strips of vegetables and the cubes in the space provided below.

_____

_____

_____

1. Julienne

2. Batonnet

3. Paysanne

4. Brunoise

5. Small dice

6. Medium dice

7. Allumette

E. True or False

For each question below, circle either True or False to indicate the correct answer.

1. A sharp knife is more dangerous than a dull one.
   True   False

2. A steel is used to sharpen knives.
   True   False

3. Tourner means "to turn" in French.
   True   False

4. A whetstone should be moistened with a mixture of water and mineral oil.
   True   False

5. Batonnet is also referred to as allumette.
   True   False

6. Paysanne is a half-inch dice that has been cut in half.
   True   False

7. One should not attempt to catch a falling knife.
   True   False

8.   Knives should not be washed in the dishwasher.
     True   False

9.   Any whetstone can be moistened interchangeably with either water or mineral oil
     True   False

10. A 40 degree angle is preferred when using a knife against a steel.
     True   False

Chapter 7

Flavours and Flavourings

The chef must understand how to flavour foods and be able to recognize flavouring ingredients and know how to use them. This chapter looks at the sense of taste and smell and the flavouring ingredients used in the professional kitchen to enhance foods. A single, complete list of kitchen staples does not exist due to the varying needs of food service establishments. Identifying common ingredients such as herbs, spices, nuts, oils and vinegars that are used as staples can enable us to set forth standards of quality and storage.

At the end of this chapter the student should be able to:

1. Understand the basic principles of the physiology of the sense of taste and smell.
2. Recognize a variety of herbs, spices, oils, vinegars and other flavourings.
3. Understand how to use flavouring ingredients to create, enhance or alter the natural flavour of a dish.

Key Terms

Flavour	Lemon grass	Paprika	Poppy seeds
Taste	Lovage	Chilli powders	Saffron
Mouth-feel	Marjoram	Crushed chiles	Sesame seeds
Aromas	Mint	Cinnamon	Tamarind
Palate	Spearmint	Cassia	Turmeric
Flavourings	Peppermint	Cloves	Wasabi
Herbs	Oregano	Coriander	Chinese five-spice powder
Aromatic	Parsley	Cumin	
Spices	Curly parsley	Fennel	Curry powder
Condiments	Italian parsley	Fenugreek	Masala
Basil	Rosemary	Ginger	Garam masala
Sweet basil	Sage	Horseradish	Herbes de Provence
Opal basil	Savory	Juniper	
Bay	Tarragon	Mustard seeds	Italian seasoning blend
Chervil	Thyme	Nutmeg	Pickling spice
Chives	Allspice	Mace	Quatre-épices
Garlic chives	Anise	Peppercorns	Seasoned salts
Cilantro	Star anise	Black peppercorns	Bouquet garni
Curry leaves	Capers	White peppercorns	Sachet
Dill	Caraway	Green peppercorns	Oignon piqué
Epazote	Cardamom		Culinary salt
Fine herbs	Chiles	Pink peppercorns	Table salt
Lavender	Cayenne	Szechuan pepper	Rock salt

Sea salt	Rancidity	Malt vinegar	Fermented black bean sauce
Kosher salt	Vegetable oils	Distilled vinegar	
Sel gris	Canola oil	Cider vinegar	Fish sauce
Fleur de sel	Nut oils	Rice vinegar	Prepared mustard
Specialty salts	Olive oil	Flavoured vinegars	Soy sauce
Smoked salt	Flavoured oils		Ketchup
Oils	Infused oils	Balsamic vinegar	
Shortenings	Vinegar	Relish	
Smoke point	Wine vinegar	Pickle	

Test Your Knowledge

The practice sets provided below have been designed to test your comprehension of the information found in this chapter. It is recommended that you read the chapter completely before attempting these questions.

A. Terminology

Fill in the blank spaces with the correct term.

1. _____ An identifiable or distinctive quality of a food, drink or other substance perceived with the combined senses of taste, touch and smell.

2. _____ The sensations, as interpreted by the brain, of what we detect when food, drink or other substances come in contact with our taste buds.

3. _____ The sensation created in the mouth by a combination of a food's taste, smell, texture and temperature.

4. _____ The sensations, as interpreted by the brain, of what we detect when a substance comes in contact with sense receptors in the nose.

5. _____ The complex of smell, taste and touch receptors that contributes to a person's ability to recognize and appreciate flavours

6. _____ From the Japanese word meaning "delicious."

7. _____ Boiling a substance until its flavour is removed.

8. _____ An item that adds a new taste to a food and alters its natural flavours.

9. _____ Recognizable combinations of spice flavours that are developed by countries and cuisines. These can be purchased as commercial blends or can be mixed by the chef as needed.

10. _____ Used to introduce flavourings, seasonings and aromatics into stocks, sauces, soups and stews; it is made by tying a selection of herbs and vegetables into a bundle with twine.

11. _____ Any item added to a dish for flavour with a modern identity of cooked or prepared flavourings such as prepared mustards, relishes, bottled sauces and pickles.

12. _____ The extraction of flavours at temperatures below boiling.

13. _____ The edible single-seed kernel of a fruit surrounded by a hard shell.

14. _____ A type of fat that remains liquid at room temperature.

15. _____ Also known as chervil.

16. _____ A parsley with flat leaves, a darker colour and coarser flavour.

17. _____ Also known as sweet laurel.

18. _____ A combination of parsley, tarragon, chervil and chives; widely used in French cuisine.

19. _____ The finest and smallest capers produced in France's Provence region.

Fill in the blank spaces with the correct definition.

20. Oignon piqué _____

21. Herb _____

22. Spice _____

23. Staples _____

24. Vinegar _____

25. Flavouring _____

26. Seasoning_____

B. Fill in the Blanks

Fill in the blank provided with the response that correctly completes the statement.

1. _____ is recognized as the fifth taste in western cuisine.

2. _____ are specialized sensory organs of taste.

3. _____ are specialized sensory organs of smell.

4.   _____ is the active ingredient in peppercorn.

5.   _____ is the active ingredient in chiles.

6.   _____, _____ and _____ are three types of vinegar.

C. Short Answer

Provide a short answer that correctly answers each of the questions below.

1.   List today's five (5) recognized tastes in the western culture.

    a._____

    b._____

    c._____

    d._____

    e._____

2.   List five (5) factors that affect one's perception of flavours.

    a._____

    b._____

    c._____

    d._____

    e._____

3.   List three (3) factors that affect one's taste perception.

    a._____

    b._____

    c._____

4.   List three (3) guidelines to follow when experimenting with the use of different herbs and spices in various dishes.

    a._____

    b._____

    c._____

5. Salt is the most basic seasoning and its use is universal. List three (3) things salt can do for food.

a._____

b. _____

c._____

6. What does smoke point refer to? Explain its importance.

_____

_____

_____

_____

7. When a fat is said to go rancid, what does it refer to?

_____

_____

_____

_____

D. Multiple Choice

1. The sharp, first flavours or aromas that provide instant impact and dissipate quickly are referred to as:
   a. Depth of flavours
   b. Roundness
   c. Top notes
   d. Low notes

2. The most dominant, lingering flavours that consist of the basic tastes are referred to as:
   a. Depth of flavours
   b. Roundness
   c. Top notes
   d. Low notes

3. The final flavour that remains in the mouth after swallowing is referred to as:
   a. Aftertaste
   b. Middle note
   c. Depth of flavour
   d. Top note

4. The second wave of flavour and aromas is referred to as:
   a. Aftertaste
   b. Middle note
   c. Depth of flavour
   d. Top note

5. Which of the following commercial sauces is made with a mixture of malt vinegar, tamarind, molasses and spices?
   a. barbecue
   b. fish
   c. Worcestershire
   d. Pikapeppa

6. Which of the following commercial sauces is made with a mixture of tomatoes?
   a. barbecue
   b. fish
   c. Tabasco
   d. hoisin

7. Which of the following commercial sauces can be described as dark, thick and salty-sweet, made from fermented soybeans, vinegar, garlic and caramel?
   a. soya
   b. fish
   c. Worcestershire
   d. hoisin

8. Which of the following commercial sauces can be described as thin, dark brown liquid made from anchovy extract and salt?
   a. oyster
   b. fish
   c. Worcestershire
   d. hoisin

9. In today's kitchen, which of the following is referred to as cooked and prepared flavourings that may be used to alter or enhance the flavour of a dish during cooking or added to a completed dish?

   a. barbecue

   b. fish

   c. Worcestershire

   d. hoisin

E. Matching

Match each of the clues in List A with the appropriate definition or explanation in List B. Each choice in List B can only be used once.

List A		*List B*
_____ 1.	Western definition of taste	a. Maintaining the proper balance of tastes in a dish or during an entire meal assists in maintaining good health and fortune.
_____ 2.	Sweet	b. Found in acidic foods, it can vary in intensity but can be made more palatable by adding varying amounts of sweet.
_____ 3.	Umami	c. Helps to finish a dish, heightening or enhancing other flavours, it may occur naturally in the food or be added by the cook.
_____ 4.	The Chinese 5-taste scheme	d. Based more on science, it identifies four tastes: sweet, sour, salty, bitter and sometimes umami.
_____ 5.	Bitter	e. The practice of arranging taste on a continuum, rating them as primary or secondary, including sweet, salty, bitter, pungent, harsh and astringent.
_____ 6.	Salty	f. Less preferred across cultures than other tastes, it is potent and easily unbalanced by other tastes like sour and salty.
_____ 7.	Sour	g. Literally means delicious, it is naturally occurring in foods that contain amino acid glutamates such as soy sauce, cheese, meats, mushrooms and tomatoes to name a few.
_____ 8.	Ayurvedic medicine	h. Created by naturally occurring sugars that can be enhanced by small amount of sour, bitter or salty tastes.
		i. The Indian way of creating dishes with the balance of 6 tastes that are based on the tastes of various herbs and spices.

Based on the two categories given, identify the items from the list below that are examples of each category. Fill in the blanks provided under each category heading with the corresponding examples.

Herb	*Spice*
1. _____	6. _____
2. _____	7. _____
3. _____	8. _____
4. _____	9. _____
5. _____	10. _____

paprika	oregano	lemon grass
cilantro	thyme	lavender
capers	garlic	coriander
black pepper	ground mustard	

F. True or False

For each question below, circle either True or False to indicate the correct answer.

1.   When preparing a recipe that calls for fresh herbs, the rule to follow when fresh herbs are unavailable is to use more dried herbs than the original fresh variety.
   True   False

2.   A standard sachet consists of peppercorns, bay leaves, parsley stems, thyme, cloves, and (optionally) garlic.
   True   False

3.   Mustard never really spoils; its flavour just fades away.
   True   False

4.   Ketchup originally referred to any salty extract from fish, fruits, or vegetables.
   True   False

5.   A shortening is a fat, usually made from animal fats, and is solid at room temperature.
   True   False

Chapter 8

Eggs and Dairy Products

Eggs, milk and milk-based products, known collectively as dairy products, are extremely versatile in numerous culinary applications. Attaining the highest quality, and maintaining freshness through proper handling and storage, are critical.

At the end of this chapter the student should be able to:

1. Describe the composition of eggs.
2. Purchase and store eggs properly.
3. Prepare whipped egg whites.
4. Identify, store and use a variety of milk-based products.
5. Explain how to clarify butter.
6. Identify, store and serve a variety of fine cheeses.

Key Terms

Shell
Yolk
Albumen
Egg white
Chalazae cords
Omega-3 eggs
Pasteurization
Dairy products
Lowfat milk
Skim milk
Evaporated milk
Sweetened condensed milk
Dry milk powder
Table cream
Half-and-half
Light cream
Coffee cream
Whipping cream
Lactose

Buttermilk
Sour cream
Crème fraîche
Yogurt
Canada 1, 2 and 3
Salted butter
Whipped butter
Whole butter
Cream cheese
Mascarpone
Ricotta
Bel paese
Brie
Boursin
Camembert
Unripened cheese
Interior ripened cheese
Surface ripened cheese
Feta

Havarti
Danish Tilsit
Port Salut
Esrom
Cheddars
Colby
Brick
English cheddar
Emmenthaler (Swiss)
Gruyère
Fondue
Gouda
Fontina
Fontina Val D'Aosta
Fontal Fontinella
Jarlsberg
Manchego
Asiago

Parmigiano-Reggiano (Parmesan)
Pecorinao Romano
Provolone
Light cheese
Blue cheeses
Gorgonzola
Roquefort
Stilton
Goat's milk cheese
Chèvre
Pasteurized processed cheese
Processed cheese food
Cold pack
Imitation cheese

Test Your Knowledge

The practice sets provided below have been designed to test your comprehension of the information found in this chapter. It is recommended that you read the chapter completely before attempting these questions.

A. Terminology

Fill in the blank spaces with the correct term.

1. _____ Constituting just over one-third of the egg and three-fourths of the calories, it also contains most of the minerals and vitamins, all of the fat and lecithin.

2. _____ These thick, twisted strands of egg white anchor the yolk in place and their prominence can be an indicator of freshness.

3. _____ The process of reducing the fat globules in size and permanently dispersing them throughout the liquid in order to ensure a uniform consistency, a whiter colour and a richer taste.

4. _____ A process performed to destroy the pathogenic bacteria by heating a liquid to a prescribed temperature for a specific period of time.

5. _____ Pasteurized skim or lowfat milk to which a bacterial culture (*Streptococcus lactis*) has been added.

6. _____ Term used to refer to milk with a fat content of no more than 1%.

7. _____ Name given to eggs from chickens fed with flaxseed.

8. Eggs contain vitamins __, __, __ and __ as well as the __ _____ vitamins.

9. Eggs are rich in minerals but also in _____ .

10. When whipping egg whites, some _____ or _____ should be added to obtain a better foam.

11. Crème fraîche is produced by combining _____ mL of _____ with _____ mL of _____ containing active cultures.

12. Sour cream is made with _____ cream while crème fraîche is made with _____ cream.

Fill in the blank spaces with the correct definition.

13. Ghee _____

14. Green cheese _____

15. Crème fraîche _____

16. Certification _____

17. Fondue _____

18. Albumen _____

19. Clarified butter_____

20. Cultured butter_____

B. Fill in the Blanks

Identify the parts of the egg indicated in the following diagram and write their names in the spaces provided.

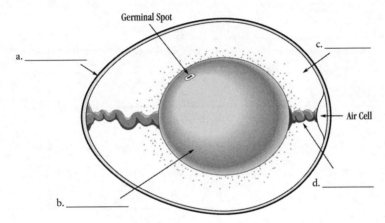

C. Short Answer

1. Describe the qualities of the primary parts of an egg in each of the grades listed below.

Primary part	Grade A	Grade B	Grade C
Albumen	_____	_____	_____
Yolk	_____	_____	_____
Shell	_____	_____	_____

2. List four (4) main points to observe to properly whip egg whites

    a._____

    b. _____

    c._____

    d. _____

3. List the ingredients of margarine.

    _____

    _____

    _____

    _____

    _____

4. Describe egg products.

    _____

    _____

    _____

    _____

    _____

5. Describe egg substitutes.

    _____

    _____

    _____

    _____

    _____

D. Multiple Choice

For each question below, choose the one response that correctly answers the question.

1. At what temperature does an egg yolk solidify (coagulate) when cooking?
    a. 57°–61°C (135°F–143°F)
    b. 49°–55°C (120°F–132°F)
    c. 71°–77°C (160°F–171°F)
    d. 65°–70°C (149°F–158°F)

2. Aside from increasing the shelf life of cream, the process of ultra-pasteurization:
    a. reduces the whipping properties
    b. thickens the consistency
    c. causes the cream to stay whipped for longer periods of time
    d. concentrates the fat content

3. What would be a good use for grade B eggs?
    a. as a compound in facial creams and other cosmetic products
    b. for baking, scrambling, or the production of bulk egg products
    c. grade B eggs are not recommended for use in food service operations
    d. for frying, poaching, or cooking in the shell

4. By law all milk must be processed by heating the milk at a temperature of 72°C (161°F) for 16 seconds. This process is called:
    a. homogenization
    b. ultra-high-temperature (UHT)
    c. pasteurization
    d. certification

5. In which of the following applications would grade A eggs be preferred?
    a. omelettes
    b. breakfast
    c. baking
    d. batters

6. Clarified butter is whole butter with the water and milk solids removed by:
    a. melting it over high heat and then straining it through cheesecloth
    b. melting it with the inclusion of whipped egg whites, bringing to a simmer, and then removing the raft and impurities
    c. melting it over low heat, then chilling it quickly in order to clarify
    d. melting it over low heat, without boiling, and then skimming

7. Evaporated milk, sweetened condensed milk, and dry milk powders are all examples of:
   a. canned milk products
   b. concentrated milk products
   c. cultured dairy products
   d. substandard milk products

8. Four hundred and fifty grams (one pound) of whole butter that is then clarified will result in what volume of clarified butter?
   a. 300 g (10 oz)
   b. 450 g (16 oz)
   c. 240 g (8 oz)
   d. 360 g (12 oz)

9. In Canada eggs are graded as:
   a. No. 1, No. 2, No. 3
   b. A, B, U and C
   c. A, B, C
   d. No. 1, No. 2

10. The temperature/time used in pasteurization of eggs is:
    a. 60°C (140°F) for 3.5 minutes
    b. 62°C (144°F) for 5 minutes
    c. 72°C (161°F) for 4 seconds
    d. 74°C (165°F) for 2 minutes

11. Milk is ultra-pasteurized at:
    a. 82°C (180°F) for 1 to 2 minutes
    b. 95°C (203°F) for 10 to 12 seconds
    c. 100°C (212°F) for 1 minute
    d. 135°C (275°F) for 3 to 4 seconds

12. To be labelled cream the product must have a minimum of _____ fat.
    a. 10%
    b. 18%
    c. 35%
    d. 32%

13. The main difference between evaporated milk and condensed milk is that:
    a. condensed milk is sweetened
    b. evaporated milk contains less moisture
    c. condensed milk is thinner than evaporated milk
    d. evaporated milk contains more fat

14. The bacterial culture used to produce buttermilk is:
    a. *Lactobacillus bulgaricus*
    b. *Streptococcus lactis*
    c. *Streptococcus thermophidus*
    d. both a and c

15. _____ is used to produce yogurt.
    a. *Lactobacillus bulgaricus*
    b. *Streptococcus lactis*
    c. *Streptococcus thermophidus*
    d. both a and c

16. Salted butter contains up to _____ salt.
    a. 15%
    b. 2%
    c. 2.5%
    d. 3%

17. Soft margarines should not be substituted for regular butter because they:
    a. are whipped
    b. contain more water
    c. contain emulsifiers
    d. contain more saturated fats

18. The protein in milk is known as
    a. casein
    b. albumen
    c. lactose
    d. whey

E. Matching Questions

I. Cheeses

Match each of the cheeses in List A with the appropriate description in List B. Each choice in List B may be used only once.

List A

_____ 1. Mozzarella

_____ 2. Cheddar

_____ 3. Parmigiano-Reggiano

_____ 4. Emmenthaler

_____ 5. Boursin

_____ 6. Stilton

_____ 7. Chèvre

_____ 8. Fontina

_____ 9. Feta

_____ 10. Havarti

List B

a. Britain's soft, blue-veined cow's milk cheese containing 45% fat.

b. A hard cow's milk cheese containing from 32% to 35% fat and produced exclusively near Parma, Italy.

c. A soft, creamy, goat's milk cheese with a short shelf life.

d. A pale yellow Danish cow's milk cheese with many small, irregular holes, often made with herbs and spices.

e. A fresh, firm, Italian cow's milk cheese very mild in flavour, and can become elastic when cooked.

f. A French, rindless, soft, triple-cream cow's milk cheese usually flavoured with garlic, herbs, or peppers.

g. A firm cow's milk cheese made primarily in the Northern United States and most of Canada with a minimum of 31% fat.

h. A cow's milk, semi-soft cheese from the Piedmont region of Italy, having a few small holes and 45% fat.

i. A fresh, Italian or Greek sheep and/or goat's milk cheese that is white and flaky, pickled, and stored in brine.

j. A firm Swiss, cow's milk cheese from Switzerland that is mellow, rich and nutty (45% fat) with natural large holes.

k. A sheep's milk cheese from central and southern Italy containing approximately 35% fat.

II. Cream:

Match each type of cream in List A with the appropriate fat content in List B. Each choice in List B may be used only once.

	List A		List B
_____ 1.	whipping cream	a.	no less than 18% milkfat
_____ 2.	table cream	b.	more than 10% but less than 18% milkfat
_____ 3.	half and half	c.	30%–35% milkfat
_____ 4.	partly skim milk	d.	7.5% milk fat
_____ 5.	evaporated milk	e.	1% to 3.2% milk fat
_____ 6.	water buffalo milk	f.	30% to 35% milk fat
_____ 7.	condensed milk	g.	More than 10% but less than 18% milk fat
_____ 8.	whole milk	h.	No less than 18% milk fat

F. True or False Questions

For each question below, circle either True or False to indicate the correct answer.

1. Shell colour has an effect on the grade of the egg, but not on flavour or nutrition.
   True   False

2. Egg whites solidify (coagulate) when cooked at temperatures between 62° and 65°C (144°F and 149°F).
   True   False

3. Eggs are a potentially hazardous food.
   True   False

4. Eggs should be stored at temperatures below 2°C (35°F) and at a relative humidity of 70–80%.
   True   False

5. All milk must be pasteurized before retail sale.
   True   False

6. To ensure maximum volume when preparing whipped egg whites, the whites should be thoroughly chilled prior to whipping.
   True   False

7. Both butter and margarine contain about 80% fat and 20% water.
   True   False

8. Yogurt is a good example of a health or diet food.
   True   False

9. Margarine is a dairy product that serves as a good substitute for butter.
   True   False

10. Aside from excess moisture, processed cheese foods are of equal quality to natural cheeses.
    True   False

11. Natural cheeses contain cholesterol.
    True   False

12. Egg substitutes can replace whole eggs in all applications.
    True   False

13. Egg products are subject to strict pasteurization standards.
    True   False

14. When whipping eggs, the colder they are, the better they foam.
    True   False

PART 3 COOKING

Chapter 9

Principles of Cooking

During the cooking process, heat energy is transferred to foods by means of conduction, convection or radiation. Understanding how cooking influences the molecular structure, appearance, aroma, flavour and texture of foods is important in order to perfect these techniques.

At the end of this chapter the student should be able to:

1. Explain how heat is transferred to foods through conduction, convection and radiation.
2. Recognize how heat affects foods.
3. Identify the procedures for using various cooking methods.

Key Terms

Conduction
Convection
Natural convection
Mechanical convection
Induction
Radiation cooking
Infrared cooking
Microwave cooking
Coagulation
Gelatinization
Caramelization

Maillard reactions
Evaporation
Melting
Cooking medium
Dry-heat cooking methods
Moist-heat cooking methods
Combination cooking methods
Steaming
Blanching

Recovery time
Standard breading procedure
Smoke point
Tempura
Basket method
Croquettes
Double-basket method
Fritters
Swimming method

Test Your Knowledge

The practice sets provided below have been designed to test your comprehension of the information found in this chapter. It is recommended that you read the chapter completely before attempting these questions.

A. Terminology

Fill in the blank spaces with the correct definition.

1. Poaching _____

2. Baking _____

3. Gelatinization _____

4. Radiation _____

5. Conduction _____

6. Blanching _____

7. Stewing _____

8. Pan-frying _____

9. Microwave cooking _____

10. Grilling _____

11. Steaming _____

12. Recovery time _____

13. Swimming method _____

14. Smoke point _____

15. Basket method _____

16. Hydrogenation _____

Fill in the blank spaces with the correct term.

17. _____ A method of cooking that usually applies to meats and poultry and is the process of surrounding a food with dry, heated air in a closed environment.

18. _____ A cooking method in which dry heat is transferred by means of conduction. The method is performed by cooking relatively small cuts of food at high temperatures in a small amount of fat or oil.

19. _____ A term associated with what happens when proteins are cooked by the application of heat. The proteins will lose moisture, shrink, and become firm.

20. _____ The transfer of heat through a fluid, which may be liquid or gas.

21. _____ The food is submerged in a liquid held at temperatures between 85°C (185°F) and 96°C (205°F) and cooked.

22. _____ A dry-heat cooking method that uses convection to transfer heat to food completely submerged in hot fat.

23. _____ A moist-heat cooking method using convection to transfer the energy from the liquid to the food. The large amount of liquid used to cook the food is brought to a rolling boil before the food product to be cooked is completely submerged.

24. _____ A combination cooking method usually performed on larger pieces of foods, especially meats, that need tenderizing by cooking for long periods of time at a relatively

low temperature. The liquid, which covers 1/3 to 1/2 of the product during cooking, is usually used to make the sauce that is served with the finished product.

25. _____ A dry-heat cooking method using radiant heat that is applied from above the food product being cooked. The food being cooked is usually placed on a metal grade and is subjected to temperatures as high as 1100°C (2000°F).

26. _____ A new form of electric cooking that works when a coil below the cook stove's surface generates a magnetic current that reacts very quickly with special cookware made of cast iron or magnetic stainless steel.

27. _____ The process of cooking sugars where through the application of dry heat they turn brown and change flavour.

28. _____ Cooking that occurs when an electric or ceramic element is heated to such a high temperature that it emits waves of radiant heat that cook the food.

29. _____ The process of browning non-sugar foods.

30. _____ A frying method used to prevent the floating of food product being cooked and therefore promote even cooking and browning.

31. Most foods to be deep-fried are first _____ or _____.

32. The most common fats used for deep-frying are _____ such as _____, _____, and _____.

33. _____ Specialized cooking method characterized by fresh ingredients combined in various dishes, vacuum packed in individual portions, cooked under vacuum and then chilled.

B. Fill in the Blanks

Fill in the spaces provided with the response that correctly completes information about each cooking method.

Cooking method		Medium	Equipment
ex:	Sautéing	fat	stove
1.	Stewing	_____	_____
2.	Deep-fat frying	_____	_____
3.	Broiling	_____	_____
4.	Poaching	_____	_____
5.	Grilling	_____	_____
6.	Simmering	_____	_____

7.   Baking   _____   _____

8.   Roasting   _____   _____

9.   Steaming   _____   _____

10.   Braising   _____   _____

C. Short Answer Questions

Provide a short response that correctly answers each of the questions below.

1.   List the four (4) major differences between braising and stewing

| *Braising* | *Stewing* |
| | |

a. _____   a. _____

b. _____   b. _____

c. _____   c. _____

d. _____   d. _____

2.   List two (2) recommendations on how to properly steam a food product.

a._____

b. _____

3.   In five (5) steps explain how to properly sauté a chicken breast.

a._____

b. _____

c._____

d. _____

e._____

4.   Describe the six (6) steps necessary for correct poaching of a food item.

a._____

b. _____

c._____

d. _____

e._____

f. _____

5.   What changes occur in food when it is heated?

_____

_____

_____

6.   What happens to protein when it's cooked?

_____

_____

_____

7.   Explain the term *gelatinization*. At what temperature does it happen?

_____

_____

_____

8.   List four (4) mediums used for cooking foods

a. _____

b. _____

c. _____

d. _____

9. Identify the elements that damage fryer fat and explain their effects on the fat.

   Element   *Effects*

   a. _____   _____

   b. _____   _____

   c. _____   _____

   d. _____   _____

   e. _____   _____

10. List two (2) reasons most fried foods are breaded or battered.

    a. _____

    b. _____

11. "The temperature of the fat is critical during frying." List two (2) reasons to support this statement.

    a. _____

    b. _____

12. List three (3) considerations when choosing fat for frying.

    a. _____

    b. _____

    c. _____

13. Explain the procedures to follow when handling cooked, large, thick items in the cook-chill system.

    _____

    _____

    _____

14. Explain the procedures to follow when reheating cook-chill products.

    _____

    _____

    _____

15. Explain the procedures to follow when handling cooked food in the cook-freeze system

_____

_____

_____

D. Multiple Choice

For each question below, choose the one response that correctly answers the question.

1. Which method refers to the transfer of heat through a fluid?
   a. convection
   b. radiation
   c. conduction
   d. induction

2. What cooking technique is an example of moist-cooking?
   a. grilling
   b. sautéing
   c. deep-fat frying
   d. steaming

3. The purpose for the shape of the wok used for stir-frying is that the rounded shape:
   a. makes it easier to pour liquids out of it.
   b. is designed to fit into the specially designed shape of the turbo gas burners.
   c. diffuses the heat and makes tossing and stirring easier.
   d. makes the cookware more durable.

4. Which of the following is an example of infrared cooking?
   a. broiling
   b. sautéing
   c. roasting
   d. baking

5. In pan-frying, how much fat or oil should be in the pan?
   a. just enough to coat the bottom of the pan
   b. 1 cup measure
   c. 1/2 to 2/3 way up on the product being cooked
   d. enough to completely cover the product

6. What cooking technique is defined as: "To briefly and partially cook a food in boiling water or hot liquid."
   a. boiling
   b. blanching
   c. frying
   d. simmering

7. Which of the following pieces of equipment cooks by radiation that penetrates the food to agitate water molecules and create energy?
   a. combi oven
   b. salamander
   c. infrared boiler
   d. microwave oven

8. Proteins coagulate at temperatures of:
   a. 50–65°C (122–149°F)
   b. 71–85°C (160–185°F)
   c. 85–95°C (185–203°F)
   e. 95–112°C (203–234°F)

9. Starches gelatinize at temperatures of:
   a. 40–50°C (104–122°F)
   b. 50–60°C (122°–140°F)
   c. 66–100°C (150–212°F)
   d. 85–120°C (185–248°F)

10. Most raw meat contains _____ water.
    a. 75%
    b. 85%
    c. 60%
    d. 40%

11. Stir-frying is a variation of:
    a. shallow frying
    b. deep frying
    c. pan-frying
    d. sautéing

12. As altitude increases, the boiling point decreases because of the drop in atmospheric pressure. By how many degrees does the boiling point decrease relative to the rise in altitude?
    a. 1°C (92°F) for every 305m (1000 feet)
    b. 2°C (3.6°F) for every 457m (1500 feet)
    c. 1°C (3.6°F) for every 152m (500 feet)
    d. 2°C (3.6°F) for every 305m (1000 feet)

13. Most foods are deep fried between:
    a. 140 and 170°C (284 and 338°F)
    b. 160 and 190°C (325 and 375°F)
    c. 170 and 200°C (338 and 392°F)
    d. 190 and 220°C (374 and 428°F)

14. What is one of the main disadvantage of sous-vide cooking?
    a. Products tend to be inconsistent.
    b. Products must be used right away.
    c. Cost of labour is high.
    d. Cost of required equipment is high.

15. In a sous-vide system, the food is:
    a. cooked on high heat first, then put under vacuum and chilled.
    b. cooked on low heat under vacuum then chilled.
    c. cooked on low heat, chilled, then put under vacuum for storage.
    d. cooked on high heat under vacuum, then frozen.

16. In a cook-chill system, if the internal temperature of food is allowed to reach 10°C (50°F), it should be:
    a. reprocessed immediately.
    b. cooled immediately in a blast chiller.
    c. heated at 74°C (165°F) for 2 minutes.
    d. destroyed.

17. Which of the following applies to a cook-chill system?
    a. foods must be cooled from 60°C to 20°C (140 °F to 68°F) within 2 hours or less.
    b. foods must be cooled from 60°C to 4°C (140 °F to 40°F) within 4 hours or less.
    c. foods must be cooled from 60°C to 4°C (140 °F to 40°F) within 2 hours or less.
    d. foods must be cooled from 60°C to 20°C (140 °F to 68°F) within 4 hours or less.

18. An essential benchmark in the cook-chill system is that the food should not stay in the danger zone for more than:
   a. 2 hours
   b. 4 hours
   c. 6 hours
   d. 8 hours

19. In a cook-chilled system, menu items cooked in trays should not exceed:
   a. 50 mm (2 in.)
   b. 100 mm (4 in.)
   c. 150 mm (6in.)
   d. 200 mm (8 in.)

20. Foods prepared in a cook-chilled system should be consumed within:
   a. 12 hours.
   b. 24 hours.
   c. 2 days.
   d. 5 days

21. In a cook-chilled system, if the food is allowed to reach internal temperatures of 5°C to 9°C (41°F to 48°F), it must be:
   a. destroyed.
   b. rethermalized within 12 hours.
   c. rethermalized immediately.
   d. blast frozen immediately for further use.

22. What is the shelf life of frozen foods prepared in a cook-freeze system?
   a. 4 weeks
   b. 6 weeks
   c. 8 weeks
   d. 10 weeks

E. Matching

I. Cooking Methods

Match each of the cooking methods in List A with the appropriate temperature in List B. Each choice in List B may be used only once.

	List A		List B
_____ 1.	boiling	a.	71°C to 82°C (160°F to 180°F)
_____ 2.	broiling	b.	85°C to 96°C (185°F to 205°F)
_____ 3.	simmering	c.	up to 1100°C (2000°F)
_____ 4.	poaching	d.	100°C (212°F) or higher (at sea level)
_____ 5.	steaming	e.	100°C (212°F) (at sea level)
_____ 6.	deep-fat frying	f.	95°C (200°F)
_____ 7.	sous-vide	g.	100°C to 104°C (212°F to 220°F)
		h.	160°C to 190°C (325°F to 375°F)

II. Effects of Heat on Foods:

Referring to the effects of heat on food, match the food categories in List A with the reactions in List B. Each choice in List B may be used only once.

	List A		List B
_____ 1.	starch	a.	caramelize
_____ 2.	water	b.	gelatinize
_____ 3.	fat	c.	melt
_____ 4.	protein	d.	evaporate
_____ 5.	sugar	e.	coagulate
		f.	permeate

F. True or False

For each question below, circle either True or False to indicate the correct answer.

1. The swimming method is best to use when large quantities of food need frying.
    True   False

2. Fryer fats are being reformulated to avoid hydrogenation, which increases trans-fats.
    True   False

3. Delicately flavoured foods should be fried separately from foods with strong flavours.
    True   False

4. Foods that are fried together can be a variety of sizes, as long as they brown evenly.
    True   False

5. Frying is a cooking application that utilizes dry heat.
    True   False

6. Vegetable oils are the most common type of fat used for deep-fat frying.
    True   False

7. Foods destined for sous-vide cooking must be of very high quality.
    True   False

8. Sous-vide cooking can be practised in any kitchen as long as a vacuum packaging machine is available.
    True   False

9. In a sous-vide system, the processed foods must be chilled rapidly and held at temperatures between 0°C and 3°C (32°F and 37°F).
    True   False

10. Foods processed in a sous-vide system must be consumed within a specific time.
    True   False

11. HACCP principles must be applied to both sous-vide and cook-chill systems.
    True   False

12. The main advantage of cook-chilled systems is increased productivity.
    True   False

13. Standardized recipes are not required in a cook-chill system, as strict safety standards are applied.
    True   False

14. Cook-chill systems are not common in large food service operations.
    True   False

Chapter 10

Stocks and Sauces

Basic stocks and sauces are the foundations upon which the creative chef can experiment and build. The importance of this chapter cannot be overemphasized as it explains the origins of sauces and how best to combine them with other flavours.

At the end of this chapter the student should be able to:

1. Prepare a variety of stocks.
2. Caramelize bones and mirepoix.
3. Deglaze a pan.
4. Reduce a stock to a glaze.
5. Cook a roux and incorporate it with a liquid.
6. Use a liaison.
7. Prepare a beurre blanc or beurre rouge.
8. Make a pan gravy and coulis.
9. Prepare salsa and relish.
10. Recognize and classify sauces.
11. Prepare a variety of classic and modern sauces.

Key Terms

White stock	Degrease	White roux	Tomato concassée
Brown stock	Deglaze	Blond roux	Hollandaise
Fish stock	Sweat	Brown roux	Emulsified
Fumet	Glaze	Slurry	Glaçage
Court bouillon	Basic sauces	Tempering	Compound butter
Vegetable stock	Derivative sauces	Reduction	Jus lié
Mirepoix	Coulis	Béchamel	Essence
Cartilage	Beurre blanc	Velouté	Tea
Connective tissue	Beurre rouge	Allemande	Nage
Collagen	Flavoured butters	Suprême	Chutney
Gelatin	Salsas	Espagnole	
Matignon	Relishes	Demi-glace	
	Pan gravy	Tomato sauce	

Test Your Knowledge

The practice sets provided on the following pages have been designed to test your comprehension of the information found in this chapter. It is recommended that you read the chapter completely before attempting these questions.

A. Terminology

Fill in the blank spaces with the correct term.

1. _____ Tissue found in the animal's body that supports muscles.

2. _____ A sauce made from a mixture of chunky vegetables and herbs, whose name is the Spanish word for sauce.

3. _____ The French term for "rewetting" a stock to reuse the bones.

4. _____ A combination of half brown sauce and half brown stock which is then reduced by half.

5. _____ A protein that is found in connective tissue and dissolves during the cooking process.

6. _____ A flavoured liquid, also known as a base.

7. _____ A sauce similar to demi-glace except that it is lighter and easier to make.

8. _____ Placing a stockpot in a sink of water to cool.

9. _____ Removing the fat from the top of a soup or stock.

10. _____ A thickened liquid used to complement and flavour foods.

11. _____ A mixture of onion, carrot, and celery used to enhance the flavour of stocks.

12. _____ A tough elastic tissue that helps give structure to an animal's body.

13. _____ A characteristic of stocks resulting from the dissolution of collagens.

14. _____ A characteristic of stocks achieved by removing impurities.

15. _____ Results from the use of appropriate herbs, spices, and mirepoix.

16. _____ Results from simmering bones and /or meat added with mirepoix, herbs and spices.

Fill in the blank spaces with the correct definition.

17. Court bouillon _____

18. Gelatin _____

19. Chutney _____

20. Refresh_____

21. Emulsification _____

22. Liaison _____

23. Deglaze _____

24. Coulis_____

25. Monter au beurre _____

26. Beurre manié _____

27. Roux _____

28. Sweat _____

29. Fumet_____

30. Collagen_____

B. Short Answer

I. General Questions
Provide a short response that correctly answers each of the questions below.

1. List the eight (8) principles of stock making.

   a. _____

   b. _____

   c. _____

   d. _____

   e. _____

   f. _____

   g. _____

   h. _____

2.   In the space below, list the essential ingredients and describe in a step-by-step manner the preparation of hollandaise sauce, using the classic method. Exact quantities are important for this exercise, and each step should be numbered for revision purposes.

Ingredients: *Procedure:*

_____

_____

_____

_____

_____

_____

_____

_____

3.   Give five (5) reasons why hollandaise sauce might separate.

a. _____

b. _____

c. _____

d. _____

e. _____

4.   List four (4) critical rules to observe for clear stock production.

a. _____

b. _____

c. _____

d. _____

5.   In general terms, what type of bones are best for the production of stocks?

_____

_____

6. List three (3) items that may cause discolouration or cloudiness or undesirable flavour in stocks.

   a. _____

   b. _____

   c. _____

7. Explain the difference between a broth and a stock.

   _____

   _____

   _____

   _____

   _____

8. List the basic procedures for blanching and refreshing bones for stock making.

   _____

   _____

   _____

   _____

   _____

9. List the basic procedures for browning bones for stock making.

   _____

   _____

   _____

   _____

   _____

10. List the basic procedures for reducing a stock to a glaze.

_____

_____

_____

_____

_____

11. Provide the reasons and the solutions related to the problems listed in the first column.

Problems	*Reasons*	*Solutions*
1. Cloudy		
2. Lack of flavour		
3. Lack of colour		
4. Lack of body		
5. Too salty		

12. List the basic procedures for making a roux.

_____

_____

_____

_____

_____

13. List the basic procedures for incorporating a liaison into a sauce or soup.

_____

_____

_____

_____

_____

14. List the basic procedures for making a beurre blanc.

_____

_____

_____

_____

15. List the basic procedures for making gravy.

_____

_____

_____

_____

16. List the basic procedures for making a coulis.

_____

_____

_____

_____

17.   List the basic procedures for making flavoured oils.

_____

_____

_____

_____

_____

II. Stock-Making Review

Stock-making is a fundamental skill. The procedure for making basic stocks should be second nature to all good chefs.

List the essential ingredients and describe in a step-by-step manner the cooking procedure for white stock, brown stock, and fish stock. Exact quantities are not important for this exercise, however, cooking times should be included and each step should be numbered for revision purposes.

1.   White Stock
      Ingredients: *Procedure:*

_____

_____

_____

_____

_____

_____

_____

_____

2.   Brown Stock
      Ingredients: *Procedure:*

      _____

      _____

      _____

      _____

      _____

      _____

      _____

      _____

3.   Fish Stock
      Ingredients: *Procedure:*

      _____

      _____

      _____

      _____

      _____

      _____

      _____

      _____

III. Sauce Review—Basic Sauces

This section reviews the makeup of the five basic sauces. In the spaces provided, fill in the name of the sauce, the thickener used, and the liquid that forms the base of the sauce. For the sauces that use a roux as a thickener, please specify the type of roux used.

	Basic Sauce	Thickener	Liquid
1.	_____	_____	_____
2.	_____	_____	_____
3.	_____	_____	_____
4.	_____	_____	_____
5.	_____	_____	_____

IV. Sauce Review—Derivative Sauces

For the following derivative sauces, identify the leading sauce that forms its base and list the main ingredients or garnishes that distinguish them from the basic sauce.

	Derivative Sauce	Ingredients Added	Basic Sauce
1.	Mornay	_____	_____
2.	Béarnaise	_____	_____
3.	Bercy	_____	_____
4.	Spanish	_____	_____
5.	Poulette	_____	_____
6.	Bordelaise	_____	_____
7.	Nantua	_____	_____
9.	Hungarian	_____	_____
10.	Aurora	_____	_____
11.	Chevreuil	_____	_____
12.	Milanaise	_____	_____

C. Multiple Choice

1. In stock-making, which ingredient will make a stock cloudy?
   a. protein
   b. sugar
   c. fibre
   d. fat

2. When making vegetable stock, starchy vegetables are not used, as they make the stocks:
   a. too thick
   b. gray
   c. too rich
   d. cloudy

3. A generally accepted proportion of bones and mirepoix for a given amount of water is:
   a. 30% bones, 5% mirepoix
   b. 10% mirepoix, 50% bones
   c. 50% bones, 10% mirepoix
   d. 40% bones, 20% mirepoix

4. When is the mirepoix best added to a meat stock?
   a. 2 to 3 hours before the end of cooking
   b. at the beginning of the cooking
   c. 1/2 hour before the end of cooking
   d. 15 minutes before the end of cooking

5. A stock made by adding water and mirepoix to a stock already drained is referred to as:
   a. weak stock
   b. remouillage
   c. estoufade
   d. light stock

6. Fish stocks or fumets are best cooked for:
   a. 10 to 20 minutes
   b. 2 to 3 hours
   c. 30 to 45 minutes
   d. 1 to 2 hours

7.   A stock made with water, mirepoix, wine or vinegar, herbs, and spices is referred to as a:
     a.   court bouillon
     b.   simple stock
     c.   lean stock
     d.   vegetarian stock

8.   The main ingredient in bases is:
     a.   flavouring
     b.   gelatine
     c.   sodium
     d.   meat

9.   Roux comes in what three flavours?
     a.   brown, white, blond
     b.   light, medium, heavy
     c.   thin, medium, thick
     d.   white, brown, dark

10. A thickening agent made with flour and water is referred to as:
     a.   white wash
     b.   slurry
     c.   white paste
     d.   beurre manié

11. When a sauce or soup is finished with a liaison, at what temperature would the yolk curdle?
     a.   55°C (131°F)
     b.   65°C (149°F)
     c.   75°C (167°F)
     d.   85°C (185°F)

12. Approximately how much flour is needed to thicken 4 litres of liquid to a medium consistency?
     a.   100 g
     b.   200 g
     c.   500 g
     d.   800 g

Match each of the basic sauces in List A with the appropriate derivative sauce in List B. Each choice in List B can only be used once.

		List A		List B
_____	1.	Espagnole	a.	Maltaise
_____	2.	Hollandaise	b.	Creole
_____	3.	Béchamel	c.	Chasseur
_____	4.	Velouté	d.	Cardinal
			e.	Soubise

E. True or False

For each question below, circle either True or False to indicate the correct answer.

1. More roux is needed for dark sauces than for light ones.
   True   False

2. To avoid lumps in sauces, add hot stock to hot roux.
   True   False

3. After adding a liaison to a sauce, simmer for 5 minutes.
   True   False

4. Nappé is a term used to describe the consistency of sauce.
   True   False

5. The combination of water and cornstarch is called slurry.
   True   False

6. A velouté is a roux-based sauce.
   True   False

7. The definition of tempering is the gradual lowering of the temperature of a hot liquid by adding a cold liquid.
   True   False

8. A reduction method is sometimes used to thicken sauces.
   True   False

9. Compound sauces come from derivative sauces.
   True   False

10. Fish stock needs to simmer for one hour in order to impart flavour.
    True   False

Chapter 11

Soups

Many of the skills learned in Chapter 10 about stocks and sauces are reused in this chapter, but some new techniques must also be acquired. Some of these specialized techniques must be learned and practised repeatedly in order to achieve successful results. The endless variation of soups that can result from experimentation with different raw materials makes this chapter especially interesting.

At the end of this chapter the student should be able to:

1. Prepare a variety of clear and thick soups, including broths and bouillons, consommés, cream soups, purée soups, bisques and chowders.

2. Garnish and serve soups appropriately.

Key Terms

Clear soups	Chowder
Broth	Cold soups
Bouillons	Garnishing
Consommé	Clearmeat
Thickened soups	Clarification
Cream soups	Onion brûlé
Purée soups	Raft
Bisques	

Test Your Knowledge

The practice sets provided below have been designed to test your comprehension of the information found in this chapter. It is recommended that you read the chapter completely before attempting these questions.

A. Terminology

Fill in the blank spaces with the correct term.

1. _____ The coagulated ingredients that rise to the surface during the clarification process of consommé.

2. _____ The burnt ingredient that is added to consommé to impart flavour and colour to the soup.

3. _____ The melting and clarification of fat.

4. _____ A shellfish soup that was traditionally thickened with rice.

5. _____ A cream soup finished with a liaison.

6. _____ Refers to a type of soup that does not demand very great precision in the apportionment of the vegetables of which it is composed.

7. _____ Another name for clearmeat.

8. _____ A subsidiary food used to add flavour or character to the main ingredient in a dish.

Fill in the blank spaces with the correct definition.

9. Clearmeat _____

10. Tomato concassé _____

11. Chowder _____

12. Broth _____

13. Consommé _____

14. Soubise _____

B. Short Answer

I. General Questions

Provide a short response that correctly answers each of the questions below.

1. List three (3) steps that can be taken to prevent cream from curdling when it is added to cream soups.

    a. _____

    b. _____

    c. _____

2. List the seven (7) common categories of soups and provide two examples of each type. Suggest an appropriate garnish for each soup.

Soup	Examples	Garnish
a. _____	_____	_____
	_____	_____
b. _____	_____	_____
	_____	_____

c. _____ _____ _____
                      _____ _____

d. _____ _____ _____
                      _____ _____

e. _____ _____ _____
                      _____ _____

f. _____ _____ _____
                      _____ _____

g. _____ _____ _____
                      _____ _____

3. Compare and contrast the following soups. Explain what they have in common, and what makes them different from one another.

a. Beef broth   Beef consommé

    _____

    _____

    _____

b. Cream of mushroom   Lentil soup

    _____

    _____

    _____

c. Gazpacho   Cold consommé

    _____

    _____

    _____

4. What differentiates a broth from a stock?

    _____

    _____

5. What differentiates a bisque from other soups?

_____

_____

6. What precautions would you take to maximize the shelf life and reduce the risk of spoilage?

_____

_____

7. List the basic procedures for making a shrimp bisque.

_____

_____

_____

_____

_____

8. List the basic procedures for making chowders.

_____

_____

_____

_____

_____

II. Consommé Preparation Review I

The procedure for making consommé is time tested. List the essential ingredients and describe in a step-by-step manner the cooking procedure for consommé. Exact quantities are important for this exercise. Each step should be numbered for revision purposes.

Ingredients: *Procedure:*

_____

_____

_____

_____

_____

_____

_____

_____

_____

III. Consommé Preparation Review II

Provide a reason for each of the following problems with consommé preparation.

1.   Cloudy _____

2.   Greasy _____

3.   Lacks flavour _____

4.   Lacks colour _____

IV. Cream Soup Preparation Review

Describe the procedure for making a cream soup using a fresh vegetable. List the essential ingredients, the quantities to be used, and suggest a garnish for the soup. Each step should be numbered for revision purposes.

Ingredients: *Procedure:*

_____

_____

_____

_____

_____

_____

_____

_____

C. Multiple Choice

1. Velouté soups are finished with:
    a. butter
    b. liaison
    c. sour cream
    d. milk

2. Bisques are thickened with:
    a. potatoes
    b. starch
    c. liaison
    d. rice

3. A chicken consommé Caroline is garnished with:
    a. royale, rice and chervil
    b. quenelles, morels and croûtons
    c. brunoise, crêpes and royale
    d. lentil royale, chervil and morels

4. A crème Dubarry is flavoured with:
    a. white onion
    b. cauliflower
    c. tomato and potato
    d. artichokes

5. A crème Solferino is flavoured with:
    a. whole onion
    b. cauliflower
    c. tomato and potato
    d. artichokes

6. A Potage Crécy is flavoured with:
    a. turnips potato and watercress
    b. green peas
    c. carrots
    d. tomato concassée

7. Potage St. Germain is flavoured with:
   a. turnips
   b. potato and watercress
   c. green peas
   d. carrots

8. A _____ chowder does not contain milk or cream.
   a. Manhattan
   b. New York
   c. Boston
   d. New England

9. What should the temperature of a cold soup be when ready for service?
   a. 0°C (32°F)
   b. 4°C (40°F)
   c. 8°C (46°F)
   d. 12°C (54°F)

10. What should the temperature of a hot soup be when ready for service?
   a. 60°C to 63°C (140°F to145°F)
   b. 80°C to 85°C (176°F to185°F)
   c. 90°C to 93°C (190°F to 200°F)
   d. 98°C to 102°C (208°F to 216°F)

D. True or False

For each question below, circle either True or False to indicate the correct answer.

1. A purée soup is usually coarser than a cream soup.
   True   False

2. A croûton is bread that has been sautéed until crisp.
   True   False

3. Consommé should be stirred after the clearmeat is added.
   True   False

4. A broth is a consommé with vegetables added to it.
   True   False

5. Cream soups are thickened with a purée of vegetables, which have been cooked in a stock.
   True   False

6.   French onion soup has only one garnish: the croûtons.
      True   False

7.   Cold soups should be served at room temperature.
      True   False

8.   A poorly clarified consommé should be discarded.
      True   False

9.   Cold soups need less seasoning than hot soups.
      True   False

10.   A roux can be used as a thickener for cold soups.
      True   False

Chapter 12

Principles of Meat Cookery

The meats offered on the menu are often the most popular items. It is therefore essential to have a full understanding of how heat transfer affects each cut of meat. This knowledge is the key to maximizing flavour for every cut of meat.

At the end of this chapter the student should be able to:

1. Identify the structure and composition of meats.
2. Explain meat inspection and grading practices.
3. Purchase meats appropriate for your needs.
4. Store meats properly.
5. Prepare meat for cooking.
6. Apply various cooking methods to meats
7. Carve a beef hip or leg of lamb.

Key Terms

Primal cuts	Fabricated cuts	Collagen	Mignonettes
Freezer burn	Barding	Jacquarding	Vacuum packaging
Carryover cooking	Cutlet	Émincé	
	Fricassee	Elastin	Subcutaneous fat
Chop	Marbling	Tumbling	Noisette
Subprimal cuts	Larding	Medallion	
Marinate	Escalope	Quality grades	
Fond	Blanquette	Needling	
Brown stew			

Test Your Knowledge

The practice sets provided below have been designed to test your comprehension of the information found in this chapter. It is recommended that you read the chapter completely before attempting these questions.

A. Terminology

Fill in the blank spaces with the correct term.

1. _____ The primary divisions of muscle, bone and connective tissue.

2. _____ The process of cutting cooked meat into individual portions.

3. _____ Otherwise known as silverskin, which will not break down during the cooking process.

4. _____ Streaks of fat which form in lean tissue.

5. _____ Covering the surface of meat with a thin layer of pork backfat.

6. _____ Another term for a medallion.

7. _____ The surface discolouration of foods that are directly exposed to below-freezing temperatures.

8. _____ The process of soaking meat in seasoned liquid to tenderize it.

9. _____ The word that is found on the round stamp of the Canada health inspection stamp.

10. _____ Inserting strips of fat into meat.

11. _____ A main component of connective tissue that breaks down during cooking.

12. _____ A veal classification term regulated only in Quebec.

13. _____ A type of cut referring to very small slices.

14. _____ A general term that refers to white or brown stews.

15. _____ A brown ragout made with lamb.

16. _____ A Hungarian stew thickened with onions, flavoured with paprika and garnished with potatoes.

17. _____ A North-African stew made with meat, poultry, fish or vegetables and spices and braised over a fire in a covered earthenware dish of the same name.

18. _____ A stew of Spanish origin in which meats are simmered with onions and spices in a savoury red chile sauce

19. _____ A stew in which the meat is first brown in hot fat

20. _____ A white ragout usually made from white meat and small game seared without browning and garnished with pearl onions and mushrooms

21. _____ A white stew in which the meat is first blanched, then added to a stock or sauce to complete the cooking process. It is then finished with a liaison.

Fill in the blank spaces with the correct definition.

22. Gelatin _____

23. Rigor mortis _____

24. Noisette _____

25. Vacuum packaging _____

26.　Butcher _____

27.　Subprimal cuts _____

28.　Dress _____

29.　Fabricate _____

30.　Subcutaneous fat _____

31.　Fabricated cuts _____

32.　Chop _____

33.　Fond _____

B. Fill in the Blank

Fill in the blank with the response that correctly completes the statement.

1.　Dry-heat cooking methods are best used for _____ cuts of meat.

2.　Once the meat is added to the sauce for stewing, the dish is cooked at a _____ temperature for a _____ time.

3.　Very rare meats should feel _____ and have a _____ colour; however, well-cooked meats should feel _____ and have a _____ colour.

4.　Sauté items are sometimes _____ before being placed in the pan.

5.　Some _____ cooking occurs when a roast item is removed from the oven. Allowing the meat to rest will help the meat to _____.

6.　When simmering smoked, cured meats, start them in _____ water.

7.　Boiling meats results in _____ and _____ products.

8.　Braised meats are best cooked in an oven set at ____˚C to ____˚C (____˚F to ____˚F).

C. Short Answer

I. General Questions

Provide a short response that correctly answers each of the questions below.

1.   List five (5) factors taken into account in the grading of meats.

   a. _____

   b. _____

   c. _____

   d. _____

   e. _____

2.   List the grades of beef available in Canada.

   a. _____

   b. _____

   c. _____

   d. _____

   e. _____

   f. _____

   g. _____

   h. _____

   i. _____

   j. _____

3.   List the respective internal temperature range for each degree of doneness:

   a. rare _____

   b. medium _____

   c. well-done _____

4. List, in proper sequence, the five (5) steps for the standard breading procedure.

a. _____

b. _____

c. _____

d. _____

e. _____

5. How can one keep the hands from becoming coated with breading during the standard breading procedure?

_____

_____

_____

6. List the basic procedures for pan-frying meats.

_____

_____

_____

_____

_____

7. List the basic procedures for sautéing meats.

_____

_____

_____

_____

_____

8.   List the basic procedures for making brown roux.

_____

_____

_____

_____

_____

9.   List the basic procedures for roasting meats.

_____

_____

_____

_____

_____

II. Cooking Methods

Briefly describe each of the following methods of cooking and provide an example of a cut of meat used in each method.

Cooking Method	Description	Example
1. Grilling		
2. Roasting		
3. Sautéing		
4. Pan-frying		
5. Simmering		
6. Braising		
7. Stewing		

D. Multiple Choice

1.   How much does a *Canada* yield class carcass of pork weigh?
   a. 70 kg (154 lbs)
   b. 60 kg (132 lbs)
   c. 50 kg (110 lbs)
   d. 40 kg (88 lb)

2. The process of piercing muscle tissue with needles to tenderize is referred to as:
   a. jacquarding
   b. needling
   c. tumbling
   d. swissing

3. The process of injecting a solution into the muscle to provide moisture and flavour is referred to as:
   a. jacquarding
   b. needling
   c. tumbling
   d. swissing

4. _____ is a process used to allow meat to absorb a prescribed percentage of its weight in liquid.
   a. jacquarding
   b. needling
   c. tumbling
   d. swissing

5. Which of the following is a ragout of ground or diced meat cooked with onions, chile peppers, cumin, and other spices?
   a. spaghetti sauce
   b. chili con carne
   c. paprikash
   d. beef stew

6. _____ is a stew thickened with onions, flavoured with paprika and garnished with potatoes.
   a. Southern beef stew
   b. Mexican chile
   c. Paprikash
   d. Navarin

7. Meats are generally simmered at temperatures of:
   a. 65–74°C (149–165°F)
   b. 82–93°C (180–200°F)
   c. 74–82°C (165–212°F)
   d. 93–100°C (199–212°F)

8. Large roasts, such as a 7.5 kg (16 lbs) prime rib, are best roasted at temperatures of:
   a. 175–190°C (350–375°F)
   b. 165–175°C (330–350°F)
   c. 135–165°C (275–330°F)
   d. 120–135°C (250–275°F)

9. Small roasts, such as rack of lamb or beef tenderloin, are best roasted at temperatures of:
   a. 175–190°C (350–375°F)
   b. 165–175°C (330–350°F)
   c. 135–165°C (275–330°F)
   d. 120–135°C (250–275°F)

10. Although the cooking time is dependent on the desired doneness and type and size of roast, a timing guideline commonly used is:
    a. 15 to 30 minutes per kg
    b. 25 to 35 minutes per kg
    c. 45 to 55 minutes per kg
    d. 30 to 50 minutes per kg

E. Matching

Match each of the stews in List A with the appropriate description in List B. Each choice in List B can only be used once.

	List A		List B
_____1.	Ragout	a.	A spicy ragout of ground or diced meat with vegetables, peppers, and sometimes beans.
_____2.	Goulash	b.	A white stew usually made with white meat and garnished with onions and mushrooms.
_____3.	Blanquette	c.	A brown ragout made with root vegetables and lamb.
_____4.	Fricassée	d.	A general term that refers to stews.
_____5.	Navarin	e.	A Hungarian beef stew made with onions and paprika and garnished with potatoes.
		f.	A white stew in which the meat is blanched and added to the sauce to finish the cooking process. This stew is finished with a liaison of cream and egg yolks.

F. True or False

For each question below, circle True or False to indicate the correct answer.

1. Fresh meats should be stored at 2–4°C (35–40°F).
    True   False

2. "Green meats" are meats that are allowed to turn mouldy.
    True   False

3. Braising and stewing are combination cooking methods.
    True   False

4. The Canada stamp on whole carcasses of meat does not ensure their quality or tenderness.
    True   False

5. Yield grades are used for beef, lamb, and pork.
    True   False

6. Wet aging occurs in a vacuum package.
    True   False

7. During dry aging, the meat may develop mould, which adds to the flavour of the meat.
    True   False

8. Under the correct conditions, commercially vacuum-packaged meat has a shelf life of 21 days.
    True   False

9. Most commercially frozen meats are frozen by blast freezing.
    True   False

Chapter 13

Beef

Beef is the most popular meat among North Americans. This chapter explains the different cuts of beef and their preparation for cooking.

At the end of this chapter the student should be able to:

1. Identify the primal, subprimal and fabricated cuts of beef.
2. Perform basic butchering procedures: cut stew, cut a strip loin, trim and cut a tenderloin and butterflying.
3. Apply the appropriate cooking methods for several common cuts of beef.

Key Terms

Square chuck	Flank
Short loin	Rib
Point brisket	Hip
Sirloin	Plate
Shank	Offal

Test Your Knowledge

The practice sets provided below have been designed to test your comprehension of the information found in this chapter. It is recommended that you read the chapter completely before attempting these questions.

A. Terminology

Fill in the blank spaces with the correct term.

1. _____ steaks, when compared to T-bone steaks, have a larger portion of tenderloin.

2. The _____ contains rib bones and cartilage and produces meaty ribs and _____ steak.

3. The primal _____ is the animal's shoulder and is made up of a portion of the backbone, five rib bones, and portions of the blade and arm bones.

4. _____ is the beef round with rump and shank partially removed; handle on

5. _____ is the hind leg of the animal which can weigh up to 90 kg (200 lbs).

6. _____ is the largest, thickest portion of the tenderloin.

7. The meat from the _____ is preferred to clarify and add flavour to consommés due to its high collagen content.

8. _____ are female cattle after the first calving.

9. _____ are male cattle usually not raised to be eaten.

10. _____ are male cattle castrated prior to maturity.

11. _____ an exclusive type of beef traditionally produced from the Wagyu cattle in Japan.

Fill in the blank spaces with the correct definition.

12. Heifer _____

13. Stag _____

14. Tenderloin _____

15. Offal _____

16. Flank _____

17. Short loin _____

18. Rib _____

19. Point brisket _____

B. Fill in the Blank

I. Primal Cuts of Beef

Identify the primal cuts of beef indicated in the following diagram and write their names in the spaces provided.

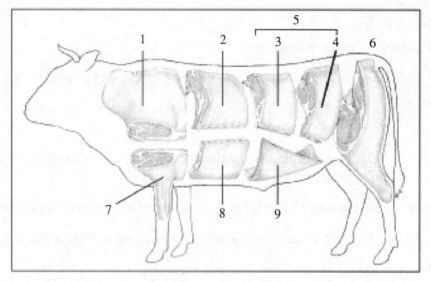

1.	_____	4.	_____	7.	_____
2.	_____	5.	_____	8.	_____
3.	_____	6.	_____	9.	_____

II. Cuts from the Round

Name the five (5) subprimal/fabricated cuts from the round and name the most appropriate cooking process or use for each cut.

	Subprimal/Fabricated Cut	*Cooking Method/Use*
1.	_____	_____
2.	_____	_____
3.	_____	_____
4.	_____	_____
5.	_____	_____

III. Cuts of Beef and Applied Cooking Methods

Name the cooking method applied to the main ingredient in each of the following beef dishes. Also, identify a subprimal and a primal cut of meat from which the main ingredient is taken.

	Name of Dish	*Cooking Method*	*Subprimal/Fabricated Cut*	*Primal Cut*
1.	Meat loaf	_____	_____	_____
2.	Beef Wellington	_____	_____	_____
3.	Chateaubriand	_____	_____	_____
4.	T-bone steak	_____	_____	_____
5.	Minute steak	_____	_____	_____
6.	London broil	_____	_____	_____
7.	Beef roulade	_____	_____	_____
8.	Prime rib	_____	_____	_____
9.	Corned beef	_____	_____	_____
10.	Beef fajitas	_____	_____	_____

117

C. Short Answer

1. List three (3) primal cuts from which grilling steak are most commonly cut.

    a. _____

    b. _____

    c. _____

2. List five (5) commonly used beef offals.

    a. _____

    b. _____

    c. _____

    d. _____

    e. _____

3. List five (5) subprimal or fabricated cuts from the chuck.

    a. _____

    b. _____

    c. _____

    d. _____

    e. _____

D. Multiple Choice

For each question below, choose the one response that correctly answers the question.

1. The outside round and the eye of the round together are called the:
    a. top round
    b. bottom round
    c. steamship round
    d. primal round

2. A carcass of beef weighs:
   a. between 270 and 428 kg (600–950 pounds)
   b. up to 450 kg (1000 pounds)
   c. from 225 to 360 kg (500–800 pounds)
   d. between 180 and 270 kg (400–600 pounds)

3. The three fabricated cuts from the tenderloin are:
   a. porterhouse steak, tournedos, and chateaubriand
   b. butt tenderloin, filet mignon, and tournedos
   c. chateaubriand, short loin, and loin eye
   d. tournedos, chateaubriand, and filet mignon

4. "Butterflying" is a preparation technique which:
   a. makes the cut of meat thinner
   b. makes the meat more tender
   c. improves the flavour of the meat
   d. improves the appearance of the meat

5. How many ribs does the chuck contain?
   a. 3
   b. 4
   c. 5
   d. 6

6. The prime rib contains _____ ribs.
   a. 5
   b. 6
   c. 7
   d. 8

7. Feather bones are found in the _____ primal.
   a. brisket
   b. rib
   c. plate
   d. short loin

8. The skirt steak is cut from the _____ primal.
    a. hip
    b. flank
    c. short loin
    d. plate

9. Club steaks are located at the _____ of the short loin.
    a. sirloin end
    b. centre
    c. rib end
    d. none of the above

10. The outside round and eye of round attached together become the:
    a. bottom round
    b. top round
    c. rump
    d. ponderosa hip

11. The ball tip is a cut from the _____ primal.
    a. knuckle
    b. short loin
    c. bottom round
    d. sirloin

12. The pin bone is found in the _____ primal.
    a. sirloin
    b. flank
    c. short hip
    d. short loin

13. The beef round, rump, and shank partially removed produce the:
    a. long hip
    b. short hip
    c. Ponderosa hip
    d. steamship hip

14. A boneless club steak is the same as
    a. ball tip steak
    b. New York steak
    c. sirloin steak
    d. rib steak

15. What is the maximum fat percentage in regular ground beef?
    a. 15%
    b. 20%
    c. 25%
    d. 30%

16. What is the maximum fat percentage in lean ground beef?
    a. 10%
    b. 12%
    c. 15%
    d. 17%

17. What is the maximum fat percentage in extra lean ground beef?
    a. 3%
    b. 5%
    c. 10%
    d. 12%

E. Matching

1. Match each of the primal cuts in List A with the appropriate description in List B. Each choice in List B can only be used once.

	List A		*List B*
____1.	Rib	a.	Produces the boneless strip loin, which can be roasted whole or cut into steaks.
____2.	Square chuck	b.	This cut is located in the hindquarter between the short loin and the round.
____3.	Short loin	c.	The eye of this cut is well exercised, quite tender, and contains large quantities of marbling. It is suitable for roasting.
____4.	Sirloin	d.	The animal constantly uses the muscle in this primal cut; therefore it is tough, contains high levels of connective tissue, and is very flavourful.
		e.	This primal cut produces the hanging tenderloin, which is very tender and can be cooked by any method.

2. Match each of the cuts in List A with the appropriate primal or secondary cut in List B. Each choice in List B can be used more than once.

List A	*List B*
___ a. Pastrami	Flank
___ b. Ball tip	Chuck
___ c. Club steak	Brisket
___ d. Tri-tip	Loin
___ e. Flat iron	Plate
___ f. Knuckle	Tenderloin
___ g. London broil	Sirloin
___ h. Skirt steak	Hip
___ i. Chateaubriand	Rib
___ j. Tournedos	
___ k. Vein steak	

F. True or False

For each question below, circle either True or False to indicate the correct answer.

1. The butt tenderloin is part of the short loin.
    True   False

2. The meat from the chuck is less flavourful than meat from the tenderloin.
    True   False

3. A porterhouse steak is a fabricated cut from the tenderloin.
    True   False

4. Prime rib of beef refers to the quality Canada grade.
    True   False

5. The subprimal and fabricated cuts from the short loin are the most tender and expensive cuts of beef.
    True   False

6. The subprimals and fabricated cuts from the sirloin are not as tender as those from the strip loin.
    True   False

7. The short loin can be cut across to produce porterhouse, T-bone, and club steaks.
    True   False

8. Pastrami is made from the meat in the short plate.
    True   False

Chapter 14

Veal

Veal is a most delicately flavoured meat and requires special care during cooking. Knowledge of the different muscles in this young animal is essential.

At the end of this chapter the student should be able to:

1. Identify the primal, subprimal and fabricated cuts of veal.
2. Perform basic butchering procedures: boning a leg of veal, cutting and pounding cutlets, cutting éminé, boning a veal loin, tying meats, cleaning and pressing sweetbreads, cleaning calves' liver and cleaning veal kidneys.
3. Apply the appropriate cooking methods to several common cuts of veal.

Key Terms

Front/Shoulder	Loin
Foreshank	Leg
Breast	Sweetbreads
Whole loin	Calves' liver
Rib	Kidneys

Test Your Knowledge

The practice sets provided below have been designed to test your comprehension of the information found in this chapter. It is recommended that you read the chapter completely before attempting these questions.

A. Terminology

Fill in the blank spaces with the correct term.

1. _____ A type of veal fed only nutrient-rich liquids

2. _____ The part of the pelvic bone in the leg primal.

3. _____ The trimmed rib and loin sections in one piece.

4. _____ This primal cut is located behind the primal rib and consists of the loin eye muscle on top of the rib bones and the tenderloin under them.

5. _____ This cut is high in cartilage, fat, and connective tissue and therefore makes a very flavourful stew.

6. _____ The meat of calves under the age of nine months.

7. _____ The primal cut that is made up of four rib bones and portions of the backbone, blade, and arms.

Fill in the blank spaces with the correct definition.

8. Sweetbreads _____

9. Foreshank _____

10. Hotel rack _____

11. Calf _____

B. Fill in the Blank

I. Common Cuts of Veal

Identify the common cuts of veal indicated in the following diagram and write their names in the spaces provided.

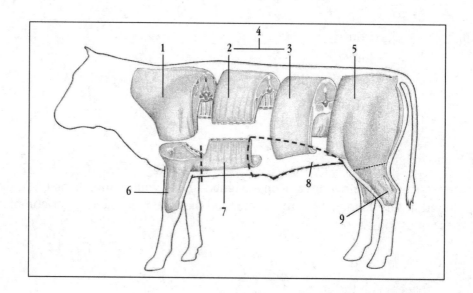

1. _____   6. _____

2. _____   7. _____

3. _____   8. _____

4. _____   9. _____

5. _____

II. Cuts of Veal and Applied Cooking Methods

Name the cooking method applied to the main ingredient in each of the following dishes. Also, identify a subprimal and a primal cut of meat from which the main ingredient is taken.

Name of Dish	*Cooking Method*	*Subprimal/Fabricated Cut*	*Primal Cut*
1. Osso buco	_____	_____	_____
2. Veal cutlets	_____	_____	_____
3. Veal fricassée	_____	_____	_____
4. Veal marsala	_____	_____	_____
5. Veal scallopini	_____	_____	_____
6. Veal medallions with green peppercorn sauce	_____	_____	_____
7. Veal tenderloin with garlic and herbs	_____	_____	_____
8. Stuffed veal breast	_____	_____	_____
9. Stuffed veal scallops	_____	_____	_____
10. Blanquette of veal	_____	_____	_____
11. Veal pojarski	_____	_____	_____
12. Kidney pie	_____	_____	_____

C. Short Answer

Provide a short response that correctly answers each of the questions below.

1. Briefly describe the eight (8) basic steps to be followed when boning a leg of veal, beginning with:

   a. Remove the shank._____

   b. _____

   c. _____

   d. _____

   e. _____

f. _____

g. _____

h. _____

2. Name the six (6) muscles in the leg of veal.

    a. _____

    b. _____

    c. _____

    d. _____

    e. _____

    f. _____

3. Name the three (3) subprimal cuts from the rib and three (3) from the loin and provide a menu example of each cut.

    Primal Cut   *Subprimal/Fabricated Cut*   *Menu Example*

    a.   Rib   _____   _____

    b.   Rib   _____   _____

    c.   Rib   _____   _____

    a.   Loin   _____   _____

    b.   Loin   _____   _____

    c.   Loin   _____   _____

4. Compare and contrast formula-fed veal with free-range veal. Discuss the advantages and disadvantages of each.

    _____

    _____

    _____

    _____

5.   Describe the foresaddle.

_____

_____

_____

_____

6.   Describe the hindsaddle.

_____

_____

_____

_____

7.   What are sweetbreads? Explain.

_____

_____

_____

_____

8.   List the basic procedures for cleaning and pressing veal sweetbreads.

_____

_____

_____

_____

9.   List the basic procedures for cleaning veal liver.

_____

_____

_____

_____

10. List the basic procedures for cleaning veal kidneys

_____

_____

_____

_____

D. Multiple Choice

1. A graded veal carcass weighs between:
   a. 50 and 100 kg (110 and 220 lbs)
   b. 60 and 120 kg (132 and 365 lbs)
   c. 80 and 160 kg (176 and 353 lbs)
   d. 100 and 190 kg (220 and 419 lbs)

2. A side of veal is separated in _____ primals.
   a. 4
   b. 5
   c. 6
   d. 9

3. The shoulder contains _____ ribs.
   a. 6
   b. 5
   c. 4
   d. 3

4. The veal rack includes _____ ribs.
   a. 6
   b. 7
   c. 8
   d. 9

5. Veal kidneys are best prepared with _____ cooking methods.
   a. braising
   b. steaming
   c. moist heat
   d. dry heat

6. When separated in primal cuts, the veal sirloin is:
   a. attached to the leg
   b. attached to the loin
   c. one of the primal cuts
   d. nonexistent

E. Matching

Match the primal cuts in List A with the appropriate definitions in List B. Each choice in List B can only be used once.

List A	List B
_____1. Leg	a. A cut of veal similar to the chuck in beef.
_____2. Shoulder	b. A primal cut of veal that is located just below the shoulder and rib section in the front of the carcass.
_____3. Foreshank and breast	c. The primal cut that produces the short tenderloin.
_____4. Loin	d. The bones in this cut are still soft, due to the immaturity of the animal.
_____5. Rib	e. The primal cut that yields the most tender meat.
	f. Made up of portions of the backbone, tail bone, hip bone, aitch bone, round bone, and shank.

F. True or False

For each question below, circle either True or False to indicate the correct answer.

1. Veal cutlets are taken from large pieces of veal and are cut on the bias, across the grain of the meat.
   True   False

2. Veal flesh begins to change colour when the animal consumes iron in its food.
   True   False

3. Sweetbreads are pressed to remove the impurities.
   True   False

4. Veal émincé are cut with the grain, from small pieces of meat.
   True   False

5. Veal cutlets are pounded in order to make them more tender.
   True   False

6. Sweetbreads become larger as the animal ages.
   True   False

7. Veal liver has a more delicate flavour than beef liver.
   True   False

8. The hindshank and foreshank of veal are prepared and cooked in the same manner.
   True   False

9. Veal is leaner than many cuts of poultry.
   True   False

10. Veal liver is often braised with onions.
    True   False

Chapter 15

Lamb

Lamb is a versatile meat that can be cooked by almost any method. This chapter outlines the various methods of preparing lamb and its accompanying sauces.

At the end of this chapter the student should be able to:

1. Identify the primal, subprimal and fabricated cuts of lamb.
2. Perform basic butchering procedures: frenching a rack of lamb, trimming and boning a lamb leg, boning a lamb loin and cutting lamb noisettes.
3. Apply the appropriate cooking methods for several common cuts of lamb.

Key Terms

Front/shoulder	Frenched rack	Hindsaddle
Flank	Loin	Saddle
Whole loin	Leg	Noisette
Rack	Foresaddle	

Test Your Knowledge

The practice sets provided below have been designed to test your comprehension of the information found in this chapter. It is recommended that you read the chapter completely before attempting these questions.

A. Terminology

Fill in the blank spaces with the correct definition.

1. Spring lamb _____

2. Blade bone _____

3. Rack _____

4. Mutton _____

Fill in the blank spaces with the correct term.

5. _____ The meat of sheep slaughtered under the age of one year.

6. _____ A method of trimming racks or chops in which the excess fat is removed and the rib bones are cleaned.

7. _____ The two loin and two racks in one piece.

8. _____ The anterior portion of the carcass severed from the rest between the 12th and 13th rib.

131

9. _____ The posterior portion of the carcass including the double loin, double leg and the kidneys.

B. Fill in the Blank

I. Primal Cuts of Lamb

Identify the primal cuts of lamb indicated in the following diagram and write their names in the spaces provided below.

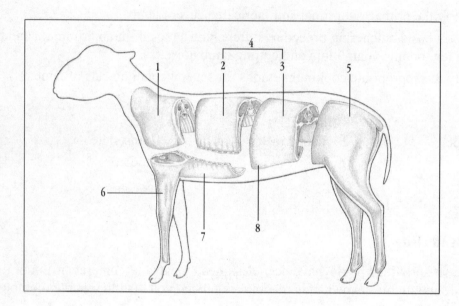

1. _____

2. _____

3. _____

4. _____

5. _____

6. _____

7. _____

8. _____

II. Subprimal or Fabricated Cuts

For each primal cut listed, name the subprimal cuts and the appropriate cooking method for each of these cuts.

	Primal Cut		*Subprimal/Fabricated Cut*	*Cooking Methods*
1.	Front/Shoulder	a.	_____	_____
		b.	_____	_____
		c.	_____	_____
2.	Breast		_____	_____
3.	Hotel Rack	a.	_____	_____
		b.	_____	_____
4.	Loin	a.	_____	_____
		b.	_____	_____
5.	Leg	a.	_____	_____
		b.	_____	_____

III. Cuts of Lamb and Applied Cooking Methods

Name the cooking method applied to the main ingredient in each of the following lamb dishes. Also, identify a subprimal and a primal cut of meat from which the main ingredient is taken.

	Name of Dish	Cooking Method	Subprimal/ Fabricated Cut	Primal Cut
1.	Shish kebabs	_____	_____	_____
2.	Lamb in coconut curry	_____	_____	_____
3.	Noisettes of lamb with garlic sauce	_____	_____	_____
4.	Lamb Navarin	_____	_____	_____
5.	Rack of lamb with mint and celeriac sauce	_____	_____	_____

C. Short Answer

Provide a short response that correctly answers the questions below.

1. Briefly describe the six (6) basic steps to be followed when "frenching" a rack of lamb.

    a. _____

    b. _____

    c. _____

    d. _____

    e. _____

    f. _____

2. Briefly describe the four (4) basic steps to be followed when trimming a leg of lamb for roasting/grilling.

    a. _____

    b. _____

    c. _____

    d. _____

3. Briefly describe the eight (8) basic steps to be followed when preparing a loin of lamb for roasting.

    a. _____

    b. _____

    c. _____

    d. _____

    e. _____

    f. _____

    g. _____

    h. _____

D. Multiple Choice

1. The shoulder primal includes _____ ribs.
   a. 3
   b. 4
   c. 5
   d. 6

2. The flank is often:
   a. grilled
   b. braised
   c. ground
   d. stuffed

3. The lamb rack includes _____ ribs.
   a. 5
   b. 6
   c. 7
   d. 8

4. The lamb loin includes _____ rib(s).
   a. 0
   b. 1
   c. 2
   d. 3

E. True or False

For each question below, circle either True or False to indicate the correct answer.

1. The lamb carcass is classified into two parts—the hindquarter and the forequarter.
   True   False

2. The term "spring lamb" applies to animals that are born between February and May.
   True   False

3. The primal cuts of both veal and lamb are broken down into bilateral halves.
   True   False

4. The primal leg of lamb is rarely left whole.
   True   False

5. The leg of lamb can be broken down to produce steaks.
   True   False

6. The chine bone runs through the loin of lamb only.
    True   False

7. A noisette of lamb is a boneless cut from the loin.
    True   False

8. The lamb flank is often marketed as flank steak.
    True   False

Chapter 16

Pork

Pork has taken on a new popularity in recent times in North America. This chapter describes the many different preparations for this versatile, flavoursome meat.

At the end of this chapter the student should be able to:

1. Identify the primal, subprimal and fabricated cuts of pork.
2. Perform basic meat-cutting procedures: boning a pork loin, tying a pork roast, cutting a chop from a loin, cutting a pocket in a pork chop and trimming a pork tenderloin.
3. Apply the appropriate cooking methods for several common cuts of pork.

Key Terms

Pork shoulder picnic	Fresh leg	Pork rib chops
Pork shoulder blade	Pork side ribs	
Belly	Pork tenderloin	
Loin	Pork backribs	

Test Your Knowledge

The practice sets provided below have been designed to test your comprehension of the information found in this chapter. It is recommended that you read the chapter completely before attempting these questions.

A. Terminology

Fill in the spaces with the correct definition.

1. Belly _____

2. Pork _____

3. Ham _____

4. Backribs _____

Fill in the spaces with the correct term.

5. _____ The ribs that are taken from the belly.

6. _____ Another term for the primal shoulder, which contains the arm and shank bones and has a relatively high ratio of bone to lean meat.

7. _____ The square cut located just above the primal shoulder also known as a cottage ham.

8. _____ Cured and smoked boneless pork loin.

137

9. _____ Trimmed rib bones from the loin.

10. _____ A small, very young whole pig.

B. Fill in the Blank

I. Primal Cuts of Pork

Identify the primal cuts of pork indicated in the following diagram and write their names in the spaces provided below.

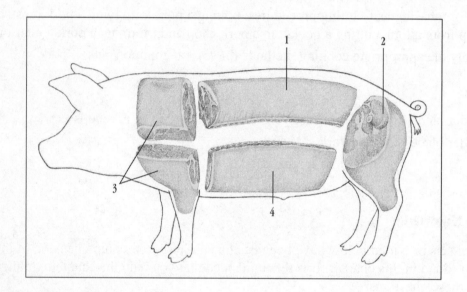

1. _____

2. _____

3. _____

4. _____

II. Subprimal or Fabricated Cuts

For each primal cut listed above, name the subprimal cuts and an appropriate cooking method. Indicate with an **X** in the appropriate column(s) whether these cuts are usually cured and smoked or used fresh (or both).

Primal Cut	Subprimal/ Fabricated Cut	Cooking Methods	Cured and Smoked	Fresh
1. Shoulder	_____	_____	____	____
	_____	_____	____	____

138

2. Belly   _____   _____   _____   _____

            _____   _____   _____   _____

3. Loin   _____   _____   _____   _____

            _____   _____   _____   _____

            _____   _____   _____   _____

            _____   _____   _____   _____

4. Leg   _____   _____   _____   _____

III. Cuts of Pork and Applied Cooking Methods

Name the cooking method applied to the main ingredient in each of the following recipes. Also identify a subprimal and a primal cut of meat from which the main ingredient is taken.

Name of Dish	Cooking Method	Subprimal/ Fabricated Cut	Primal Cut
1. Stuffed pork chops	_____	_____	_____
2. Smoked loin of pork, hazelnut and syrup crust, apple cider sauce	_____	_____	_____
3. Breakfast bacon	_____	_____	_____
4. Cassoulet	_____	_____	_____
5. Barbecue ribs	_____	_____	_____
6. Chinese barbecued pork	_____	_____	_____
7. Pork with apricots and prunes	_____	_____	_____
8. Mie Goreng	_____	_____	_____

C. Short Answer

Provide a short response that correctly answers the questions below.

1. Briefly describe the three (3) basic steps to be followed when boning a pork loin.

   a. _____

   b. _____

   c. _____

2. Name six (6) fabricated cuts that are most often smoked and cured.

   a. _____

   b. _____

   c. _____

   d. _____

   e. _____

   f. _____

D. Multiple Choice

1. The pork foreshank is called the:
   a. thigh
   b. feet
   c. hock
   d. leg

2. The pork shoulder contains _____ ribs.
   a. 2
   b. 3
   c. 4
   d. 5

3. In pork, the hip bone is located in the _____ primal.
   a. leg
   b. sirloin
   c. loin
   d. long hip

4. The pork loin includes a portion of the:
   a. cervical vertebrae
   b. arm bone
   c. breast bone
   d. blade bone

E. Matching

Match the primal cuts in List A with the appropriate definitions in List B. Each choice in List B can only be used once.

List A	List B
_____1. Shoulder blade	a. A primal cut that is very fatty with strips of lean meat.
_____2. Picnic shoulder	b. The primal cut from which the most tender portion of pork is taken.
_____3. Belly	c. A primal cut that contains large muscles and relatively small amounts of connective tissue. It may be smoked and cured or cooked fresh.
_____4. Loin	d. A primal cut with a good percentage of fat to lean meat—ideal when a solid piece of pork is required for a recipe.
_____5. Fresh ham	e. A single, very tender eye muscle that can be braised/roasted/sautéed.
	f. One of the toughest cuts of pork. It has a relatively high ratio of bone to lean meat, is relatively inexpensive and widely available.

F. True or False

For each question below, circle either True or False to indicate the correct answer.

1. The shoulder blade is located in the hindquarter.
   True   False

2. Pork is unique because the ribs and loin are considered one primal cut.
   True   False

3. Cooking pork to well done is not recommended in Canada.
   True   False

4. The foreshank is also known as the ham hock.
   True   False

5. Centre-cut pork chops are chops that are split open to form a pocket.
   True   False

6. The belly is used to make Canadian bacon.
   True   False

7. Backfat is the layer of fat between the skin and the lean muscle of the pork loin.
   True   False

8. The two primal cuts that produce ribs are the loin and the belly.
   True   False

9. Hogs are bred to produce short loins.
   True   False

10. Picnic ham is made from the hog's hind leg.
    True   False

11 The average weight of a carcass of pork is 55 to 95 kg (129 to 210 lb).
   True   False

12. The shoulder blade primal is tough and contains a higher proportion of fat to lean.
    True   False

13. In Canada, trichinosis from domestic pork has virtually been eradicated.
    True   False

14. The pork loin primal contains a portion of the sirloin.
    True   False

Chapter 17

Poultry

Poultry is perhaps the most versatile and least expensive main dish food. This chapter discusses the many different types of poultry, the safety precautions to be taken so that food-borne illness may be avoided, and the cooking methods applied to poultry.

At the end of this chapter the student should be able to:

1. Recognize the structure and composition of poultry.
2. Identify various kinds and classes of poultry.
3. Explain poultry inspection and grading practices.
4. Purchase poultry appropriate for your needs.
5. Store poultry properly.
6. Prepare poultry for cooking.
7. Apply various cooking methods to poultry.
8. Carve a turkey, capon, or other large bird, or a chicken or other small bird.

Key Terms

Kinds of birds	Duck	Foie gras
Classes of poultry	Duckling	Ratites
Game hen	Goose	Frogs
Broiler/fryer	Guinea	Inspection
Roaster	Pigeon	Grading
Capon	Turkey	Truss
Fowl	Giblets	Dressing

Test Your Knowledge

The practice sets provided below have been designed to test your comprehension of the information found in this chapter. It is recommended that you read the chapter completely before attempting these questions.

A. Terminology

Fill in the spaces with the correct definition.

1. Giblets _____

2. Trussing _____

3. Capon _____

4. Suprême _____

5. Kinds _____

6. Classes _____

7. Poulet _____

8. Duckling _____

9. Guinea _____

Fill in the spaces with the correct term.

10. _____ The French term for the degree of doneness, i.e., when the juices show traces of pink.

11. _____ The young or immature progeny of Cornish chickens or of a Cornish chicken and a White Rock chicken.

12. _____ The enlarged liver of a duck or goose.

B. Fill in the Blank

Fill in the blank provided with the response that correctly completes the statement.

1. The colour difference between the legs and wings of chicken and turkey is due to a higher concentration of the _____ called _____ in the tissue.

2. The recommended internal temperature of fully cooked poultry is _____.

3. The most commonly used duck in food service operations is a _____. Its meat is different from chicken in two ways: the flesh is _____ and has large amounts of _____ and _____.

4. Chicken is often marinated in a mixture of _____
   _____.
   A common example of a chicken marinade is _____ sauce.

C. Short Answer

Provide a short response that correctly answers each of the questions below.

1. List five (5) important guidelines for stuffing poultry.

   a. _____

   b. _____

   c. _____

   d. _____

   e. _____

Name one (1) similarity and one (1) major difference between poultry and red meats.

Similarity: _____

Difference: _____

3. Poultry is a highly perishable product and improper storage can lead to food poisoning. Discuss the guidelines for storing poultry products under the following headings. *Include *exact* temperatures and times in this answer.

Storage under refrigeration: _____

_____

Freezing: _____

_____

Thawing: _____

_____

Reheating: _____

_____

4. List five (5) differences between the rearing and sale of free-range chicken compared to traditionally reared chicken.

a. _____

b. _____

c. _____

d. _____

e. _____

5. What are the nine (9) categories of poultry?

a. _____

b. _____

c. _____

d. _____

e. _____

f. _____

g. _____

h. _____

i. _____

6. For each of the following cooking methods, give a recipe example and accompaniment for the poultry item.

Cooking Method	*Recipe Example*	*Accompaniment*
Sauté	_____	_____
Pan-fry	_____	_____
Simmer/Poach	_____	_____
Braise/Stew	_____	_____

7. Describe five (5) ways to prevent cross-contamination when handling poultry.

a. _____

b. _____

c. _____

d. _____

e. _____

8. Describe the six (6) steps for portioning poultry into 8 pieces.

a. _____

b. _____

c. _____

d. _____

e. _____

f. _____

9. Describe the poultry kind "ratites." List some examples.

_____

_____

_____

10. Describe the meat from ratites.

_____

_____

11. List two (2) classes of ducks, two (2) classes of pigeons and two (2) classes of turkeys. Indicate the approximate age and range of size.

_____

_____

_____

_____

_____

_____

12. List the basic procedures for boning a chicken leg.

_____

_____

_____

_____

13. List the basic procedures for broiling or grilling poultry.

_____

_____

_____

_____

14. List the basic procedures for trussing poultry.

_____

_____

_____

_____

15. List the basic procedures for roasting poultry.

_____

_____

_____

_____

16. List three (3) reasons why it is not recommended to stuff larger birds for cooking.

a. _____

b. _____

c. _____

17. List the basic procedures for sautéing poultry.

_____

_____

_____

_____

18. List the basic procedures for making a sauce in a sauté pan.

_____

_____

_____

_____

19. List the basic procedures for pan-frying poultry.

_____

_____

_____

_____

20. List the basic procedures for poaching poultry.

_____

_____

_____

_____

21. List the basic procedures for stewing and poêléing poultry.

_____

_____

_____

_____

D. Multiple Choice

For each question below, choose one response that correctly answers the question.

1. Poultry should be refrigerated at:
   a. −1 to 2°C (30 to 35°F)
   b. 1 to 3°C (33 to 36°F)
   c. 0 to 2°C (32 to 35°F)
   d. −1 to 3°C (30 to 38°F)

2. Which of the following groups do not fall into the "poultry" category?
   a. chicken, duck, pigeon
   b. duck, pheasant, goose
   c. pigeon, guineas, chicken
   d. none of the above

3. The poultry that is sold in wholesale or retail outlets must:
   a. be subject to health inspection (fit for human consumption)
   b. be subjected to an air-dry chilling system
   c. be headless
   d. be fresh-frozen

4. Most whole poultry sold wholesale or retail is:
   a. grade A or U
   b. grade A, B or U
   c. grade A
   d. grade A, B, C or U

5. The tenderness of poultry is usually indicated by its:
   a. size
   b. grade
   c. class
   d. both size and grade

6. A frenched breast of chicken is also known as a:
   a. supreme
   b. boneless breast
   c. hotel breast
   d. fancy breast

7. The maximum weight of a broiler/fryer is:
   a. 1.5 kg
   b. 2 kg
   c. 2.5 kg
   d. 1 kg

8. Roasters weigh
   a. 1.6 kg (3.5 lb) and over
   b. 1.5 to 2.5 kg (3.3 to 5.5 lbs)
   c. 2 kg (4 lbs) and over
   d. 1.2 to 2 kg (2.6 to 4 lbs)

9. A chicken that weighs 1.2 kg and has a firm breastbone is probably a:
   a. Cornish game hen
   b. capon
   c. broiler/fryer
   d. fowl

'0. Livers, gizzards, hearts, and necks are commonly referred to as:

a. inners

b. offal

c. giblets

d. guts

11. Most ratites are slaughtered at _____ months of age.

a. 4–7

b. 9–12

c. 10–13

d. 14–16

12. The thigh from ratites is marketed as the:

a. leg

b. fan

c. round

d. oyster

13. For best results poultry should be poached at a temperature of:

a. 75–80°C (165–175°F)

b. 60–71°C (140–160°F)

c. 82–93°C (180–200°F)

d. 90–100°C (194– 212°F)

E. Matching

Match each of the terms in List A with the appropriate letter definition in List B. Each choice in List B can only be used once.

	List A		List B
_____1.	Hen/stewing	a.	Young tender meat, smooth skin, breastbone less flexible than a broiler's (3–5 months).
_____2.	Broiler/fryer	b.	A duck breast
_____3.	Roaster	c.	Young immature progeny of Cornish chicken, very flavourful (5–6 weeks).
_____4.	Capon	d.	A domesticated musk duck with a rich flavour and tender texture
_____5.	Game hen	e.	Young with soft, smooth skin, lean with flexible breastbone (6–8 weeks).
_____6.	Magret	f.	Mature female, less tender meat, nonflexible breastbone (over 10 months).

_____ 7.   Muscovy

g.   Rich, tender dark meat with large amounts of fat, soft windpipe (6 months or less).

h.   Surgically castrated male, tender meat, smooth skin, high proportion of light to dark meat, relatively high fat content (under 8 months).

F. True or False

For each question below, circle either True or False to indicate the correct answer.

1.   Poultry fat has a higher melting point than other animal fats.
      True   False

2.   Duck and goose must be roasted at a higher temperature in order to render as much fat from the skin as possible.
      True   False

3.   Myoglobin is a protein that stores oxygen.
      True   False

4.   The longer chicken is left in a marinade, the better the flavour.
      True   False

5.   Dark meat takes less time to cook than light meat.
      True   False

6.   Poultry should not be frozen below 0°F (−18°C).
      True   False

7.   The skin colour of poultry is partly affected by the amount of sunlight it is exposed to.
      True   False

8.   Quality grades do not reflect the tenderness of poultry.
      True   False

9.   Older male birds have more flavour than female birds.
      True   False

10.   When foie gras is overcooked, it becomes tough.
      True   False

11.   A young pigeon is called a yearling.
      True   False

12.   The gizzard is a term used to describe the chicken's neck.
      True   False

Chapter 18

Game

Game has become more popular and available in North America since farm-raising techniques have been perfected. This chapter outlines the many different types of game and discusses the most appropriate cooking methods for them.

At the end of this chapter the student should be able to:
1. Identify a variety of game.
2. Explain how to disjoint a rabbit.
3. Explain game inspection practices.
4. Purchase game appropriate for your needs.
5. Store game properly.
6. Prepare game for cooking.
7. Apply various cooking methods to game.

Key Terms

Furred game	Venison	Partridge
Ground game	Rabbit	Pheasant
Antelope	Wild boar	Quail
Bison	Feathered game	Hanging
Deer	Winged game	

Test Your Knowledge

The practice sets provided below have been designed to test your comprehension of the information found in this chapter. It is recommended that you read the chapter completely before attempting these questions.

A. Terminology

Fill in the spaces with the correct term.

1. _____ Animals that are hunted for sport or food.

2. _____ The process used to tenderize the flesh and strengthen the flavour of game.

3. _____ The Hungarian and chukar of Europe introduced in North America in the 19th century.

4. _____ About 1/2 the size of deer, ranch-raised, it has almost no body fat but retains a high amount of moisture.

5. _____ French for white-tailed deer.

6. _____ The term used to describe deer meat.

7. _____ Animals that used to room the prairies and almost became extinct during the 19th century.

B. Short Answer

Provide a short response that correctly answers the questions below.

1. List three (3) uses for tougher cuts of game.

   a. _____

   b. _____

   c. _____

2. Explain the process and purpose of hanging wild game.

   Process: _____

   Purpose: _____

   _____

3. Describe the characteristics of wild boar.

   _____

   _____

   _____

4. Describe the guidelines for refrigeration and freezing of game.

   _____

   _____

   _____

5. Describe the characteristics of venison.

   _____

   _____

   _____

6. Describe the characteristics of pheasant.

_____

_____

_____

7. Describe the characteristics of rabbit.

_____

_____

_____

8. Describe the characteristics of partridge.

_____

_____

_____

9. Describe the characteristics of quail.

_____

_____

_____

10. List six (6) upland birds.

a. _____

b. _____

c. _____

d. _____

e. _____

f. _____

11. List two (2) waterfowl.

    a. _____

    b. _____

12. For each of the following game animals listed below, list the respective commonly purchased cuts, their cooking methods and their suggested use.

Animal	Commonly Purchased Cuts	Cooking Method	Suggested Use
Antelope	_____	_____	_____
Bison	_____	_____	_____
Deer	_____	_____	_____
Rabbit	_____	_____	_____
Wild boar	_____	_____	_____

C. Multiple Choice

For each question below, choose the one response that correctly answers the question.

1. Which of the following cannot be categorized as furred game?
   a. antelope
   b. pheasant
   c. bison
   d. rabbit

2. Due to the lean nature of game birds, they are barded and cooked:
   a. medium
   b. rare
   c. medium rare
   d. well done

3. Which one of the following is *not* a member of the deer family?
   a. elk
   b. bison
   c. mule deer
   d. moose

. Feathered game includes:
  a. pheasant, quail, woodcock
  b. partridge, pheasant, pigeon
  c. turkey, lark, squab
  d. guinea, goose, duck

5. Quail weighs approximately:
  a. 285–340 g (10–12 ounces)
  b. 454–908 g (1–2 pounds)
  c. 1800–4500 g (4–5 pounds)
  d. none of the above

6. The most popular game bird is:
  a. quail
  b. partridge
  c. pheasant
  d. woodcock

7. In general, game meat is _____ than other meats.
  a. fatter
  b. lighter
  c. leaner
  d. higher in calories

8. What is the average weight of a rabbit?
  a. 0.75–1.2 kg (1.7–2.5 lbs)
  b. 1.2–1.4 kg (2.5–3 lbs)
  c. 1.3–1.6 kg (2.9–3.5 lbs)
  d. none of the above

9. Which of the following is not commercially farmed?
  a. quails
  b. wild turkey
  c. muscovy duck
  d. pheasant

10. Reptiles have a texture similar to:
  a. lobster
  b. chicken
  c. fish
  d. veal

11. Game birds are often:
    a. cooked well done
    b. braised
    c. cooked on low heat
    d. barded

12. "Faisan à la Saint Alliance" is stuffed with:
    a. woodcock
    b. foie gras
    c. partridge
    d. quail

13. The average dressed weight of pheasant is:
    a. 500–750 g (1.1–1.65 lbs)
    b. 1–1.2 kg (2.2–2.6 lb)
    c. 680 g–1 kg (1.5–2 lbs)
    d. none of the above

14. Compared to beef, most game meat has approximately _____ calories.
    a. ⅓ less
    b. ¼ more
    c. ½ less
    d. ¼ less

15. Generally game meat is not graded except for:
    a. antelope
    b. musk ox
    c. deer
    d. bison

16. Boar can often be substituted in recipes for:
    a. beef or veal
    b. chicken or rabbit
    c. venison or pork
    d. bison or antelope

D. True or False

For each question below, circle either True or False to indicate the correct answer.

1. Most farmed deer is not slaughtered or processed in the slaughterhouse.
    True   False

2. Wild antelope, venison, and rabbit are not subject to inspection under federal law.
    True   False

3. A mature boar (1–2 years old) has a better flavour than a younger animal.
    True   False

4. True wild game can be purchased by request from most butchers.
    True   False

5. Wild boar is closely related to the domestic pig.
    True   False

6. Game is higher in fat and vitamins than most other meats.
    True   False

7. Venison is very moist due to the marbling through the tissue.
    True   False

8. Large game animals are usually sold in primal portions.
    True   False

9. Farm-raised furred game meat has a milder flavour than their wild cousins.
    True   False

10. The aroma, texture, and flavour of game are affected by the lifestyle of the animal.
    True   False

Chapter 19

Fish and Shellfish

Fish and shellfish have always been an important food source, but they have become increasingly popular in recent years. The development of fish farms has improved the availability and quality of seafood. A knowledge of the numerous varieties of fish, their seasonability, perishability, flavour characteristics, and the best preparation techniques is essential in the modern kitchen.

After studying this chapter the student should be able to:

1. Describe the structure and composition of fish and shellfish.
2. Identify a variety of fish and shellfish.
3. Purchase fish and shellfish appropriate to your needs.
4. Store fish and shellfish properly.
5. Prepare fish and shellfish for cooking.
6. Apply various appropriate cooking methods to fish and shellfish.

Key Terms

Round fish	Eels	Wahoo
Flatfish	Grouper	Whitefish
Mollusks	Herring	Trash fish
Univalves	Sardines	Flounder
Bivalves	John Dory	English sole
Cephalopods	Mackerel	Petrale sole
Crustaceans	Mahi-mahi	Domestic Dover sole
Anadromous	Monkfish	Lemon sole
Aquafarming	Orange roughy	Halibut
Bass	Red snapper	Sole
Black sea bass	Salmon	Dover sole
Striped bass	Atlantic salmon	Turbot
Catfish	Chinook (or king) salmon	Abalone
Fiddlers	Coho (or silver) salmon	Conch
Arctic char	Gravlax	Snails
Cod	Lox	Clams
Atlantic cod	Nova	Atlantic hard-shell clams (or quahogs)
Scrod	Sharks	Littlenecks
Haddock	Swordfish	Cherrystones
Pacific cod	Tilapia	Topnecks
Pollock	Trout	Chowders
Surimi	Tuna	

Soft-shell clams	Squid	Drawn
Surf clams	Crayfish	Dressed
Pacific clams	Crabs	Pan-dressed
Manila clams	King crabs	Butterflied
Geoducks	Dungeness crabs	Fillet
Red River clams	Blue crabs	Steak (darne)
Cockles	Snow (or spider) crabs	Wheel (centre-cut)
Mussels	Stone crabs	Fresh
Blue mussels	Lobsters	Chilled
Greenshell mussels	Atlantic lobsters	Flash frozen
Oysters	Spiny lobsters	Fresh frozen
Atlantic oysters	Slipper lobsters	Frozen
European flat oysters	Lobsterettes	Glazed
Olympias	Squat lobsters	Fancy
Pacific oysters	Shrimp	En papillote
Hamma-hamma oysters	Prawn	Submersion poaching
Scallops	Langoustine	Shallow poaching
Octopus	Whole (round)	Cuisson

Test Your Knowledge

The practice sets provided below have been designed to test your comprehension of the information found in this chapter. It is recommended that you read the chapter completely before attempting these questions.

A. Terminology

Fill in the blank spaces with the correct term.

1. _____ A method of steaming achieved by wrapping the fish or shellfish in parchment paper with other flavouring ingredients and baking in the oven.

2. _____ Shellfish with soft, unsegmented bodies with no internal skeleton.

3. _____ The business, science, and practice of raising large quantities of fish and shellfish in tanks, ponds, or ocean pens.

4. _____ The viscera and gills are removed, the fish scaled and fins and tails trimmed. The heads of small fish may remain, and then the fish is pan-fried.

5. _____ These swim in a vertical position and have eyes on both sides of their heads.

6. _____ Shellfish with hard outer skeleton or shell and jointed appendages.

7. _____ Usually from a large round fish, it is a cross-section slice with a small portion of the backbone attached.

8. _____ The most common way of purchasing fish; viscera is removed.

9. _____ The liver of lobsters.

10. _____ The roe of lobsters.

11. _____ The internal shell (cartilage) of cephalopods.

Fill in the blank spaces with the correct definition.

12. Black sea bass _____

13. Arctic char _____

14. Haddock _____

15. Fillet _____

16. Escalope or tranche _____

17. Dressed _____

18. Flatfish _____

19. Wheel or centre cut _____

B. Fill in the Blanks

1. The fish and shellfish used in food service operations can be divided into three categories: _____, _____ and _____.

2. The body of round fish may be truly _____, _____ or _____.

3. Compared to meat, fish does not contain a large amount of _____ _____.

4. Smoked cod is also known as _____.

5. Pacific cod, also known as _____, are found in the Northern Pacific Ocean.

6. There are hundreds of oyster species on the market; however, there are only two that have a market significance: the _____ and the _____.

7. Crayfish are called _____ in the North and _____ in the South.

8. Blue crabs are available as _____ or _____.

9. The most important concern about storing fish is _____.

10. All fish should be _____ lightly with _____ or _____ before being placed on the grill.

11. Sharks are not actually fish; rather they are _____.

12. Monk fish is also known as _____ or _____ or _____ or _____.

13. Mahi-mahi is also known by its Spanish name _____.

14. John Dory is also known as _____ fish.

15. Pollock are often frozen at sea and reprocessed as _____.

C. Short Answer

Provide a short response that correctly answers each of the questions below.

1. Give two (2) reasons why fish fillets and steaks are the best market forms to bake.

   a. _____

   b. _____

2. List the four (4) guidelines for determining the doneness of fish and shellfish.

   a. _____

   b. _____

   c. _____

   d. _____

3. Explain the proper procedures for storing fresh fish.

   _____

   _____

   _____

   _____

4. List four (4) cooking methods that would be appropriate for preparing an escalope or tranche of salmon.

a. _____

b. _____

c. _____

d. _____

5. List two (2) oily and two (2) lean fish that grill well.

       oily   *lean*

a. _____   c. _____

b. _____   d. _____

6. Name four (4) types of shellfish good for sautéing.

a. _____

b. _____

c. _____

d. _____

7. List three (3) dishes that exemplify why shellfish are good for baking.

a. _____

b. _____

c. _____

8. Explain two (2) reasons why combination cooking methods are not traditionally used to prepare fish and shellfish.

a. _____

b. _____

9. List four (4) of the seven (7) quality points used to determine the freshness of fish.

a. _____

b. _____

c. _____

d. _____

10. List two (2) poaching methods, explaining the principles for each.

   a. _____

   _____

   b. _____

   _____

11. List five (5) varieties of tuna commonly used in the food service.

   a. _____

   b. _____

   c. _____

   d. _____

   e. _____

12. List the proper procedures for skinning a true sole.

   _____

   _____

   _____

   _____

13. List the proper procedures for broiling and grilling fish.

   _____

   _____

   _____

   _____

14. List the proper procedures for baking fish.

_____

_____

_____

_____

15. List the proper procedures for sautéing fish.

_____

_____

_____

_____

16. List the proper procedures for pan-frying fish.

_____

_____

_____

_____

17. List the proper procedures for deep-fat frying fish.

_____

_____

_____

_____

18. List the proper procedures for stewing fish.

_____

_____

_____

_____

19. List the proper procedures for preparing and cooking red snapper en papillote.

_____

_____

_____

20. List the proper procedures for shallow poaching.

_____

_____

_____

_____

21. List the proper procedures for preparing Fillets of Sole Bonne Femme; amount of ingredients is not required.

_____

_____

_____

_____

22. List the proper procedures for preparing Clams Casino; amount of ingredients is not required.

_____

_____

_____

23. List the proper procedures for preparing Seviche; amount of ingredients is not required but include times as required.

_____

_____

_____

_____

D. Multiple Choice

For each question below, choose the one response that correctly answers the question.

1. To maintain optimum freshness, fish and shellfish should be stored at what temperature?
    a. 4°C (40°F)
    b. −1 to 2°C (30 to 34°F)
    c. 4 to 7°C (40 to 45°F)
    d. 3 to 4°C (38 to 40°F)

2. In Canada fish are graded:
    a. Prime, Choice, Select, or Utility
    b. Type 1, Type 2, Type 3
    c. Premium, Commercial Grade
    d. There is no grading protocol for fish in Canada.

3. Clams, mussels, and oysters should be stored:
    a. at 2°C (36°F)
    b. on ice and in refrigeration
    c. in boxes or net bags
    d. at 20% humidity

4. Univalves and bivalves are both examples of:
    a. mollusks
    b. cephalopods
    c. clams
    d. crustaceans

5. The "universal" meaning of *prawn* refers to:
    a. shrimp sautéed in garlic and butter
    b. all shrimp, freshwater or marine variety
    c. shrimp from the Gulf of Mexico
    d. a freshwater variety of shrimp only

6. In terms of the market forms of fish, *dressed* refers to:
    a. viscera removed
    b. viscera, gills, fins, and scales removed
    c. as caught, intact
    d. viscera, fins, and gills removed, scaled, and tail trimmed

7. The most important commercial variety of salmon is:
   a. Atlantic
   b. Pacific
   c. Chinook
   d. King

8. Which type of sole cannot be caught off the coastline of Canada?
   a. Lemon
   b. English
   c. Petrale
   d. Dover

9. Mackerel, herring, sardines, and salmon have similar characteristics in that:
   a. the colour of their flesh is the same
   b. they all migrate
   c. their flesh is moderately to highly oily
   d. their geographic availability is the same

10. All clams are examples of:
    a. cephalopods
    b. crustaceans
    c. univalves
    d. bivalves

11. The best-selling fish in Canada is:
    a. Atlantic salmon
    b. lemon sole
    c. Atlantic cod
    d. ahi tuna

12. When cooking fish fillets with the skin on, what can be done to prevent the fillet from curling?
    a. Cook fillet at a high temperature, short time.
    b. Cook fillet at a low temperature, longer time.
    c. Score the skin of the fish before cooking.
    d. Flatten the fillet by weighing down with a semi-heavy object during cooking.

E. Matching

Market Forms of Fish

Identify the market forms indicated in the following diagram and write their names in the spaces provided below.

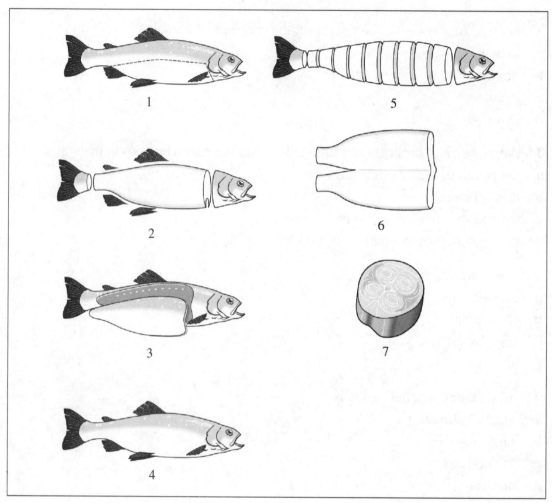

1. _____

2. _____

3. _____

4. _____

5. _____

6. _____

7. _____

F. True or False

For each question below, circle either True or False to indicate the correct answer.

1.   All fish must be purchased from approved sources only.
     True   False

2.   Agriculture Canada is responsible for fish inspection.
     True   False

3.   A lobster is an example of a crustacean.
     True   False

4.   Fatty fish are especially good for baking.
     True   False

5.   The only difference between Atlantic lobsters and spiny lobsters is the geographic location
     where they're caught.
     True   False

6.   Atlantic hard-shell clams are also known as geoducks.
     True   False

7.   Fillet of halibut is a good fish to pan-fry.
     True   False

8.   Cooking fish or shellfish en papillote is an example of baking.
     True   False

9.   Shellfish has as much cholesterol as lamb.
     True   False

10. A cuisson is a classic accompaniment to poached salmon.
     True   False

11. Chinook and smoked salmon are the same fish.
     True   False

Chapter 20

Charcuterie

Over the years, charcuterie has developed from pork preparations of pâtés, terrines, and galantines to include game, poultry, fish, shellfish, and even vegetables. The increased versatility of these items on menus has reflected the art and science of such preparations.

At the end of this chapter the student should be able to:

1. Prepare a variety of forcemeats.
2. Assemble and cook a variety of pâtés, terrines, and sausages.
3. Explain the proper methods for salting, brining, curing, and smoking meats and fish.
4. Identify several cured pork products.

Key Terms

Forcemeat	Quenelles	Chopped chicken liver	Cold smoking
Fat	Pâté		Hot smoking
Panada	Terrine	Ballotine	Pan smoking
Curing salt	Pâté en croûte	Sausage	Side bacon
Pâté spice	Galantine	Fresh sausages	Canadian bacon
Country-style forcemeat	Liver terrines	Smoked and cooked sausages	Pancetta
Dominant meat	Foie gras terrines	Dried or hard sausages	Fresh ham
5/4/3 forcemeat	Vegetable terrines		Boneless or formed ham
Gratin-style forcemeat	Brawns	Natural casings	Country ham
Straight forcemeat	Aspic terrines	Collagen casings	Prosciutto
Mousseline forcemeat	Mousse	Salt-curing	Westphalian ham
	Rillettes	Brining	
	Confit	Smoker	

Test Your Knowledge

The practice sets provided below have been designed to test your comprehension of the information found in this chapter. It is recommended that you read the chapter completely before attempting these questions.

A. Terminology

Fill in the blank spaces with the correct term.

1. _____ Hot or cold; salt curing, brining or not, this preparation imparts distinctive flavour to the food.

2. _____ A "marinade" with approximately 20% salinity, sugar, herbs, and sometimes nitrites.

3. _____ Forcemeats stuffed into casings.

4. _____ The most versatile of all forcemeats, it is smoother and more refined than country-style.

5. _____ Preserved pork and fatty poultry that has been seasoned and slow-cooked in large amounts of its own fat. Cooked until falling off the bone, the meat is then mashed and pressed into crocks or terrines with additional fat.

6. _____ A preparation more basic than pâté, it consists of coarsely ground and highly seasoned meats baked in an earthenware mould and always served cold.

7. _____ Preserved pork and fatty poultry that is often lightly salt-cured before being cooked in large amounts of its own fat; usually served hot.

8. _____ Small dumpling-shaped portions of a mousseline forcemeat poached in an appropriately flavoured stock.

9. _____ An aspic terrine made from simmered meats packed into a terrine and covered with aspic.

10. _____ A preparation made from uncooked ground meats, poultry, fish, or shellfish, seasoned and emulsified with fat.

11. _____ The meat that gives the forcemeat its name and essential flavour.

12. _____ Panada and eggs are the two principal types.

13. _____ is produced by brining and cold smoking pork belly.

14. _____ is produced from a boneless pork loin trimmed of its fat, then brined and smoked.

15. _____ is an Italian pork belly, salt-cured, peppered, but not smoked.

16. _____ This term means ham in Italian. This product is actually known as _____ in Italy.

Fill in the blank spaces with the correct definition.

17. Pâté spice _____

18. 5/4/3 forcemeat _____

19. Country-style forcemeat _____

20. Curing salt _____

21. Galantine _____

22. Pâté en croûte _____

23. Aspic jelly _____

24. Pâté _____

25. Mousseline forcemeat _____

26. Ballottine _____

27. Panada _____

B. Short Answer

Provide a short response that correctly answers each of the questions below.

1. Name three (3) kinds of forcemeat can be used to make a pâté en croûte.

    a. _____

    b. _____

    c. _____

2. If a forcemeat will not emulsify in a warm kitchen, what can be done?

    _____

    _____

    _____

3. Compare and contrast a galantine and a ballottine.
    galantine   *ballottine*

    a. _____

    b. _____

    c. _____

    d. _____

    e. _____

    f. _____

4. What are three (3) steps one can take to ensure proper emulsification of a forcemeat?

    a. _____

b. _____

c. _____

5. List five (5) reasons for using an aspic jelly.

   a. _____

   b. _____

   c. _____

   d. _____

   e. _____

6. List the procedures for making a mousseline forcemeat.

   a. _____

   b. _____

   c. _____

   d. _____

   e. _____

   f. _____

7. Compare a pâté and a terrine.

   _____

   _____

   _____

   _____

   _____

8. Describe a foie gras terrine. How is it different from other terrines?

_____

_____

_____

_____

_____

9. Describe the basic procedures for preparing a Country-Style Forcemeat.

_____

_____

_____

_____

_____

10. Describe the basic procedures for preparing a Terrine.

_____

_____

_____

_____

_____

11. Describe the basic procedures for preparing Aspic-Jelly-Coated Chilled Mousse.

_____

_____

_____

_____

_____

12. Describe the basic procedures for preparing Chaud-Froid.

_____

_____

_____

_____

_____

13. Describe the basic procedures for coating foods with chaud-froid.

_____

_____

_____

_____

_____

14. Describe the basic procedures for cold-smoking foods.

_____

_____

_____

_____

15. Describe the basic procedures for hot-smoking foods.

_____

_____

_____

_____

C. Multiple Choice

For each question below, choose the one response that correctly answers the question.

1. When making a forcemeat, ingredients as well as equipment temperatures should be kept at what level throughout preparation?
    a. below 4°C (40°F)
    b. as cold as possible
    c. room temperature, but not to exceed 16°C (60°F)
    d. 5–7°C (42–45°F)

2. Which of the following is *not* true about salt curing? It:
    a. inhibits bacterial growth
    b. dehydrates the food
    c. is quick and easy
    d. can take the place of cooking

3. Meat-based galantines, terrines, and pâtés en croûte should be cooked to an internal temperature of:
    a. 60°C (140°F)
    b. 52°C (125°F)
    c. 66°C (150°F)
    d. 71°C (160°F)

4. When meats are cold-smoked, what process is usually performed prior to the smoking?
    a. salt-curing and brining
    b. trimming
    c. barding
    d. marinated

5. What gives ham, bacon, and other smoked meats their pink colour?
    a. Red dye #7 is added to the curing process.
    b. The meat is cooked to a medium-rare state of doneness.
    c. Smoking, when performed slowly, maintains the natural colour of meats.
    d. Nitrites are added to the cure.

6. Which of the statements is *not* true about a panada?
    a. Aids in emulsification.
    b. Adds significant flavour.
    c. Should not make up more than 20% of the forcemeat.
    d. It is a binder.

7. Which of the following is an Italian pork belly bacon that is not smoked?
   a. Italian bacon
   b. sopressata
   c. mortadella
   d. pancetta

8. The main characteristic that differentiates country hams from others is that it is:
   a. dry cure
   b. wet cure
   c. made in the country
   d. made on the farm

9. In Canada, parma crudo is known as:
   a. prosciutto
   b. pancetta
   c. mortadella
   d. raw ham

10. Hot smoking is done at temperatures ranging from:
    a. 60–80°C (110–176°F)
    b. 70–100°C (158–212°F)
    c. 93–121°C (200–250°F)
    d. 120–150°c (248–302°F)

11. Cold smoking is done at temperatures ranging from:
    a. 5–15°C (41–59°F)
    b. 10–29°C (50–85°F)
    c. 20–40°C (68–104°F)
    d. 40–60°C (104–140°F)

12. A very spicy smoked pork sausage popular in Cajun cuisine is known as:
    a. mortadella
    b. sopressata
    c. chorizo
    d. andouille

13. The ratio of time to weight for dry curing is:
    a. 1 day per kg (2 lb)
    b. 1.5 days per 450 g (1 lb)
    c. 2 days per 650 g (1.5 lb)
    d. 1.5 days per kg (2 lbs)

14. Which of the following statement is *true* regarding collagen casings?
    a. They are superior as they are 100% natural.
    b. They are inferior in taste and texture.
    c. They require soaking before filling.
    d. They can be fairly uneven in size.

15. Which of the following statements is *not true*? Casings from hog:
    a. are considered the finest
    b. come in different sizes
    c. are the most popular
    d. are used to make hot dogs

16. Salami, pepperoni and landjäger are examples of:
    a. cooked sausages
    b. fresh sausages
    c. hard sausages
    d. smoked sausages

D. Matching

Match each of the terms in List A with the appropriate letter definition in List B. Each choice in List B can only be used once.

List A

_____1. Mousse

_____2. Country-style forcemeat

_____3. Brawn

_____4. Forcemeat

_____5. Mousseline forcemeat

_____6. Pâté en croûte

_____7. Galantine

_____8. Quenelle

_____9. Terrine

List B

a. Pâté cooked in pastry dough.

b. A cooked, light, airy, delicately flavoured forcemeat.

c. A poached dumpling of mousseline forcemeat.

d. Meat, fish, or poultry, bound, seasoned, with or without garnishes.

e. A terrine made from highly simmered gelatinous cuts of meat, wine, and flavouring.

f. A purée of fully cooked meats, poultry, game, fish, shellfish, or vegetables, lightened with cream and bound with aspic.

g. A whole poultry item boned, stuffed, and reshaped, poached and served cold.

h. A deboned, stuffed poultry leg, poached or braised and usually served hot.

i. A hearty, highly seasoned, coarse-textured forcemeat.

j. A coarse forcemeat cooked in an earthenware mould.

E. True or False

For each question below, circle either True or False to indicate the correct answer.

1. It is possible to make a vegetable mousseline forcemeat.
   True   False

2. The best type of mould to use to make a pâté en croûte is a metal loaf pan.
   True   False

3. Sausages are forcemeat stuffed into casings.
   True   False

4. Pork bellies are usually made into bacon.
   True   False

5. Galantines are always served cold.
   True   False

6. Any type of forcemeat can be used to make a terrine.
   True   False

7. A fresh ham is made from the hog's shoulder.
   True   False

8. A mousseline forcemeat can be served hot or cold.
   True   False

9. Only hams made in rural areas can be called country hams; all others must be called country-style hams.
   True   False

10. Brining and curing use the same procedure.
    True   False

Chapter 21

Buffet Presentation

In this chapter, the word *buffet* refers to both the event where all the dishes from a menu are served at once and the table on which these foods are displayed. Food service professionals have the opportunity to exercise creativity by identifying themes and then creating menus along with attractive displays and decorations.

At the end of this chapter the student should be able to:

1. Understand the basic principles of buffet presentation.
2. Use a variety of techniques to create and maintain appealing buffets.

Key Terms

Theme	Height
Menu	Negative space
Kosher	Flow
Halal	Risers
Grosse piece	Butler service

Test Your Knowledge

The practice sets provided below have been designed to test your comprehension of the information found in this chapter. It is recommended that you read this chapter completely before attempting these questions.

A. Terminology

Fill in the blank spaces with the correct term.

1. Theme _____

2. Menu _____

3. Chafing dish_____

4. Grosse piece_____

5. Risers _____

Fill in the blank spaces with the correct definition.

6. _____ A diet requiring that only foods from animals that chew their cud and have split hooves can be eaten.

7. _____ Refers to the food that can be eaten by observant Muslims.

8. _____ Refers to the placement of foods in a logical order that affords the diner to construct a meal in the same order as one that would be served to him or her.

9. _____ Refers to area left unused to prevent overcrowding.

10. _____ Restaurant service in which servers pass foods or drinks arranged on trays.

11. _____ Scandinavian word for buffet.

B. Short Answer

Provide a short response that correctly answers each of the questions below.

1. Describe the four (4) guidelines for avoiding repetition on a buffet.

   a. _____

   b. _____

   c. _____

   d. _____

2. Explain why each of the following aspect of presentation are important when preparing buffets.

   a. Height: _____

   _____

   b. Pattern: _____

   _____

   c. Colour: _____

   _____

   d. Texture: _____

   _____

   e. Negative space: _____

   _____

3. Describe three (3) styles of buffet setup designed to promote efficient service of large groups.

   a. _____

   b. _____

   c. _____

4. Describe four (4) guidelines for presenting hot food on buffets.

   a. _____

   b. _____

   c. _____

   d. _____

5. Describe the kosher diet principles.

   _____

   _____

   _____

   _____

6. Describe the halal diet principles.

   _____

   _____

   _____

   _____

7. Describe the type of linens and dinnerware appropriate for a business luncheon.

   a. Linens: _____

   _____

   b. Dinnerware: _____

   _____

8. Describe the type of linens and dinnerware appropriate for a Mexican fiesta.

    a. Linens: _____

    _____

    b. Dinnerware: _____

    _____

9. Describe the type of linens and dinnerware appropriate for a barbecue.

    a. Linens: _____

    _____

    b. Dinnerware: _____

    _____

10. Describe five (5) steps to follow to ensure safety in addition to keeping foods at the proper temperatures.

    a. _____

    b. _____

    c. _____

    d. _____

    e. _____

11. Describe two (2) things that can be done to keep cold foods cold on a buffet.

    a. _____

    b. _____

C. Multiple Choice

For each question below, choose the one response that correctly answers the question.

1. On a buffet, hot foods are served on/in:
    a. platters
    b. bowls
    c. chafing dishes
    d. mirrors

2. Which of the following best describes the logical flow for a buffet table?

    a. appetizers, entrées, plates, vegetables

    b. plates, soups, entrées, desserts

    c. plates, entrées, vegetables, appetizers

    d. desserts, vegetables, entrées, appetizers

3. Which of the following items are appropriate to use as a centrepiece on a buffet table?

    a. flowers

    b. ice carvings

    c. whole turkey

    d. all of the above

4. Having servers stationed behind the buffet is called:

    a. waiter service

    b. buffet service

    c. butler service

    d. restaurant service

5. Which of the following is *not* a safe procedure to follow when dealing with food safety?

    a. Provide clean utensils regularly.

    b. Do not add new foods to old foods in a serving dish.

    c. Reheat foods in a chaffing dish.

    d. Provide an ample supply of clean plates.

D. Matching

Match each of the buffet themes in List A with the appropriate décor or ambiance item in List B. Each choice in List B can only be used once.

	List A		List B
_____ 1.	Mexican fiesta	a.	calla lilies and white orchids
_____ 2.	Western barbecue	b.	no music
_____ 3.	Formal wedding	c.	fresh chiles and brightly coloured flowers
_____ 4.	Business luncheon	d.	horse shoes, cow bells and hay bales

E. True or False

For each question below, circle either True or False to indicate the correct answer.

1. More guests help themselves to little portions of every item on a buffet rather than gorging themselves on one or two items.
    True   False

2. Cost is *not* a factor when preparing buffet menus.
    True   False

3. When designing a buffet, the food tables should be located as far away from the kitchen as possible for ease of traffic flow.
    True   False

4. The start of the buffet should be located near the entrance of the room.
    True   False

5. A buffet table with ten (10) items should measure approximately ten (10) feet (3 m) long.
    True   False

6. Dishes containing sauces should be positioned at the back of the table.
    True   False

7. Dead space on a buffet should never be filled with decorations or props.
    True   False

8. Guests will generally take larger portions of foods at the beginning of the buffet than at the end.
    True   False

9. Spaghetti is an appropriate choice of hot food to serve on a buffet.
    True   False

10. Dishes of food on a buffet should be replenished when they are two-thirds empty.
    True   False

11. The word "buffet" is used to describe the event as well as the table on which the food is served.
    True   False

12. The chef should not plan one portion of each food item on the buffet for each guest.
    True   False

Chapter 22

Vegetables

The relatively newfound popularity of vegetables is a direct result of the demands of health-conscious patrons. Chefs have had to become responsive to such demands by using a greater variety of vegetables more frequently on the menu.

At the end of this chapter the student should be able to:

1. Identify a variety of vegetables.
2. Purchase vegetables appropriate for your needs.
3. Store vegetables properly.
4. Explain how vegetables are preserved.
5. Prepare vegetables for cooking or service.
6. Apply various cooking methods to vegetables.

Key Terms

Vegetable

Brassica

Bok choy

Broccoli

Brussels sprouts

Cauliflower

Green and red cabbages

Kale

Napa cabbage

Savoy cabbage

Avocado

Eggplant

Capsicum

Sweet or bell peppers

Hot peppers or chiles

Tomatillo

Tomato

Sun-dried tomatoes

Cucumber

Chayote

Winter squashes

Summer squashes

Mustard greens

Sorrel

Spinach

Swiss chard

Turnip greens

Mushrooms

Truffles

Bulb onions

Fennel

Garlic

Kohlrabi

Leeks

Scallions

Shallots

Corn

Legumes

Pulses

Fresh beans

Dried beans

Peas

Okra

Beets

Carrots

Celery root

Jicama

Parsnips

Radishes

Rutabagas

Turnips

Water chestnuts

Artichokes

Asparagus

Fiddleheads

Bamboo shoots

Celery

Nopales

Baby vegetables

Cellulose

Irradiation

Blanching

Parboiling

Refreshing or shocking

Test Your Knowledge

The practice sets provided below have been designed to test your comprehension of the information found in this chapter. It is recommended that you read the chapter completely before attempting these questions.

A. Terminology

Fill in the blank spaces with the correct term.

1. _____ Chilling just-cooked vegetables quickly in ice water to stop the cooking process and maintain degree of doneness.

2. _____ A complex carbohydrate found in the cell wall of plants; is edible but indigestible for humans.

3. _____ The same as blanching, but the cooking time is longer.

4. _____ Known as merliton or vegetable pear.

5. _____ The pads of the prickly pear cactus.

6. _____ A legume that grows underground as a tuber.

7. _____ Any herbaceous plant that can be partially or wholly eaten.

8. _____ A Canadian delicacy with a flavour resembling asparagus and broccoli; grown in New Brunswick and Nova Scotia.

9. _____ A type of green bean with a long slender pod with an intense flavour and tender texture.

10. _____ The pigment in broccoli.

11. _____ The pigment in tomatoes.

12. _____ The pigment in cauliflower.

13. _____ The pigment in red cabbage.

Fill in the blank spaces with the correct definition.

14. Concassée _____

15. Blanching _____

16. Irradiation _____

17. Brassica _____

18. Capsicum _____

B. Short Answer

1. List four (4) chilies by their fresh and dried name

    Fresh   **Dried**

    a. _____   _____

    b. _____   _____

    c. _____   _____

    d. _____   _____

2. For each of the following pigments, identify the changes in colour and texture when **acid** is added.

Pigment Family	Effect on Colour	Effect on Texture
a. Chlorophyll		
b. Carotenoids		
c. Anthoxantins		
d. Anthocyanins		

3. For each of the following pigments, identify the changes in colour and texture when **alkali** is added.

Pigment Family	Effect on Colour	Effect on Texture
a. Chlorophyll		
b. Carotenoids		
c. Anthoxantins		
d. Anthocyanins		

4. Explain the procedure used for roasting peppers.

    _____

    _____

    _____

5. Describe the procedure for coring jalapeños. Explain the importance of doing so.

_____

_____

_____

_____

6. Explain the basic procedures for cutting and pitting avocadoes.

_____

_____

_____

_____

7. Explain the basic procedures for cutting pepper julienne.

_____

_____

_____

_____

8. Explain the basic procedures for making tomato concassée.

_____

_____

_____

_____

9. Explain the basic procedures for soaking dry beans.

_____

_____

_____

_____

10. Explain the basic procedures for **quick** soaking dry beans.

_____

_____

_____

_____

11. Explain the basic procedures for sautéing vegetables.

_____

_____

_____

_____

12. Explain the basic procedures for preparing beer-battered onion rings.

_____

_____

_____

_____

13. Explain the basic procedures for boiling vegetables.

_____

_____

_____

_____

14. Explain the basic procedures for cooking dry beans.

_____

_____

_____

_____

15. Explain the basic procedures for preparing tempura batter. List all ingredients; amounts are not required.

_____

_____

_____

_____

16. Explain the basic procedures for preparing braised romaine lettuce.

_____

_____

_____

_____

17. Explain the basic procedures for preparing a vegetable stew such as ratatouille.

_____

_____

_____

_____

C. Multiple Choice

For each question below, choose the one response that correctly answers the question.

1. A braised vegetable dish differs from a stewed vegetable dish in that it:
   a. contains an acid product
   b. is usually prepared with only one vegetable
   c. has a longer cooking time
   d. is served with a reduction of the cooking liquid

2. Grades for all vegetables include:
   a. Canada Fancy, Canada Choice
   b. Grade A, Grade B, Grade C
   c. Canada Fancy, Canada No. 1, Canada No. 2, Canada Domestic Grade
   d. Canada Recommended, Canada Approved

3. Vegetables are considered savoury because:
   a. they are an herbaceous plant that can be partially or wholly eaten
   b. they have less sugar than fruit
   c. they have little or no woody tissue
   d. they are usually eaten cooked, not raw

4. Tofu is:
   a. used as a principal ingredient in the Chinese culture
   b. available in four different types
   c. high in nutritional value, low in cost, low in fat and sodium
   d. a fermented soybean paste stored in water with limited applications

5. The biggest disadvantage of freezing as a preservation method is that it does not maintain:
   a. flavour
   b. colour
   c. nutritional value
   d. texture

6. Which of the following vegetables is *not* suitable for roasting or baking?
   a. eggplant
   b. potatoes
   c. spinach
   d. peppers

7. To preserve nutrients, colour, and texture, you should:
   a. cut vegetables into uniform shapes before cooking
   b. cook vegetables whole, then peel and cut
   c. add acid to the cooking liquid
   d. cook vegetables as little as possible

8. When steaming vegetables:
   a. overcooking is less likely to occur
   b. cover the cooking apparatus
   c. more nutrients are lost than in other techniques
   d. choose only vegetables with a firm texture

9. Which of the following is true concerning microwave cooking?
   a. It is a good substitute for all cooking techniques except broiling and grilling.
   b. It can be used as a substitute for traditional steaming.
   c. It is dangerous to use in large-scale food service operations.
   d. Its cooking process, agitating water molecules within food, depletes nutrients.

10. Common sweet peppers are also known as:
    a. bell peppers
    b. green peppers
    c. chiles
    d. Anaheim peppers

11. Hot peppers are also known as:
    a. mulattos
    b. red peppers
    c. chiles
    d. jalapeños

12. A dish containing potatoes is often named:
    a. Parmentier
    b. Dubarry
    c. Crecy
    d. Augustin

13. Consider the following statements. Which one is true?
    a. Hubbard squash is a summer squash.
    b. Acorn squash does not require peeling.
    c. Most summer squashes can be eaten raw.
    d. Crooknecks should be peeled before cooking.

14. The crossbreed of cabbage and turnip results in a vegetable known as:
    a. taproot
    b. nopale
    c. chayote
    d. kohlrabi

15. Consider the following statements. Which one is *not* true?
    a. Most vegetables contain 80% water.
    b. Most vegetables contain a high amount of fibre.
    c. Stem-type vegetables tend to have lots of cellulose.
    d. Fibre is digested and very nutritious.

16. Potatoes are best stored at:
    a. 1–3°C (34–37°F)
    b. 2–4°C (34–40°F)
    c. 4– 16°C (40–60°F)
    d. 10–20°C (50–68°F)

17. Consider the following statements. Which one is *not* true?
    a. Irradiation is not yet approved for fruits and vegetables.
    b. Frozen vegetables are not graded.
    c. There are three grades of canned vegetables.
    d. Drying is not commonly used with vegetables.

18. Which of the following makes fibre resist softening?
    a. flour and salt
    b. vinegar and baking soda
    c. baking soda
    d. lemon juice and sugar

19. To improve the colour of red cabbage, a little _____ should be added.
    a. acid
    b. sugar
    c. salt
    d. baking soda

D. Matching

Match each vegetable in List A with the appropriate letter in List B. Each choice in List B can only be used once.

List A

_____ 1. Artichokes

_____ 2. Swiss chard

_____ 3. Okra

_____ 4. Bok choy

_____ 5. Pumpkin

_____ 6. Tomatillos

_____ 7. Leeks

_____ 8. Truffles

List B

a. A winter squash variety that is popular especially in October.

b. A type of beet only used for its greens.

c. Husk tomatoes with a crisp, tart flesh.

d. Tubers that grow near oak or beech tree roots.

e. Immature flowers of a thistle plant often canned or marinated.

f. From Arab and African cuisines, often used for thickening.

g. A sweet, onion-flavoured vegetable with flat, wide leaves.

h. A white-stemmed variety of southern Chinese cabbage.

i. The immature stalks of bulb onions.

E. True or False

For each question below, circle either True or False to indicate the correct answer.

1. Puréed vegetables are usually prepared by first sautéing, steaming, or boiling.
    True   False

2. Winter squash is commonly braised or stewed due to its dense texture.
    True   False

3. Food is irradiated by exposing it to gamma rays to sterilize it, slow the ripening process, or prevent sprouting.
    True   False

4. Eggplants, peppers, and tomatoes are considered "fruit-vegetables."
    True   False

5. Examples of legumes are dried beans and peas.
    True   False

6. The grading of vegetables is required by the Canadian Food Inspection Agency.
    True   False

7. Potatoes, onions, shallots, and garlic are best stored at 2–4°C (34–40°F).
   True   False

8. Depending on the vegetable cooked, exposure to acidity can either harm or help retain colour.
   True   False

9. Flavonoids are found mainly in beets, cauliflower, and winter squash.
   True   False

10. Timing a vegetable as it cooks is the best way to determine doneness.
    True   False

Chapter 23

Potatoes, Grains and Pasta

Potatoes, grains, and pastas are a great source of energy. These starchy carbohydrates are also low in fat, making them especially attractive to the health-conscious consumer. Chefs especially appreciate their versatility, variety, and ease of preparation. No menu would be complete without them.

At the end of this chapter the student should be able to:

1. Identify a variety of potatoes.
2. Apply various cooking methods to potatoes.
3. Identify a variety of grains.
4. Apply various cooking methods to grains.
5. Identify pasta products.
6. Make fresh pasta.
7. Cook pasta: to order, in advance.

Key Terms

Fingerlings

Purple potatoes

Red potatoes

Russet potatoes

White potatoes

Sweet potatoes

Yams

Mealy potatoes

Waxy potatoes

Tossing method

Still-frying method

Hull

Bran

Endosperm

Germ

Cracking

Grinding

Hulling

Pearling

Cornmeal

Hominy

Masa harina

Grits

Long-grain rice

Medium-grain rice

Short-grain rice

Brown rice

White rice

Converted rice

Instant or quick-cooking rice

Arborio rice

Basmati rice

Wild rice

Wild pecan rice

Berry

Bulgur

Couscous

Durum wheat

Barley

Buckwheat

Groat

Kasha

Oats

Risotto

Pilaf

Extrusion

Macaroni

Semolina

Dumplings

Wheat noodles

Rice noodles

Bean starch noodles

Buckwheat noodles

Sfoglia

Al dente

Test Your Knowledge

The practice sets provided below have been designed to test your comprehension of the information found in this chapter. It is recommended that you read the chapter completely before attempting these questions.

A. Terminology

Fill in the blank spaces with the correct term.

1. _____ Grasses that bear edible seeds.

2. _____ The most basic form of pasta; a thin, flat sheet of dough.

3. _____ The process of forcing pasta dough through perforated plates to create various shapes.

4. _____ A milling process in which all or part of the hull, bran, and germ are removed from the grain.

5. _____ Small, immature red potatoes usually marketed during early summer.

6. _____ Potatoes with a high starch content and a thick skin, also known as "bakers."

7. _____ A classic Northern Italian dish that can be made from short-grain starchy rice such as arborio, oats, or barley. When cooked, the grains should be creamy and tender, but still al dente in the centre.

8. _____ The milling process in which grains are broken open.

9. _____ Raw grains are lightly sautéed, usually with onions and seasonings, and then hot liquid is added. The mixture is then covered and simmered until tender and the liquid is absorbed.

10. _____ Foods that are cooked firm to the bite.

11. _____ Name of a standard baking potato.

12. _____ A toxic substance found in potatoes with green patches.

13. _____ A potato preparation in which mashed baked potato pulp is combined with butter and seasonings, shaped, and pan-fried.

14. _____ Made with duchesse and tomato concassée.

15. _____ Made with duchesse and pâte-à-choux.

16. _____ Turned potatoes cooked in clarified butter until brown and tender.

17. _____ Duchesse, shaped, breaded and deep-fried

18. _____ Small spheres of raw potato sautéed in clarified butter, finished with glace de viande and garnished with parsley.

Fill in the blank spaces with the correct definition.

19. Grinding_____

20. Masa harina _____

21. Waxy potatoes _____

22. Macaroni _____

23. Durum wheat _____

24. Hulling_____

25. Dumplings _____

26. Gratin Dauphinois _____

B. Short Answer

Provide a short response that correctly answers each of the questions below.

1. Complete the table below by identifying the content of starch, moisture and sugar with "high" or "low."

Potato	Starch	Moisture	Sugar
a. Russet	_____	_____	_____
b. White Rose	_____	_____	_____
c. Red	_____	_____	_____
d. Purple	_____	_____	_____
e. Bintje	_____	_____	_____
f. Yukon Gold	_____	_____	_____

2. What type of potatoes is best suited for the following:

a. Dry heat cooking methods: _____

b. Dry heat cooking methods: _____

3.   Briefly explain the procedure for making french fries.

_____

_____

_____

4.   Explain the basic procedure for making Duchesse potatoes.

_____

_____

_____

5.   Explain the basic procedures for baking potatoes en casserole.

_____

_____

_____

6.   Explain the basic procedures for sautéing and pan-frying potatoes.

_____

_____

_____

7.   Explain the basic procedures for boiling potatoes.

_____

_____

_____

8. Explain the basic procedures for preparing Lyonnaise potatoes.

_____

_____

_____

_____

9. Complete the table below by indicating the recommended ratio of water to rice and the approximate simmering time.

Type of Rice	Ratio Water:Rice	Simmering Time
a. Arborio	_____	_____
b. Basmati	_____	_____
c. Brown (long grain)	_____	_____
d. Converted	_____	_____
e. White (long, regular)	_____	_____
f. Wild	_____	_____

10. Explain the basic procedure for preparing risotto. List all ingredients; amounts are not required.

_____

_____

_____

_____

11. Explain the basic procedures for preparing rice pilaf. List all ingredients; amounts are not required.

_____

_____

_____

_____

12. Explain the basic procedures for preparing gnocchi (with potato). List all ingredients; amounts are not required.

_____

_____

_____

_____

13. Explain the basic procedures for preparing spaetzle. List all ingredients; amounts are not required.

_____

_____

_____

_____

14. Explain the basic procedures for preparing rösti. List all ingredients; amounts are not required.

_____

_____

_____

_____

15. Define cornmeal.

_____

_____

_____

16. Although there are many varieties of rice, it is classified into three main types based on its size. List the three types.

a. _____

b. _____

c. _____

17. Why is it so important to use ample water when cooking pasta?

_____

_____

_____

18. Why shouldn't a baked potato be cooked by wrapping in foil or microwaving?

   a. _____

   b. _____

19. Name three (3) dishes that are traditionally made with short-grain rice.

   a. _____

   b. _____

   c. _____

20. The finest commercial pastas are made with pure semolina flour. Why?

_____

_____

_____

21. Identify the three (3) main shapes of Italian pasta.

   a. _____

   b. _____

   c. _____

22. What are the three (3) basic cooking methods for grains?

   a. _____

   b. _____

   c. _____

3. Give three (3) reasons for soaking dried Asian noodles in hot water before cooking.

a. _____

b. _____

c. _____

C. Multiple Choice

For each question below, choose the one response that correctly answers the question.

1. What is the difference between cooking fresh pasta and dry, factory-produced pasta?
   a. Fresh pasta takes significantly less time to cook.
   b. Dried pasta should be cooked to order.
   c. Dried pasta takes significantly less time to cook.
   d. Fresh pasta contains different ingredients.

2. Which of the following grains can be used to make risotto?
   a. barley
   b. oats
   c. buckwheat
   d. arborio rice

3. American-grown rice does not need to be rinsed before cooking because:
   a. all of the starch will be washed away
   b. the rice will become soggy before cooking
   c. rinsing will result in a sticky rice
   d. such rice is generally clean and free of insects

4. When boiling pasta, "ample water" is defined by the measurements:
   a. 1 litre (1 quart) of water to 454 g (1 pound) of pasta
   b. 2 litres (2 quarts) of water to 454 g (1 pound) of pasta
   c. 15:1 ratio of water to pasta
   d. 4 litres (1 gallon) of water to 454 g (1 pound) of pasta

5. Which of the following is *not* true about converted rice? It:
   a. tastes the same as regular milled white rice.
   b. retains more nutrients than regular milled white rice.
   c. has been pearled in order to remove the surface starch.
   d. cooks more slowly than regular milled white rice.

6. Why is long-grain rice more versatile and popular than other rice? Long-grain rice:
    a. has a higher nutritional content than short- or medium-grain rice.
    b. remains firm and separate when cooked properly.
    c. is more affordable for food service operations.
    d. is easier and faster to cook than the other rice.

7. Which type of potato is best suited for making Potatoes Berny?
    a. Mealy potatoes
    b. Waxy potatoes
    c. New potatoes
    d. Sweet potatoes

8. Which statement is *not* true about the nutritional content of grains?
    a. They contain all of the essential amino acids.
    b. They are high in fat.
    c. They are a good source of dietary fibre.
    d. They are a good source for vitamins and minerals.

9. Which of the following flours is used to make Asian noodles?
    a. potato
    b. bean
    c. corn
    d. oat

10. A dried corn that has been soaked in hydrated lime or lye is known as:
    a. cornmeal
    b. hominy
    c. grits
    d. semolina

11. Ground hominy is referred to as:
    a. cornmeal
    b. corn flour
    c. masa harina
    d. grits

12. This rice is one of the finest in the world and it is grown in the Himalayan foothills.
    a. arborio
    b. Thai
    c. basmati
    d. brown

13. A unique long-grain rice from the Bayou country in Louisiana is known as:
    a. basmati rice
    b. jasmine rice
    c. wild rice
    d. wild pecan rice

14. Wheat berry that has had the bran removed, then steamed, dried, and ground is known as:
    a. cracked wheat
    b. bulbar
    c. couscous
    d. durum wheat

15. Which of the following describes couscous?
    a. Steamed durum wheat, pressed and dried
    b. Steamed wheat berry, dried and ground
    c. Whole wheat kernel broken in small pieces
    d. Buckwheat kernel, steamed, pressed, dried and ground

16. The pasta that has the shape of a shell is known as:
    a. conchiglie
    b. farfalle
    c. rotelle
    d. rigatoni

17. The pasta that is extruded to have the shape of a grain of rice is:
    a. spira
    b. capellini
    c. orzo
    d. ziti

D. Matching

Match each vegetable in List A with the appropriate letter in List B. Each choice in List B can only be used once.

List A

_____1. Artichokes

_____2. Swiss chard

_____3. Okra

_____4. Bok choy

_____5. Pumpkin

_____6. Tomatillos

_____7. Leeks

_____8. Truffles

List B

a. A winter squash variety that is popular especially in October

b. A type of beet only used for its greens.

c. Husk tomatoes with a crisp, tart flesh.

d. Tubers that grow near oak or beech tree roots.

e. Immature flowers of a thistle plant often canned or marinated.

f. From Arab and African cuisines, often used for thickening.

g. A sweet, onion-flavoured vegetable with flat, wide leaves.

h. A white-stemmed variety of southern Chinese cabbage.

i. The immature stalks of bulb onions.

E. True or False

For each question below, circle either True or False to indicate the correct answer.

1. Grains cooked by the risotto or pilaf method are first coated with hot fat.
    True   False

2. Medium-grain rice is best served freshly made and piping hot.
    True   False

3. The only grain that can be eaten fresh as a vegetable is corn.
    True   False

4. Making dough with semolina flour makes it softer, more supple, and easier to work with.
    True   False

5. Asian noodle dough can be used to make dumplings.
    True   False

6. "Yam" is an industry term for sweet potato.
   True   False

7. Potatoes should be stored at 0–4°C (32–40°F).
   True   False

8. The best applications for mealy potatoes are sautéing and pan-frying.
   True   False

9. A wonton is a dumpling.
   True   False

10. For best results, fresh pasta should be cooked to order.
    True   False

11. Quinoa is not used a lot on menus because it is known to have poor nutritional values.
    True   False

12. The term "macaroni" technically refers to pastas made with flour and water.
    True   False

Chapter 24

Vegetarian Cooking

Vegetarianism can be seen as a kind of self-expression, but whether it is for religious, ethics, or environmental concerns, more and more people are opting for a vegetarian diet. A wide variety of fruits, vegetables, salads and other products either grown here or imported from neighbouring countries are increasingly available. Learning about these motivations and products makes it a lot easier for a chef to understand the vegetarian philosophy and include vegetarian dishes in the daily meal plans.

At the end of this chapter the student should be able to:

1.   Understand the range of vegetarian diets and motivations supporting vegetarianism.
2.   Use a variety of protein products as alternatives to meat, poultry, fish and dairy.
3.   Create interesting, varied and balanced vegetarian dishes, meals and menus.

Key Terms

Strict-vegetarian	Demi-vegetarian	White miso
Vegan	Macrobioticist	Red miso
Raw foodist	Soy-milk	Tempeh
Fruitarian	Tofu	Textured soy protein
Ovo-vegetarian	Cotton tofu	Seitan
Ovo-lacto-vegetarian	Silken tofu	
Lacto-vegetarian	Miso	

Test Your Knowledge

The practice sets provided below have been designed to test your comprehension of the information found in this chapter. It is recommended that you read the chapter completely before attempting these questions.

A. Terminology

Fill in the blank spaces with the correct term.

1.   _____ Made from soybeans that are soaked, cooked and ground, then simmered in water and strained.

2.   _____ Soybean curd.

3.   _____ A type of bean cake made from fermented whole soybeans mixed with grains such as rice or millet.

4.   _____ A defatted soy protein that is dried and then compressed into granules or chunks or extruded into shapes.

5.   _____ A form of wheat gluten with a firm, chewy texture and a blend of flavours.

6. _____ Fresh green soybeans.

7. Cotton tofu comes in three styles:_____ , _____ and _____ .

8. Tofu comes from processing_____ into _____, which is then_____ and formed into a cake.

Fill in the blank spaces with the correct definitions.

9. Pythagoreans_____

10. Strict or pure vegetarian_____

11. Living foodist_____

12. Macrobioticist_____

13. Silken tofu_____

14. Miso_____

15. Analogous foods_____

16. Cotton tofu_____

B. Short Answer

Provide a short response that correctly answers each of the questions below.

1. Name the one vitamin not found in vegetables, which therefore requires a supplement.

   _____

2. Name the one mineral that is either not found in vegetables or the type found in the plant food is not readily absorbed by the body, therefore requiring a supplement.

   _____

3. List four (4) reasons why one might choose a vegetarian lifestyle.

   a._____

   b._____

   c._____

   d._____

4.   Frances Moore Lappé's 1971 publication supported vegetarianism from what perspective?

_____

_____

5.   Dieticians recommend that vegans include linolenic acids in their diet so as to compensate for fatty acids that may be deficient. What four (4) ingredients offer a good supply of such acids?

a._____   c._____

b._____   d._____

6.   Australian ethics professor Peter Singer wrote a book in 1975 that helped spark the United States-based PETA (People for the Ethical Treatment of Animals). What two (2) things does this organization stand for?

a._____

b._____

7.   What makes vegetarian diets so hard for a chef to understand when trying to appeal to guests' desires?

_____

_____

_____

_____

8.   Vegans can meet the calcium requirements in their diets by consuming what four (4) things?

a._____   c._____

b._____   d._____

9.   Explain the difference between white and red miso.

_____

_____

_____

0. Explain the procedures for making soy-milk.

_____

_____

11. Explain the procedures for making seitan.

_____

_____

12. List three (3) groups of food listed in the Vegetarian Diet Pyramid that should be consumed at every meal.

a._____   c._____

b._____

13. List three (3) groups of food listed in the Vegetarian Diet Pyramid that should be consumed daily.

a._____   c._____

b._____

14. Name one (1) group of food listed in the Vegetarian Diet Pyramid that should be consumed weekly.

_____

15. List eight (8) suggestions that a chef can follow to plan and prepare to add vegetarian dishes to a restaurant menu.

a._____

b._____

c._____

d._____

e._____

f._____

g._____

h._____

C. Matching

Below is a list of numbered beliefs related to vegetarianism and major world religions. Under each numbered fact, list the letter of the religion(s) that prescribe to the belief. More than one religion may be matched with each belief.

List A   **List B**

_____ 1. Some follow a religious and ethical standard of ahimsa.   a. Hinduism

_____ 2. Practices can vary by geographic location grouping such as   b. Buddhism
China and Vietnam; Japan and Korea; Sri Lanka and
Southeast Asia.

_____ 3. Majority live in India.   c. Jainism

_____ 4. Approximately 800 million observe this faith worldwide.   d. Judaism and
Christianity

_____ 5. Eating meat is common.

_____ 6. Based on Vedas, sacred texts approximately 4000 years old.

_____ 7. Vegetarianism is common, but not followed by all.

_____ 8. Some follow ancient texts that believe Buddha ate meat
because he didn't want to offend those who brought him
charitable offerings.

_____ 9. Some prepare for the coming of the Messiah by practising
vegetarianism.

_____ 10. Combines Hinduism and Buddhism.

_____ 11. Try to practise as pure a form of ahimsa as possible,
sweeping the ground before they walk on it and wearing
gauze masks so as not to tread or breathe on insects and harm
them.

_____ 12. Some believe they can eat meat.

_____ 13. All follow the Dalai lama, the spiritual leader worldwide.

_____ 14. Most observers abstain from eating the sacred cow.

_____ 15. Predominant religion in India.

D. True or False

For each question below, circle either True or False to indicate the correct answer.

1. A growing number of people are choosing to forgo some or all animal products in their diet.
    True   False

2. It is estimated that 25% of Canadian adults follow a vegetarian diet.
    True   False

3. Vegetarians who consume dairy and/or eggs generally have an easier time meeting their nutrient needs compared to a fruitarian.
   True   False

4. Tossed salads are a good source of quality protein.
   True   False

5. Eggs are consumed by ovo-vegetarians as well as vegans.
   True   False

6. Grains can be consumed by people observing all types of vegetarian diets.
   True   False

7. The same quantity of soy-milk can be substituted for dairy milk in all recipes.
   True   False

8. Peas, most nuts and seeds, as well as oats, are the only plant-based foods that are equivalent to animal proteins.
   True   False

9. Once opened, soy-milk that is sold in aseptic packaging (stored at room temperature) is good for one year as long as it is refrigerated.
   True   False

10. Nuts and seeds can be consumed by all types of vegetarians.
    True   False

11. Tempeh should be cooked prior to eating, which tempers its pronounced flavour.
    True   False

12. Of all the vegan protein ingredients, tofu has a texture similar to wheat.
    True   False

13. Many of the world's major religions promote meatless diets.
    True   False

14. Although there are brown, black and green varieties of soybeans, the majority are brown.
    True   False

15. Silken tofu should be boiled for ten (10) minutes for safety purposes.
    True   False

16. Miso should never be boiled.
    True   False

Chapter 25

Salads and Salad Dressings

Today more than ever before, salads are being revitalized on the North American menu. Based on the demands of the clientele, chefs are using new and different salad ingredients.

At the end of this chapter the student should be able to:
1.   Identify and prepare a variety of salad greens.
2.   Prepare a variety of salad dressings.
3.   Prepare a variety of salads.
4.   Present salads attractively.

Key Terms

Salad	Radicchio	Green salads
Boston lettuce	Arugula	Emulsification
Iceberg lettuce	Dandelion	Tossed salad
Leaf lettuce	Mâche	Composed salad
Romaine lettuce	Sorrel	Bound salad
Mesclun	Spinach	Vegetable salads
Micro greens	Sprouts	Fruit salads
Chicory	Watercress	Base
Belgian endive	Edible flowers	Body
Curly endive	Vinaigrette	Garnish
Escarole	French dressing	Dressing

Test Your Knowledge

The practice sets provided below have been designed to test your comprehension of the information found in this chapter. It is recommended that you read the chapter completely before attempting these questions.

A. Terminology

Fill in the blank spaces with the correct definition.

1.   Composed salad _____

2.   Tossed salad _____

3.   Vinaigrette _____

4.   Cos _____

5. Witloof _____

6. Escarole _____

7. Arugula _____

8. Mâche _____

Fill in the blank spaces with the correct term.

9. _____ The bringing together of two liquids that do not ordinarily form a stable mixture, with the aid of an emulsifying agent.

10. _____ A salad created by combining cooked meats, poultry, fish, shellfish, potatoes, pasta, grains and/or legumes with a dressing and garnishes.

11. _____ A mixture of several kinds of baby lettuce.

12. _____ A cold emulsified sauce consisting of vinegar, egg yolks, oil and flavourings.

13. _____ The first true leaves of any edible greens.

B. Fill in the Blanks

Fill in the blanks provided with the response that correctly completes the statement.

1. An emulsified vinaigrette is a standard vinaigrette dressing emulsified with _____, _____ or _____.

2. The emulsifier in mayonnaise is _____, which is a protein found in _____.

3. The higher the proportion of vinegar in the mayonnaise, the _____ it will be.

4. There are two types of green salads: _____ and _____.

5. The basic ingredients of Waldorf salad are _____, _____, _____ and _____.

6. A preparation made by simmering vegetables in a marinade, flavoured with olive oil and lemon juice and served cold, is referred to as _____.

7. There are usually four (4) components in a composed salad; they are _____, the _____, the _____ and the _____.

C. Short Answer

Provide a short response that correctly answers each of the questions below.

1. List three (3) edible flowers.

    a. _____

    b. _____

    c. _____

2. Briefly explain the procedure used to remove the midrib from spinach.

    _____

    _____

    _____

3. Explain the procedure for washing salad greens.

    _____

    _____

    _____

    _____

4. What are three (3) things that should be avoided when making a nutritionally balanced salad? The overuse of:

    a. _____

    b. _____

    c. _____

5. Give two (2) reasons why greens should be stored separately from tomatoes and apples.

    a. _____

    b. _____

6. List five (5) of the ingredients that may be included in mayonnaise-based dressing.

    a. _____   c. _____   e. _____

    b. _____   d. _____

7. List the four (4) components of composed salad:

    a. _____   c. _____

    b. _____   d. _____

8. List four (4) possible ingredients for a fruit salad dressing.

    a. _____   c. _____

    b. _____   d. _____

9. Describe the procedure for making mayonnaise.

    _____

    _____

    _____

10. Explain the procedure for storing salad greens.

    _____

    _____

    _____

    _____

11. Explain the procedure for preparing a composed salad.

    _____

    _____

    _____

12. Explain the procedure for washing salad greens.

    _____

    _____

    _____

    _____

D. Multiple Choice

For each question below, choose the one response that correctly answers the question.

1. What is the best type of oil to use when making mayonnaise?
   a. Nut oil
   b. Vegetable oil
   c. Seed oil
   d. Olive oil

2. What are the *two* forms in which lettuce grows?
   a. Bunch and leaf
   b. Leaf and head
   c. Head and stalks
   d. Stalks and bunch

3. Lettuces and salad greens should be stored in protective containers at what temperature?
   a. -1–1°C (30–32°F)
   b. 0–1°C (32–34°F)
   c. 1–3°C (34–38°F)
   d. 4–10°C (40–50°F)

4. What type of an emulsion is a basic vinaigrette?
   a. permanent
   b. semi-permanent
   c. temporary
   d. semi-temporary

5. Approximately how much oil can one egg yolk emulsify?
   a. 60 mL (2 ounces)
   b. 120 mL (4 ounces)
   c. 250 mL (1 cup)
   d. 210 mL (7 ounces)

6. The four types of salads are:
   a. tossed, green, composed, fruit
   b. fruit, vegetable, meat, dairy
   c. starch, vegetable, composed, bound
   d. green, vegetable, fruit, bound

7. In a composed salad, the green would serve as the:
    a. base
    b. body
    c. garnish
    d. dressing

8. Tomato and asparagus salad with fresh mozzarella would be considered a:
    a. fruit salad
    b. composed salad
    c. vegetable salad
    d. bound salad

9. Traditional potato salad is considered a:
    a. green salad
    b. composed salad
    c. vegetable salad
    d. bound salad

10. Due to the flavour characteristics of mâche, what *would not* be an appropriate green to toss with this in a salad?
    a. Boston lettuce
    b. radicchio
    c. bibb lettuce
    d. iceberg lettuce

11. One of the most popular types of butter leaf lettuce is:
    a. Boston
    b. iceberg
    c. leaf
    d. romaine

12. Chicory is a family of salad greens that includes:
    a. sorrel and leaf
    b. iceberg and Belgian endive
    c. arugula and curly endive
    d. escarole and radicchio

13. Consider the following statements. Which one is *not* true?
    a. Salad greens are high in vitamins A and C, iron, and fibre.
    b. Greens should be stored with the tomatoes.
    c. Flowers grown from bulbs can be toxic.
    d. Fresh herbs can be used to add flavour to salads.

14. Consider the following statements. Which one is true?
    a. Storing greens with apples will help prolong their shelf life.
    b. Greens have a low nitrate content.
    c. Lettuces are usually packed in cases of 24 heads.
    d. Because they spoil rapidly, greens are not available precut and washed.

15. What is basic French dressing?
    a. mayonnaise and wine vinegar
    b. oil, vinegar, and French mustard
    c. oil, vinegar, salt, and pepper
    d. mayonnaise, blue cheese, and cream

E. Matching

Match the type of dressing in list B with the appropriate type of salad in List B. Choices in List B may be used more than once.

List A	List B
_____ 1. Any greens	a. Vinaigrette dressing made with vegetable oil and wine vinegar
_____ 2. Delicate greens	b. Vinaigrette dressing made with nut oil and balsamic vinegar
_____ 3. Hardy greens	c. Emulsified vinaigrette dressing
	d. Mayonnaise-based dressing such as blue cheese or Green Goddess

F. True or False

For each question below, circle either True or False to indicate the correct answer.

1. Salad greens are not necessarily green.
   True   False

2. Mesclun is the name of a type of lettuce originally grown in France.
   True   False

3. Micro greens are the first true leaves of any edible greens.
   True   False

4. Many flowers grown from bulbs are toxic.
   True   False

5. Radicchio is a type of red cabbage.
   True   False

6. Cauliflower and broccoli are examples of vegetables that contain high levels of nitrate and nitrite as compared to cured meats.
   True   False

7. Lettuce is often packed in cases of 30 heads.
   True   False

8. When working with products that will not be cooked, the use of single-use gloves is recommended.
   True   False

9. The standard ratio of oil to vinegar in a French dressing is 3 parts of vinegar to 1 part of oil.
   True   False

10. An emulsion is always made with eggs.
    True   False

11. Mayonnaise is best made with neutral flavoured oil such as safflower oil.
    True   False

12. Aïoli is a type of mayonnaise made with olive oil.
    True   False

13. Vinaigrette dressings can be emulsified by using whole eggs.
    True   False

14. A vinaigrette dressing made with nut oil is a good choice for a Belgian endive salad.
    True   False

15. Blue cheese dressing is an appropriate addition to a mesclun salad.
    True   False

Chapter 26

Fruits

The versatility of fruit in cooking is astounding. Learning product identification, handling and storage techniques, and flavour combinations that enhance the characteristics of fruit are valuable references for kitchen application.

At the end of this chapter the student should be able to:

1. Identify a variety of fruits.
2. Purchase fruits appropriate for your needs.
3. Store fruits properly.
4. Explain how fruits are preserved.
5. Prepare fruits for cooking or service.
6. Apply various cooking methods to fruits.

Key Terms

Ripe	Cape gooseberries	Santa Claus melons	Mangoes
Blackberries	Lychees	Watermelons	Papayas
Blueberries	Mangosteens	Pomes	Papain
Cranberries	Figs	Apples	Passion fruits
Currants	Persimmons	Pears	Pineapples
Raspberries	Pomegranates	Quince	Respiration rate
Strawberries	Prickly pears	Pectin	Acidulation
Zest	Rhubarb	Stone fruits	Juice
Grapefruits	Star fruits	Apricots	Nectar
Kumquats	Red flame grapes	Cherries	Cider
Lemons	Thompson seedless	Peaches	Concentrate
Limes	grapes	Nectarines	Jam
Oranges	Concord grapes	Plums	Jelly
Tangerines	Cantaloupes	Bananas	Marmalade
Hybrids	Casaba melons	Dates	Preserve
Varieties	Crenshaw melons	Kiwis	

Test Your Knowledge

The practice sets provided below have been designed to test your comprehension of the information found in this chapter. It is recommended that you read the chapter completely before attempting these questions.

A. Terminology

Fill in the blank spaces with the correct term.

1. _____ A citrus jelly that also contains unpeeled slices of citrus fruit.

2. _____ A fruit gel made from fruit juice and sugar.

3. _____ An enzyme found in papayas that breaks down proteins; used as the primary ingredient in meat tenderizers.

4. _____ A fruit gel made from fruit pulp and sugar.

5. _____ The stage where fruit is at its full size, its pulp or flesh becomes soft and tender, its colour changes, the acid content declines, and the starches convert to sugar, providing sweetness, flavour, and aroma.

6. _____ A fruit gel that contains large pieces or whole fruits.

7. _____ Cross breeding of fruits from different species that are genetically unalike.

8. _____ Fruits characterized by a thick rind most of which is a bitter white pith.

9. _____ Sometimes referred to as mandarins.

10. _____ Tart fruits that grow on shrubs in grape-like clusters, the most common variety being beautiful, almost translucent red

11. _____ Fruits that grow on low vines cultivated in swamps and are rarely eaten raw.

12. _____ Native to North America and cultivated in almost all provinces of Canada with the Lac St. Jean region being the most famous.

13. _____ A hybrid of orange and pummelo.

14. _____ This variety of fruit is essential in the production of Curaçao and Grand-Marnier.

15. _____ Also known as Physalis or ground cherries.

16. _____ The most important variety of this fruit is the Calimyrna.

17. _____ Also known as Carambolas.

Fill in the blank spaces with the correct definition.

18. Supreme _____

19. Kaki _____

20. Pectin _____

21. Zest _____

22. Ethylene gas _____

23. Concentrate _____

24. Acidulation _____

B. Fill in the Blanks

Fill in the blanks provided with the response that correctly answers the statement.

1. _____ is the most common method of cooking pears.

2. In classic dishes, the term *à la Normande* refers to the use of _____.

3. Pumpkins, cucumbers, and melons are all members of the _____ family.

4. _____ are the single largest fruit crop in the world.

5. When deep-fat frying fruits, the best results are achieved by first dipping the fruit slices in _____ before submerging in the fat.

6. Melons are members of the _____ family.

7. Virtually all the fine wine made in the world comes from varieties of _____ from a single species known as _____.

8. Peaches have a _____ covered with _____, while nectarines have a _____, _____ skin.

9. Bananas grow in bunches known as _____ and are actually the _____ of a large tropical herb.

10. Kiwis are also known as _____ _____.

11. Papayas are also known as _____.

12. Papayas contain an _____ called _____ and can be added to meat marinades to _____ them.

13. The cross-breeding of fruits from different species results in a _____ fruit.

14. The breeding of fruits from the same species results in a _____ of that species

15. The concentrated juice of _____ is used to make grenadine syrup

16. Although botanically not a fruit, _____ is most often prepared as a fruit. Its pinkish-red stems are very acidic.

C. Short Answers

Provide a short response that correctly answers the questions below.

1. Describe the procedure for segmenting citrus fruits.

    _____

    _____

2. List eight (8) common varieties of apples.

    a. _____   e. _____

    b. _____   f. _____

    c. _____   g. _____

    d. _____   h. _____

3. List four (4) common varieties of pears.

    a. _____   c. _____

    b. _____   d. _____

4. List the four (4) fruits that emit ethylene gas.

    a. _____   c. _____

    b. _____   d. _____

5. What is an indicator of cold damage to bananas?

    _____

6. Fruits are varied in their content of vitamins and minerals. Identify the fruits that are plentiful in the elements listed below.

Vitamin C	*Vitamin A*	*Potassium*
a. _____	b. _____	c. _____
_____	_____	_____
_____	_____	_____

7. List four (4) uses for lower grades of fruit.

    a. _____   c. _____

    b. _____   d. _____

8. List five (5) methods of fruit preservation.

    a. _____   d. _____

    b. _____   e. _____

    c. _____

9. Name four (4) fruits that benefit from acidulation.

    a. _____   c. _____

    b. _____   d. _____

10. Name five (5) fruits that maintain their texture when sautéed.

    a. _____   d. _____

    b. _____   e. _____

    c. _____

11. Fruits are divided into eight (8) categories; list them.

    a. _____   e. _____

    b. _____   f. _____

    c. _____   g. _____

    d. _____   h. _____

12. Describe the basic procedures for trimming and slicing pineapple.

    _____

    _____

    _____

    _____

13. Describe the basic procedures for baking fruit.

_____

_____

_____

_____

14. Describe the basic procedures for sautéing fruit.

_____

_____

_____

_____

15. Describe the basic procedures for poaching fruit.

_____

_____

_____

_____

16. Describe the basic procedures for making fruit preserves.

_____

_____

_____

_____

17. Describe the basic procedures for making apple sauce.

_____

_____

_____

_____

18. List the essential ingredients of jellies and explain the procedures for preparing jellies; identify the most important points.

_____

_____

_____

_____

D. Multiple Choice

For each question below, choose the one response that correctly answers the question.

1. Citrus fruits are known to be high in:
   a. vitamin D
   b. fibre
   c. vitamin A
   d. vitamin C

2. Fresh fruit grades in Canada are:
   a. Canada No. 1, Canada No. 2 and Canada Domestic
   b. Canada No. 1, Canada No. 2 and Canada No. 3
   c. Canada Fancy, Canada Choice, Canada Standard
   d. Canada Prime, Canada Standard

3. Consider the following statements. Which one is true?
   a. Figs arc picked green and ripen with ethylene gas.
   b. Figs do not continue to ripen after picking.
   c. Figs will keep well if picked under-ripe.
   d. Figs will ripen nicely in a cool storage room.

4. The addition of an acidic solution to fruits is referred to as:
   a. acidulation
   b. brining
   c. antioxidizing
   d. wet packing

5. In solid-pack cans:
   a. 5% juice is added
   b. 10% water is added
   c. some fruit juice is added
   d. the only liquid is from the fruit's natural moisture

6. Compared to solid-pack, water-pack cans have:
   a. somewhat better yield
   b. some yield
   c. lesser yield
   d. much better yield

7. Frozen fruit grades in Canada are:
   a. the same as fresh fruit
   b. Canada Fancy, Canada Choice, Canada Standard, Canada Substandard
   c. the same as fresh vegetables
   d. the same as frozen vegetables

8. Which of the following is highest in pectin?
   a. quince
   b. pear
   c. peach
   d. grape

9. A good choice of fruit for baking is:
   a. cherries and peaches
   b. apple and pears
   c. kiwis and melons
   d. star fruit and quince

10. A good choice of fruit for frying is
    a. oranges, bananas, peaches
    b. mango, cherries, pears
    c. strawberries, kiwis, carambolas
    d. bananas, apples, pineapples

D. True or False

For each question below, circle either True or False to indicate the correct answer.

1. Carryover cooking occurs with fruit.
   True   False

2. Sulfur dioxide is added to dried fruits to maintain their flavour during storage.
   True   False

3. Freezing is the best method for preserving the fresh appearance of fruit.
   True   False

4. Most fruit purchased for food service operations is Canada Fancy.
    True   False

5. Pineapples do not ripen after picking.
    True   False

6. Irradiation maintains fruit's flavour and texture while slowing the ripening process.
    True   False

7. Papayas are also known as carambola.
    True   False

8. Tropical fruit flavours complement rich or spicy meat, fish, and poultry dishes.
    True   False

9. Fruits naturally contain varying amounts of pectin.
    True   False

PART 4 BAKING

Chapter 27

Principles of the Bakeshop

Preparing bakeshop food products requires precise measurements and careful attention. Knowledge of the nature of the ingredients and the chemistry of baking are key responsibilities for those who work in this area.

At the end of this chapter the student should be able to:

1. Recognize and select ingredients used in a bakeshop.
2. Control the development of gluten.
3. Cook sugar correctly.
4. Control the baking process.
5. Recognize many of the specialized tools and equipment used in the bakeshop.

Key Terms

Formula	Bloom	Gelatin
Raw sugar	Dough	Eau de vie
Cocoa butter	Patent flour	Gluten
Kneading	Simple syrups	Emulsions
Flour	Liquor	Beating
Demerara sugar	Batter	Leavener
Cocoa powder	Clear flour	Extracts
Sifting	Cooked syrups	Blending
Sugar	Liqueur	Vanillin
Granulated white sugar	Staling	Creaming
Conching	All-purpose flour	Sucrose
Stirring	Hydrometer	Nib
Fats	Wine	Cutting
Hygroscopic	Starch retrogradation	Refined or table sugar
Couverture	Gelatinization	Chocolate liquor
Whipping	Interferents	Folding
Flavouring	Brandy	Molasses
Sugar syrups	Fermentation	Chocolate mass

Test Your Knowledge

The practice sets provided below have been designed to test your comprehension of the information found in this chapter. It is recommended that you read the chapter completely before attempting these questions.

A. Terminology

Fill in the blank spaces with the correct definition.

1. Whipping _____

2. Liquor _____

3. Simple syrup _____

4. Cocoa butter _____

5. Blending _____

6. Dough _____

7. Wine _____

8. Sucrose _____

9. Bloom _____

10. Folding _____

11. Batter _____

12. Cocoa powder _____

13. Interferents _____

14. Emulsions _____

15. Starch retrogradation _____

Fill in the blank spaces with the correct term.

16. _____ A large, coarse crystal structure that prevents it from dissolving easily.

17. _____ The all-purpose sugar used throughout the kitchen.

18. _____ Regular refined sugar with some molasses returned to it.

19. _____ A tool used to measure the specific gravity of sugar syrups.

20. _____ A high-quality chocolate containing 32% cocoa butter.

21. _____ Grayish-white spots that are the result of the migration of cocoa butter crystals to the surface when temperature changes.

22. _____ Also known as ground nuts.

23. _____ Incorporating solid fat into dry ingredients until lumps of the desired size remain.

24. _____ The tough, rubbery substance created when wheat flour is mixed with water.

25. _____ A common thickener in the bakeshop, it is a natural product derived from the animal protein collagen.

26. _____ Passing one or more dry ingredients through a wire mesh to remove lumps as well as combine and aerate ingredients.

27. _____ An alcoholic beverage made from distilling the fermented mash of grapes or other fruits.

28. _____ A strong, sweet, syrupy alcoholic beverage made by mixing or redistilling neutral spirits with fruits, flowers, herbs, spices, or other flavourings.

29. _____ Mixtures of flavouring oils and ethyl alcohol.

30. _____ Vigorously agitating foods to incorporate air or develop gluten.

31. _____ Gently mixing ingredients until blended.

32. _____ Working a dough to develop gluten.

33. _____ Also known as chocolate mass, it is the result of further roasting nibs and crushing into a thick (nonalcoholic) paste.

34. _____ Vigorously combining fat and sugar while incorporating air.

35. _____ A gas produced by baking powder reacting with acid or heat.

36. _____ Gaseous form of water used as a leavening agent.

37. _____ A protein found in flour, responsible for the formation of gluten.

38. _____ The cultivated form of hazelnut.

B. Fill in the Blank

1. A product extracted from wheat flour and averaging 75% protein content is known as

_____ _____ _____.

2. Wheat is classified as _____ and _____ depending on the kernel's hardness.

3. To produce a more acceptable product, rye flour is often _____ with a _____ wheat flour.

4. The sugar most often used in the kitchen is _____.

5. The uncrystallized liquid by-product from the production of sugar is _____.

6. Demerara sugar, sometimes called _____ sugar is the closest consumable product to _____ sugar.

7. _____ is a granulated sugar with smaller size crystals and is also known as _____ sugar.

8. _____ is made by grinding granulated sugar crystals through varying degree of fine screens. It is also known as _____ sugar and is widely available in three degree of fineness: _____, _____ and _____.

9. Corn syrup is a _____ sweetener, which means it will _____ (retain) water.

10. Light syrup is made with _____ of water to _____ of sugar by weight.

11. Medium syrup is made with _____ of sugar to _____ of water by weight.

12. Heavy syrup is made with _____ of sugar to _____ of water by weight.

13. Vanilla beans may develop a white coating, which are crystals known as _____.

14. Chocolate mass contains _____ known as _____.

15. Indicate the protein content of the flours listed below:

a. Pastry _____

b. All purpose _____

c. Patent or clear _____

16. Unsweetened chocolate is also known as _____ chocolate; it contains approximately _____ % cocoa butter

17. Small round pieces of chocolate referred to as _____ or _____ are often made with the finest chocolate.

18. A native of the Mississippi Valley, _____ are perhaps the most popular nut in America.

19. A native of Central Asia, _____ are unique for the green colour of their meat.

C. Short Answer

1. Briefly explain the importance of aging and bleaching flour.

_____

_____

_____

_____

2. What is the purpose of emulsified shortenings?

_____

_____

_____

_____

3. List four (4) factors that should be evaluated when selecting chocolate.

a. _____

b. _____

c. _____

d. _____

4. List two (2) important rules to follow when melting chocolate.

a. _____

b. _____

5. Describe the proper procedures for tempering chocolate.

_____

_____

_____

D. Multiple Choice

For each question below, choose the one response that correctly answers the question.

1. All fats are considered to be shortenings in baking because they tenderize the product and:
    a. leaven
    b. strengthen the gluten strands
    c. give good colour
    d. shorten the gluten strands

2. Composite flours are:
    a. made from corn, soybeans, and rice
    b. categorized as non-wheat flours
    c. naturally high in protein
    d. made with the bran intact

3. Sanding sugar is primarily used for:
    a. a granulated sugar substitute
    b. making light, tender cakes
    c. decorating cookies and pastries
    d. making icings and glazes for decorating

4. What is the most frequently used and therefore most important ingredient in the bakeshop?
    a. granulated sugar
    b. wheat flour
    c. shortening
    d. yeast

5. Whole-wheat flour, which includes the bran and germ, is also called:
    a. wheat germ
    b. composite flour
    c. whole flour
    d. graham flour

6. Which of the following is *not* true about the role of sugar and sweeteners in the bakeshop?
    a. They act as a crisping agent.
    b. They serve as a preservative.
    c. They tenderize products.
    d. They act as a creaming agent.

7. A baked good's final texture is determined by the rise, which is caused by the _____, _____ and _____ in the dough or batter.
   a. temperature, sugar, yeast
   b. protein, gluten, strands
   c. glutenin, gliadin, water
   d. carbon dioxide, air, steam

8. Seventy-one degrees Celsius (160°F) is the temperature at which gluten, dairy, and egg proteins:
   a. brown
   b. soften
   c. crystallize
   d. solidify

9. A change in a baked good's texture and starch granule structure results in:
   a. staling
   b. browning
   c. leavening
   d. gluten development

10. _____ is the brown powder left after the _____ is removed.
   a. Unsweetened chocolate, sugar
   b. Cocoa powder, sugar
   c. Milk chocolate, dairy solids
   d. Cocoa powder, cocoa butter

11. Semi-sweet chocolate contains a minimum of _____ chocolate liquor.
   a. 47%
   b. 35%
   c. 55%
   d. 32%

12. Which of the following nuts is the main ingredient in marzipan?
   a. Almonds
   b. Chestnuts
   c. Hazelnuts
   d. Pine nuts

13. Which of the following nuts is small, creamy white and teardrop shaped, commonly used in dishes from Spain?

   a. Almonds

   b. Chestnuts

   c. Hazelnuts

   d. Pine nuts

E. Matching

I. Mixing Methods

Match each of the terms in List A with the appropriate letter in List B. Each choice in List B can only be used once.

List A	List B
_____1. Blending	a. Use a spoon or electric mixer with paddle attachment.
_____2. Cutting	b. Use a whisk or electric mixer with whip attachment.
_____3. Sifting	c. Use a rubber spatula.
_____4. Whipping	d. Use a spoon, rubber spatula, whisk, or electric mixer with paddle attachment.
_____5. Folding	e. Use an electric mixer with paddle attachment on medium speed.
_____6. Creaming	f. Use a rotary or drum sifter or mesh strainer.
_____7. Beating	g. Use a whisk, spoon, or rubber spatula.
_____8. Kneading	h. Use a flat cake spatula or metal spatula.
_____9. Stirring	i. Use pastry cutters, fingers, or an electric mixer with paddle attachment.
	j. Use hands or an electric mixer with dough hook attachment.

II. Alcoholic Beverages.

_____1. Liquor

_____2. Liqueur

_____3. Wine

_____4. Brandy

_____5. Eau de Vie

a. An alcoholic beverage made from the fermented juice of grapes.

b. Fruit spirits made by distilling fruits.

c. An alcoholic beverage made by distilling grains, vegetables or other foods.

d. An alcoholic beverage made by mixing wine with fruits, flowers, herbs, spices or other flavourings.

e. A strong, sweet, syrupy alcoholic beverage made by mixing or redistilling neutral spirits with fruits, flowers, herbs, spices or other flavourings.

f. An alcoholic beverage made by distilling wine or the fermented mash of grapes or other fruits.

F. True or False

For each question below, circle either True or False to indicate the correct answer.

1. Self-rising flour is bread flour with salt and baking powder added to it.
    True   False

2. Glutenin and gliadin contain the gluten necessary to create a quality dough or batter.
    True   False

3. Chocolate as we know it today did not exist in Europe until Columbus brought the first cacao beans back to Spain from the New World.
    True   False

4. Unsweetened chocolate is pure hardened cocoa liquor.
    True   False

5. It is the milk solids that make milk chocolate milder and sweeter than other chocolates.
    True   False

6. Cocoa butter melts at just below body temperature.
    True   False

7. Gluten provides structure in dough by enabling the gases from fermentation to be retained.
    True   False

8. Flour derived from the portion of the endosperm closest to the germ is coarser.
    True   False

9. Whole-wheat flour has a shorter shelf life due to its fat content.
   True   False

10. Unopened bags of flour can be stored anywhere as long as the location is relatively cool and free of moisture.
    True   False

11. Beets and sugar cane are the two main sources for sugar.
    True   False

12. Unsalted butter is usually preferred to salted butter in baking because the salt may interfere with the product formula.
    True   False

13. "Carryover" cooking is a phenomenon that occurs in the bakeshop as well as the kitchen.
    True   False

14. A batter generally contains more fat, sugar, and liquid than a dough.
    True   False

15. 4X sugar is finer than 10X sugar.
    True   False

16. Icing sugar contains 3% cornstarch.
    True   False

17. Milk chocolate should be tempered at slightly higher temperatures than dark chocolate.
    True   False

18. White chocolate contains 13% chocolate solids.
    True   False

Chapter 28

Quick Breads

Quick breads are popular due to their ease of preparation, versatility of application, and variety of flavour possibilities. The availability of ingredients as well as the use of chemical leaveners make quick breads an ideal option for busy food service operations.

At the end of this chapter the student should be able to:

1. Use chemical leavening agents.
2. Prepare a variety of quick breads using the biscuit, muffin and creaming methods.

Key Terms

Baking soda

Baking powder

Single-acting baking powder

Double-acting baking powder

Biscuit method

Muffin method

Creaming method

Tunnelling

Pancakes

Waffles

Test Your Knowledge

The practice sets provided below have been designed to test your comprehension of the information found in this chapter. It is recommended that you read the chapter completely before attempting these questions.

A. Terminology

Fill in the blank spaces with the correct term.

1. _____ Items such as baking soda and baking powder, which do not require fermentation, but instead release gases through chemical reactions between acids and bases contained in the formula.

2. _____ A method used to produce a tender batter with an even shape and distribution of fruits, nuts, or other ingredients. Overmixing should be avoided with this method to prevent tunnelling.

3. _____ This method is very similar to the technique used for making flaky pie doughs, creating a dough that is light, flaky, and tender.

4. _____ A crumbly mixture of fat, flour, sugar, and sometimes nuts and spices; used to top baked goods.

5. _____ An alkaline compound (a base), which releases carbon dioxide gas if both an acid and moisture are present.

6. _____ A simple quick bread found in many Canadian Native cultures.

7. _____ The cutting, shaping, and forming of dough products before baking.

8. _____ The interior of bread or cake; may be elastic, aerated, fine or coarse grained.

Fill in the blank spaces with the correct definition.

9. Tunnelling _____

10. Baking powder _____

11. Creaming method _____

12. Scones _____

13. Aluminum sulphate _____

14. Sodium bicarbonate _____

15. Cream of tartar _____

B. Fill in the Blank

1. Chemical leavening agents release _____ through chemical reactions between _____ and _____.

2. Sources of acid commonly used with baking soda are _____, _____, _____, _____, _____ and _____

3. Baking aroma or _____ is also used as a _____ in some baked goods.

4. Quick breads are generally mixed using the _____, _____ or _____ methods.

5. The biscuit mixing method is similar to the technique used in mixing _____.

6. Single-acting baking powder releases _____ _____ gas in the presence of _____ only.

7. Double-acting baking powder releases some _____ _____ gas upon contact with _____ and more when _____ is applied.

C. Short Answer

Provide a short response that correctly answers each of the questions below.

1. Describe the type and texture of fat used in the production of quick breads using the following methods:

a. Muffin method: _____

b. Biscuit method: _____

c. Creaming method: _____

2. Why might a recipe call for both baking soda and baking powder?

_____

_____

_____

3. What situation might call for the use of double-acting baking powder?

_____

_____

_____

4. What does the higher fat content in the creaming method do to the gluten in a mixture, and therefore for the final product?

_____

_____

_____

5. Explain why the fat is softened in recipes using the creaming method.

_____

_____

_____

6. Describe the procedure for making Bannock; list all ingredients but amounts are not required.

_____

_____

_____

_____

7.   What is the basic difference between a scone and a biscuit?

_____

_____

_____

_____

8.   Describe the procedure for mixing muffins.

_____

_____

_____

_____

9.   Describe the procedure for mixing biscuits.

_____

_____

_____

_____

10. Describe the procedure for mixing muffins using the creaming method.

_____

_____

_____

_____

11. Describe the procedure for making up biscuits.

_____

_____

_____

_____

12. Describe the procedure for making up muffins.

_____

_____

_____

_____

D. Matching

Match each of the "Problems" in List A with the appropriate letter "Causes" in List B. There may be more than one cause to a problem. Causes may be attributed to more than one problem.

List A: Problems	List B: Causes
_____1. Soapy or bitter taste	a. Overmixing
_____2. Elongated holes (tunnelling)	b. Oven temperature too high
_____3. Crust too thick	c. Chemical leaveners not properly mixed into batter
_____4. Flat top with only a small pick in the centre	d. Damaged leavening agents
_____5. Cracked, uneven top	e. Oven temperature too low
_____6. No rise, uneven top	f. Too much baking soda
	g. Too much sugar
	h. Old batter

E. True or False

For each question below, circle either True or False to indicate the correct answer.

1. Bread flour is used to make biscuits.
    True   False

2. The creaming method is comparable to the mixing method used for many butter cakes.
    True   False

3. Honey, molasses, fresh fruit, and buttermilk are all examples of acids that may be used with baking soda.
    True   False

4. Baking powder requires an acid ingredient in the formula in order to create the chemical reaction.
    True   False

5. Some quick breads use yeast as the leavening agent.
    True   False

6. Too much kneading toughens biscuits.
    True   False

7. Fats used in the muffin method should be in a solid form.
    True   False

8. A quick bread made using the creaming method must be mixed with extra care as this method tends to produce tougher products.
    True   False

9. When carbon dioxide is trapped within a batter or dough, it expands when heated, causing the product to rise.
    True   False

10. Batters and dough made with single-acting baking powder do not need to be baked immediately, as long as the product is refrigerated immediately.
    True   False

Chapter 29

Yeast Breads

Although making yeast breads may intimidate the novice baker, mastering a few basic techniques can result in a quality baked product. Beautiful breads made in-house are quickly becoming a thing of the past in the food service industry due to a lack of understanding of these elementary skills.

At the end of this chapter the student should be able to:

1. Select and use yeast.
2. Perform the 10 steps involved in yeast bread production, including kneading by hand.
3. Mix yeast doughs using the straight dough method and sponge method.
4. Prepare rolled-in doughs.

Key Terms

Yeast	Rounding
Fermentation	Bagel
Fresh yeast	Bun
Active dry yeast	Club roll
Instant dry yeast	Kaiser roll
Sourdough starter	Rope infection
Straight dough method	Proof box
Sponge method	Oven spring
Rolled-in doughs	Wash
Proofing	Slashing
Punching down	

Test Your Knowledge

The practice sets provided below have been designed to test your comprehension of the information found in this chapter. It is recommended that you read the chapter completely before attempting these questions.

A. Terminology

Fill in the blank spaces with the correct definition.

1. Sponge method _____

2. Proofing _____

3. Oven spring _____

4. Yeast _____

5. Fermentation _____

Fill in the blank spaces with the correct term.

6. _____ Improving the shape and appearance of some breads by cutting their tops with a sharp knife or razor just before baking; also known as docking.

7. _____ A crust is made shiny or matte, hard or soft, darker or lighter, garnished with seeds or grains, by using this glaze before or after proofing. Egg wash, water, egg and milk, and even plain flour are examples.

8. _____ A type of dough steeped in history since its "starter" was relied on by bakers to leaven the dough prior to the commercial production of yeast.

9. _____ A procedure performed with machine or by hand, to develop the gluten which gives the dough its structure, shape, and texture.

10. _____ The simplest and most common method for yeast doughs in which all of the ingredients are simply combined and mixed.

11. _____ A dough in which the fat is incorporated through a process of rolling and folding, giving the dough a distinctive flaky texture due to the repeated layering of fat throughout the dough. During baking, moisture is released from the fat in the form of steam, causing the layers of dough to rise and separate.

B. Fill in the Blank

1. Compressed yeast is also referred to as _____. It is a mixture of yeast and _____ with a moisture content of _____%.

2. Instant or _____ dry yeast is also available. It must be blended with the _____ ingredients in the formula. It is then activated with hot water at _____°C to _____°C (_____ to _____°F).

3. Yeast doughs are usually mixed using the _____ method or the _____ method.

4. Fermentation is the process by which yeasts convert _____ into _____ and _____.

5. Fermentation is complete when the dough has _____ in size and no longer _____ when pressed gently with two fingers.

6. An infection caused by the hay bacilli bacteria and known as _____ infection causes the crumb to lose _____ and become _____ and _____.

7. Fresh compressed yeast can be interchanged with _____ the amount of instant yeast or _____ the amount of active dry yeast.

8. Yeast becomes dormant at temperatures below _____ °C (_____°F) and dies at temperatures above _____ °C (____°F).

C. Short Answer

Provide a short response that correctly answers each of the questions below.

1. Explain the two (2) steps involved in the sponge method.

    a. _____

    b. _____

2. Why is the organism in active dry yeast considered dormant?

    _____

    _____

3. List four (4) factors for determining the doneness of a baked yeast-leavened product.

    a. _____

    b. _____

    c. _____

    d. _____

4. List three (3) examples of a rolled-in dough product.

    a. _____

    b. _____

    c. _____

5. How is the quantity of dry yeast determined when it is being substituted for compressed yeast?

    _____

    _____

    _____

6. Describe the method for producing a straight method dough.

_____

_____

_____

7. Briefly list the ten (10) sequential stages of yeast bread production.

a. _____   f. _____

b. _____   g. _____

c. _____   h. _____

d. _____   i. _____

e. _____   j. _____

8. For each of the washes listed, identify their respective use.

a. whole egg and water _____

b. whole egg and milk _____

c. egg white and water _____

d. water _____

e. flour _____

f. milk or cream _____

9. List three (3) principal differences between the making of yeast dough and the making of rolled-in dough.

a. _____

b. _____

c. _____

10. Describe the procedure for making rolled-in dough.

a. _____

b. _____

c. _____

d. _____

e. _____

f. _____

11. Describe how bread is judged.

_____

_____

_____

_____

D. Multiple Choice

For each question below, choose the one response that correctly answers the question.

1. Which is an example of a rich dough?
    a. biscuits
    b. Italian bread
    c. challah bread
    d. muffins

2. Quick-rise dry yeast uses _____°C (_____°F) water in order to activate the fermentation process.
    a. 58°C (138°F)
    b. 35°C (95°F)
    c. 38–43°C (100–110°F)
    d. 52–54°C (125–130°F)

3. When yeast is combined with carbohydrates, the result is alcohol and:
    a. oxygen
    b. gas
    c. carbon dioxide
    d. water

4. The disadvantage of using butter in roll-in doughs is that it:
    a. has a high moisture content
    b. cracks and breaks
    c. adds too much salt to the dough
    d. needs to be clarified before using

5. Yeast products should be cooled to approximately what temperature?
   a. 0–1°C (32–34°F)
   b. 16–21°C (60–70°F)
   c. 7–10°C (45–50°F)
   d. 27–32°C (80–90°F)

6. Which of the following is *not* important when considering the amount of flour used in a yeast bread?
   a. percentage of salt in the formula
   b. flour storage conditions
   c. humidity level
   d. measuring accuracy of other ingredients

7. Commercial baking yeast was not made available in stores until:
   a. 1654
   b. 1857
   c. 1910
   d. 1868

8. There are primarily two market forms of baker's yeast. They are:
   a. compressed and active dry
   b. brewer's and compressed
   c. quick-rise dry and instant
   d. fresh and compressed

9. The primary chemical function of rounding is to:
   a. smooth the dough into round balls
   b. stretch the gluten into a smooth coating
   c. help retain the gases from fermentation
   d. proof the dough

10. When is "punching" performed?
   a. after initial fermentation
   b. after proofing
   c. during proofing
   d. after initial mixing of dough

E. Matching

Match each of the "Problems" in List A with the appropriate letter "Causes" in List B. There may be more than one cause to a problem. Each cause may be attributed to more than one problem.

List A: Problems	List B: Causes
_____ 1. Cannonball of dough	a. Too much liquid
	b. Not enough fermentation time
_____ 2. Crust too pale	c. Insufficient kneading
	d. Dough improperly shaped
_____ 3. Crust too dark	e. Too much flour forced into the dough
	f. Too much sugar in dough
_____ 4. Top crust separates from rest of loaf	g. Bread expanded after crust had formed
	h. Too much yeast
_____ 5. Sides of loaf are cracked	i. Insufficient rising time
	j. Dough over-proofed
_____ 6. Dense texture	k. Improper shaping
	l. Oven temperature too low
_____ 7. Ropes of undercooked dough running through the product	m. Oven temperature too high
_____ 8. Free formed loaf spreads and flattens	n. Too much salt
	o. Dough dried out during proofing
_____ 9. Large holes in bread	p. Inadequate punch-down
	q. Over-kneaded
_____ 10. Blister on crust	r. Crust not slashed properly
	s. Too much steam in oven
	t. Dough too soft
	u. Not enough yeast

F. True or False

For each question below, circle either True or False to indicate the correct answer.

1. Punching down occurs before the proofing process.
    True   False

2. Soft yeast dinner rolls are an example of a product made using the straight dough method.
    True   False

3. Washes can be applied before or after proofing occurs.
    True   False

4. Under-proofing may result in a sour taste, poor volume, and a paler colour after baking.
    True   False

5. Rich doughs are baked without steam.
    True   False

6. When properly stored, compressed yeast has a shelf life of two to three weeks.
    True   False

7. Instant yeast can be substituted measure for measure for regular dry yeast.
    True   False

8. There is very little difference between the flavour of dry yeast and the flavour of compressed yeast.
    True   False

9. Rope infection can be prevented by washing equipment with a vinegar solution.
    True   False

10. The bacteria that causes rope infection lives in the soil.
    True   False

11. Too much sugar will kill yeast.
    True   False

12. Instant dry yeast is the same as active dry yeast.
    True   False

13. Direct contact with milk will kill instant dry yeast.
    True   False

Chapter 30

Pies, Pastries and Cookies

The making of pastries involves a variety of techniques that, if mastered, can result in wonderful creations to grace any menu. Viewing these techniques as a series of building blocks or elements, one can study classical pastries to better understand the complexities of the art, which can result in the creation of a new repertoire of unique desserts.

At the end of this chapter the student should be able to:

1. Prepare a variety of pie crusts and fillings.
2. Prepare a variety of classic pastries.
3. Prepare a variety of meringues.
4. Prepare a variety of cookies.
5. Prepare a variety of dessert and pastry items, incorporating components from other chapters.

Key Terms

Pie	Cooked fruit	Éclairs	Ice-box cookies
Tart	Cooked juice	Paris-Brest	Bar cookies
Flaky dough	Baked fruit	Beignets	Cut-out cookies
Mealy dough	Custard	Churros	Rolled cookies
Crumbs	Puff pastry	Crullers	Pressed cookies
Sweet or short paste	Pâte feuilletée	Soft meringue	Wafer cookies
Bake blind	Détrempe	Hard meringue	
Pâte brisée	English method	Japonaise	
Mealy dough	Blitz method	Common meringue	
Pâte sucrée	Bouchées	Swiss meringue	
Docking	Vol-au-vents	Italian meringue	
Cream filling	Feuilletés	Cookies	
Fruit filling	Pâte à choux	Creaming method	
Custard filling	Cream puffs	One-stage method	
Chiffon filling	Profiteroles	Sponge method	
Tempering	Croquembouche	Drop cookies	

Test Your Knowledge

The practice sets below have been designed to test your comprehension of the information found in this chapter. It is recommended that you read the chapter completely before attempting these questions.

A. Terminology

Fill in the blank spaces with the correct term.

1. _____ A filling that is created by adding gelatin to a stirred custard or a fruit purée.

2. _____ A paste made with flour and water during the first stage of preparing a pastry dough.

3. _____ Small puff pastry shells often used for hors d'oeuvres or appetizers.

4. _____ Larger, deeper shells, often filled with savoury mixtures for a main course.

5. _____ Baked rounds of éclair paste cut in half and filled with pastry cream, whipped cream, fruit, or other filling.

6. _____ Small baked rounds of éclair paste filled with ice cream and topped with chocolate sauce.

7. _____ A pyramid of small puffs, each filled with pastry cream and held together with caramelized sugar and decorated with spun sugar or marzipan flowers.

8. _____ An item composed of a sweet or savoury filling in a baked crust.

9. _____ Similar to a pie except that it is made in a shallow, straight-sided pan, often with fluted edges.

10. _____ A dough that produces a very flaky baked product containing little or no sugar.

11. _____ A sweet dough that is rich and non-flaky, used for sweet tart shells.

12. _____ A rich cake in which all or part of the flour is replaced with finely chopped nuts or bread crumbs.

Fill in the blank spaces with the correct definition.

13. Pâte à choux _____

14. Pâte feuilletée _____

15. Bake blind _____

16. Dock _____

17. Éclairs _____

18. Paris-Brest _____

19. Beignets _____

20. Churros _____

21. Crullers _____

22. Meringue _____

23. Cookies _____

B. Fill in the Blank

1. A chiffon filling is created by adding _____ to a _____ or a fruit purée. _____ are then folded into the mixture. The filling is placed in a _____ crust and _____ until firm.

2. If the crust shrinks, it is probably caused by _____, _____ or _____.

3. Freezing baked pies is not recommended unless _____ starch has been used for the filling.

4. A tough crust can be caused by _____ or _____.

5. A runny filling is most likely caused by _____ or _____.

6. A quick puff pastry is also called _____.

7. Puff pastry boxes of various shapes and sizes are called _____.

8. An equal amount of sugar in ratio to egg white creates a _____ meringue while _____ the amount of sugar in ratio to egg whites produces a hard meringue.

9. Common meringues are made by whipping egg white to _____, adding the _____ and continue beating to firm peaks.

10. With Italian meringues, _____ cooked at _____°C (_____°F) is poured onto the _____ egg white.

11. Cookies may be leavened with _____, _____, _____ or _____.

12. Icebox cookies are made from dough that is shaped into _____ or _____, chilled, sliced and baked as needed.

13. Bar cookie dough is _____ or _____ in shallow pans and cut after baking.

14. The texture of cookies can be controlled by changing the proportion of sugar, fat, and liquid. For each of the desired textures indicate whether each of these ingredients is high or low.

Texture	Fat	Sugar	Liquid
Crispness	_____	_____	_____
Softness	_____	_____	_____
Chewiness	_____	_____	_____
Spread	_____	_____	_____

C. Short Answer

Provide a short response that correctly answers each of the questions below.

1. List three (3) types of fillings that are used to fill prebaked pie crusts.

   a. _____   c. _____

   b. _____

2. List four (4) types of fillings that are appropriate for filling a crumb crust.

   a. _____   c. _____

   b. _____   d. _____

3. Name two (2) types of fillings that are cooked by baking them *in* the crust.

   a. _____   b. _____

4. List three (3) reasons for using a flaky dough to prepare pies.

   a. _____

   b. _____

   c. _____

5. Why is a sweet dough (or pâte sucrée) better for making tarts?

   _____

   _____

260

6. When is it appropriate to use a mealy crust?

_____

_____

7. Why is hand mixing best when making small to moderate quantities of flaky dough?

_____

_____

8. What makes pâte à choux unique among dough?

_____

_____

9. What determines whether a meringue is hard or soft?

_____

_____

10. List four (4) uses for puff pastry.

a. _____   c. _____

b. _____   d. _____

11. What are sweet pastes? What are they used for?

_____

_____

12. Describe the procedure for making sweet paste.

_____

_____

13. List five popular choices used to produce crumb crusts.

a. _____

b. _____

c. _____

d. _____

e. _____

14. Describe the procedure for making pastry cream.

_____

_____

_____

_____

_____

15. Describe the procedure for making basic pie dough.

_____

_____

_____

_____

_____

16. Describe the procedure for making and baking blind baked pie crust; list temperatures.

_____

_____

_____

_____

_____

17. Describe the procedure for making cooked juice pie filling.

_____

_____

_____

_____

18. Describe the procedure for making baked fruit pie.

_____

_____

_____

_____

_____

19. Describe the procedure for making puff pastry.

_____

_____

_____

_____

_____

_____

_____

20. Describe the procedure for making choux paste.

_____

_____

_____

_____

21. Describe the procedure for making meringues.

_____

_____

_____

_____

_____

D. Multiple Choice

For each question below, choose the one response that correctly answers the question.

1. What is the most common method for preparing cookie dough?
    a. beating
    b. whipping
    c. blending
    d. creaming

2. Which is *not* a use for pâte à choux?
    a. profiteroles
    b. palmiers
    c. éclairs
    d. Paris-Brest

3. What do all meringues have in common?
    a. the ratio of egg whites to sugar
    b. whipped egg whites and sugar
    c. the flavouring ingredient used
    d. the method of preparation

4. Lacy pecan cookies are a cookie variety classified as:
    a. a pressed cookie
    b. an icebox cookie
    c. a wafer cookie
    d. a drop cookie

5. Egg whites will whip better if _____ before whipping:
    a. a small amount of salt is added
    b. they are well chilled
    c. a portion of the sugar is added
    d. they are at room temperature

6. _____ is a short pastry with a low (10–12%) sugar content.
    a. pâte sablée
    b. pâte sèche sucrée
    c. pâte a foncer
    d. pâte a choux

7. Which of the following is made with 65% butter and 35% powdered sugar?
    a. pâte sablée
    b. pâte sèche sucrée
    c. pâte a foncer
    d. pâte a choux

8. Which of the following is not an ingredient of sweet paste?
    a. sugar
    b. flour
    c. eggs
    d. water

9. When used in cream pies, pastry cream should be thickened with:
    a. cornstarch
    b. modified starch
    c. flour
    d. arrowroot

10. Which of the following would not be used in the cooked juice filling method?
    a. frozen berries
    b. pineapple
    c. blueberries
    d. pears

E. Matching

I. Trouble Shooting Pies

Match each of the "Problems" in List A with the appropriate letter "Causes" in List B. There may be more than one cause to a problem. Each cause may be attributed to more than one problem.

List A: Problems	List B: Causes
_____1. Crust shrinks	a. Starch insufficiently cooked
	b. Too much fat
_____2. Soggy crust	c. Overmixing
	d. Wrong dough used
_____3. Crumbly crust	e. Overworking dough
	f. Not enough liquid
_____4. Tough crust	g. Oven temperature too low
	h. Eggs overworked
_____5. Runny filling	i. Filling overcooked
	j. Starch not incorporated properly
_____6. Lumpy cream filling	k. Insufficient starch
	l. Too many eggs
_____7. Custard filling weeps or separates	m. Not enough fat
	n. Not baked long enough

II. Trouble Shooting Meringues

Match each of the "Problems" in List A with the appropriate letter "Causes" in List B. There may be more than one cause to a problem. Each cause may be attributed to more than one problem.

List A: Problems	List B: Causes
_____1. Weeps or beads of sugar syrup are released	a. Not baked long enough
	b. Moisture in the air
_____2. Fails to attain any volume or stiffness	c. Too much sugar added too quickly
	d. Not enough sugar
_____3. Lumps	e. Old eggs
	f. Overwhipping
_____4. Not shiny	g. Fat present
	h. Not enough sugar
	i. Egg whites overwhipped
	j. Sugar added too soon
	k. Browning too rapidly

F. True or False

For each question below, circle either True or False to indicate the correct answer.

1. A baked meringue containing ground nuts is a japonaise.
    True   False

2. Cherries and apples are appropriate fruits to use for a cooked juice filling.
    True   False

3. A cream filling is basically a flavoured pastry cream.
    True   False

4. Pumpkin pie is a good example of a custard filling.
    True   False

5. The ratio for making a crumb crust is one part sugar to four parts crumbs to two parts melted butter.
    True   False

6. Rice or beans can be used for blind baking.
    True   False

7. Any dough can be used to make a tart shell as long as it tastes good and has a good appearance.
    True   False

8. Italian and Swiss meringues work equally well in buttercreams.
    True   False

9. Unbaked fruit pies or unbaked pie shells may be frozen for up to 6 months.
    True   False

10. Custard, cream and meringue-topped pies freeze well for up to 2 months.
    True   False

11. Crumb crust is for unbaked pies.
    True   False

Chapter 31

Cakes and Frostings

Cake making is a science. Once the formulas and techniques are understood, the only other necessary ingredient is a vivid imagination. This chapter describes the batters, mixing methods, and presentation necessary for the perfect cake.

After studying this chapter the student should be able to:
1.   Prepare a variety of cakes.
2.   Prepare a variety of frostings.
3.   Assemble cakes using basic finishing and decorating techniques.

Key Terms

Cake	Italian (or meringue) buttercream
Creamed fat	French (or mousseline) buttercream
Whipped eggs	Foam frosting or boiled icing (or 7-minute frosting)
Butter cakes	Fudge frosting
Creaming method cakes	Fondant
High-ratio cakes	Glucose
Genoise	Glaze
Sponge cake	Flat icing or water icing
Angel food cakes	Royal (or decorator's) icing
Chiffon cakes	Ganache
Creaming	Side masking
Frosting or icing	Stencils
Simple buttercream	Cake or baker's comb

Test Your Knowledge

The practice sets provided below have been designed to test your comprehension of the information found in this chapter. It is recommended that you read the chapter completely before attempting these questions.

A. Terminology

Fill in the blank spaces with the correct term.

1.   _____ An icing that is similar to flat icing, except it is much stiffer and becomes hard and brittle when dry.

2.   _____ A cake that relies on creamed fat to create the structure of the cake.

3. _____ A light, smooth, fluffy mixture made of sugar, fat, and sometimes egg yolks or egg whites.

4. _____ A design cut out from paper, cardboard, or thin plastic which is used to create a design on the cake.

5. _____ Another term for a frosting that is applied as a filling and on the outside of the cake to improve the cake's appearance and shelf life.

6. _____ A cake similar to angel food cake, except for the addition of egg yolks and vegetable oil.

7. _____ A cake made by whipping egg yolks and other ingredients and then adding whipped egg whites.

8. _____ A thick sweet syrup made from cornstarch, for which light corn syrup can be substituted.

Fill in the blank spaces with the correct definitions.

9. Fondant _____

10. Ganache _____

11. Poundcakes _____

12. High-ratio cakes _____

13. Side masking _____

14. Genoise _____

15. Angel food cakes _____

B. Fill in the Blank

Fill in the blank with the response that correctly completes the statement.

1. The amount of leavening should be _____ at higher altitudes and the eggs in the mixture should be _____. Temperatures should also be _____ by _____ °F at altitudes over 1050 metres (3500 feet).

2. The two cake mixing categories are (a) _____, which uses _____, and (b) _____, which uses _____ to create a structure for the cake.

3. Most cakes are baked at temperatures between _____ and _____.

4. Royal icing is also known as _____.

5. Pan coating consists of equal parts _____, _____ and _____.

6. When the tiny air pockets in beaten eggs expand when heated, _____ occurs.

7. When the proteins in eggs coagulate, they provide _____.

8. _____ derives from the high water content of eggs.

9. Egg yolks contain _____, an emulsifier which contributes to _____ batter and better _____.

10. Examples of creamed fat cakes are _____, _____, _____ and _____.

11. Cakes based on whipped egg foams include _____, _____, _____ and _____.

12. The main difference between a génoise and a sponge cake is that in the génoise method _____ are _____ with _____ and in the sponge method _____ are whipped separately from the _____.

13. _____ is a smooth dough made with sugar and gelatin.

14. _____ is made with almond paste and sugar.

15. _____ is the technique of coating only the sides of a cake.

C. Short Answer

I. General

1. Eggs are critical in the success of many bakery products. List seven (7) functions of eggs.

    a. _____

    b. _____

    c. _____

    d. _____

    e. _____

    f. _____

    g. _____

2. Describe poundcakes; explain how they relate to today's butter cake.

_____

_____

_____

_____

_____

II. Basic Cake Mixes Review

Describe the basic steps for the preparation of the following cake mixes and give a menu example of each type of cake. Number each step in the process for revision purposes. Exact quantities are not important for this exercise.

Example: **Chiffon Cake**
a. Whip egg whites with a little sugar until stiff.
b. Add liquid ingredients, including oil, to sifted dry ingredients.
c. Fold in egg whites.
d. Bake in ungreased pan.

Menu example: Lemon chiffon cake

1. Butter cake:

_____

_____

_____

_____

2. High-ratio cake:

_____

_____

_____

_____

3.   Genoise cake:

_____

_____

_____

_____

_____

4.   Sponge cake:

_____

_____

_____

_____

_____

5.   Angel food cake:

_____

_____

_____

_____

_____

III. Frostings Review

Describe the basic steps for the preparation of the following frostings. Number each step in the process for revision purposes. Exact quantities are not important for this exercise.

1.   Simple buttercream:

_____

_____

2. Italian buttercream:

_____

_____

3. French buttercream:

_____

_____

4. Flat icing:

_____

_____

5. Royal icing (glaze):

_____

_____

6. Chocolate ganache:

_____

_____

D. Multiple Choice

1. Which of the following does not belong to génoise cakes?
    a. eggs
    b. baking powder
    c. sugar
    d. butter

2. Which of the following does not belong to angel food cakes?
    a. flour
    b. egg white
    c. sugar
    d. fat

3. Sponge cakes are baked at:
   a. 140°C (28°F)
   b. 160°C (320°F)
   c. 190°C (375°F)
   d. 210°C (410°F)

4. When mixing a cake batter, overmixing will result in:
   a. poor flavour
   b. shrinkage after baking
   c. coarse texture with open grain
   d. uneven shape

5. When baking a cake, an oven too hot will result in:
   a. coarse texture with open grain
   b. shrinkage after baking
   c. uneven shape
   d. crust burst and cracked

6. To use, fondant should be heated at:
   a. 38°C (100°F)
   b. 45°C (110°F)
   c. 62°C (145°F)
   d. 78°C (170°F)

7. Which of the following does not belong to Italian buttercream?
   a. egg yolk
   b. egg white
   c. sugar
   d. butter

8. Which of the following does not belong to French buttercream?
   a. egg yolk
   b. egg white
   c. sugar
   d. butter

E. Matching

I. Cake Ingredients

Match each of the classification headings in List A with the appropriate ingredients in List B. Each choice in List B can only be used once.

	List A		List B
_____ 1.	Flavouring	a.	Flour, milk, eggs
_____ 2.	Toughener	b.	Flour, butter, water
_____ 3.	Leavener	c.	Sugar, fats, yolks
_____ 4.	Tenderizer	d.	Flour, starches, milk solids
_____ 5.	Drier	e.	Baking powder, baking soda
_____ 6.	Moistener	f.	Cocoa, chocolate, spices, sour cream
		g.	Water, milk, juice, eggs

II. Cake Mixing Categories

Two of the cake categories are creamed fat and whipped egg. From the list below, identify the creamed fat mixes with the letter *A* and the whipped egg mixes with the letter *B*.

A = Creamed Fat
B = Whipped Egg

____ 1.	Chiffon cake	____ 6.	Yellow cake
____ 2.	Continental brownies	____ 7.	Carrot cake
____ 3.	Devil's food cake	____ 8.	Gateau Benoit
____ 4.	Chocolate sponge cake	____ 9.	Vanilla raspberry layer cake
____ 5.	Sacher torte	____ 10.	Sour cream coffeecake

F. True or False

For each question below, circle True or False to indicate the correct answer.

1. The best way to cool a cake is to leave it in an area where there is a cool breeze.
   True   False

2. Frostings should be made carefully using quality ingredients.
   True   False

3. As a general guide for setting oven temperatures for cakes, the greater the surface area, the higher the temperature.
   True   False

4. For baked cakes, pans should be filled 1/2 to 2/3 with cake mix for the best results.
   True   False

5. Angel food cake is ideal for frosting.
   True   False

6. Solid shortening is better than butter for coating pans, since it does not contain any water.
   True   False

7. Package mixes are inferior in quality to cakes that are made from scratch.
   True   False

8. The fat used in high-ratio cake mixes can be either butter or shortening.
   True   False

9. Foam icing is also known as 7-minutes icing.
   True   False

10. Boiled icing and Italian icing are the same.
    True   False

11. Pastillage is made of sugar and gelatin.
    True   False

12. Gum paste is made of sugar, cornstarch and gelatin.
    True   False

Chapter 32

Custards, Creams, Frozen Desserts and Dessert Sauces

This chapter discusses some miscellaneous items, such as custards, dessert sauces and ice creams, that do not fall into the general dessert categories, but that are essential components of the chef's repertoire.

At the end of this chapter the student should be able to:

1.   Prepare a variety of custards and creams.
2.   Prepare a variety of ice creams, sorbets and frozen dessert items.
3.   Prepare a variety of dessert sauces.
4.   Use these products in preparing and serving other pastry and dessert items.
5.   Plan and prepare assembled desserts.

Key Terms

Custard	Bread pudding	Semifreddi
Stirred custard	Steep	Overrun
Baked custard	Soufflé	Sundae
Vanilla custard sauce	Bavarian cream	Baked Alaska
Pastry cream	Chiffon	Bombe
Lemon curd	Mousses	Coupe
Sabayon	Crème Chantilly	Parfait
Crème brûlée	Charlotte Royale	Marquise
Pudding	Charlotte Russe	Neapolitan
Mousseline	Ice cream	Coulis
Crème Chiboust	Gelato	Base
Tempering	Sorbet	Filling
Crème caramel	Sherbet	Garnish
Cheesecake	Granité	

Test Your Knowledge

The practice sets provided below have been designed to test your comprehension of the information found in this chapter. It is recommended that you read the chapter completely before attempting these questions.

A. Terminology

Fill in the blank spaces with the correct term.

1.   _____ A gooey concoction of ice cream, sauces, toppings and whipped cream.

2. _____ The process of slowly adding a hot liquid to eggs to raise their temperature without causing them to curdle.

3. _____ A frozen dessert made from puréed fruit, fruit juice and sugar.

4. _____ The process of soaking food in a hot liquid in order to extract flavour into the liquid or to soften the food item.

5. _____ A dessert made with ice cream set on a layer of sponge cake and encased in meringue, then baked until the meringue is warm and golden.

6. _____ A foamy, stirred custard sauce made by whisking eggs, sugar and wine over low heat.

7. _____ The term used to describe the amount of air churned into an ice cream.

8. _____ A custard base that is lightened with whipped egg whites and then baked.

9. _____ A dessert made with two or more layers of ice cream or sherbet in a spherical mould.

10. _____ The term used to describe heavy cream that has been whipped to soft peaks, and flavoured with sugar and vanilla.

Fill in the blank spaces with the correct definitions.

11. Coupe _____

12. Pastry cream _____

13. Gelato _____

14. Custard _____

15. Parfait _____

16. Mousse _____

17. Marquis _____

18. Charlotte _____

19. Neapolitan _____

20. Bavarian cream _____

21. Chiffon _____

B. Fill in the Blank

Fill in the blanks with the response that correctly completes the statement.

1. _____ is another name for a sabayon.

2. Pastry cream can be lightened by folding in whipped cream to produce a _____ or by adding _____ to produce a crème Chiboust.

3. Some creams such as _____ and _____ are thickened with gelatin, but others such as _____ and _____ are not, and are therefore softer and lighter.

4. When preparing a soufflé, the custard base and egg whites should be at room temperature because

   a. _____

   _____

   and

   b. _____

   _____

C. Short Answer

Provide a short response that correctly answers the questions below.

1. Eggs are a high-protein food and can easily be contaminated. List and describe the seven (7) sanitary guidelines for handling eggs.

   a. _____

   b. _____

   c. _____

   d. _____

   e. _____

   f. _____

   g. _____

2. Describe the basic steps and essential ingredients for the preparation of vanilla custard sauce. Number each step in the process for revision purposes.

Ingredients _____

_____

_____

_____

_____

3. Describe the basic procedures for making sabayon.

_____

_____

_____

_____

_____

4. Describe the basic procedures for making baked soufflé.

_____

_____

_____

_____

_____

5. Describe the basic procedures for making Bavarian cream.

_____

_____

_____

_____

_____

6. Describe the basic procedures for making chiffon cream.

_____

_____

_____

_____

_____

7. Describe the basic procedures for making ice cream.

_____

_____

_____

_____

8. Describe the basic procedures for making caramel sauce.

_____

_____

_____

_____

_____

9. Describe nine (9) guidelines for assembling desserts.

a. _____

b. _____

c. _____

d. _____

e. _____

f._____

g._____

h._____

i._____

10. List four (4) examples of stirred custards.

    a._____

    b._____

    c._____

    d._____

11. List four (4) examples of baked custards.

    a._____

    b._____

    c._____

    d._____

12. List four (4) types of creams.

    a._____

    b._____

    c._____

    d._____

D. Multiple Choice

1. Any liquid thickened by the coagulation of egg yolk is referred to as a:
   a. Bavarian cream
   b. cream
   c. pudding
   d. custard

2. Which of the following does not normally belong in crème brûlée?
   a. sugar
   b. egg yolk
   c. cream
   d. milk

3. Crème Chiboust is a derivative of:
   a. pastry cream
   b. crème anglaise
   c. Italian meringue
   d. whipped cream

4. Pastry cream added with whipped cream makes cream:
   a. brûlée
   b. Chiboust
   c. mousseline
   d. Bavarian

5. Italian-style cheesecake is:
   a. light and fluffy
   b. soft but rich
   c. dense and rich
   d. creamy and soft

6. Bavarian cream is thickened with:
   a. cornstarch
   b. gelatin
   c. flour
   d. modified starch

7. A chiffon is different from other creams in that it contains:
   a. flour
   b. cornstarch
   c. whipped cream
   d. whipped egg whites

8. A Charlotte Royale is lined with:
   a. caramelized apple slices
   b. jelly roll slices
   c. sponge cake
   d. lady fingers

9.	Vanilla-flavoured whipped cream is referred to as:
	a.	cream Chiboust
	b.	crème chantilly
	c.	French cream
	d.	vanilla cream

10.	The overrun in ice cream should be:
	a.	50%
	b.	40%
	c.	30%
	d.	10%

E. True or False

For each question below, circle True or False to indicate the correct answer.

1.	Once vanilla custard is curdled, it should be discarded.
	True	False

2.	A frozen soufflé is not really a soufflé in the true sense.
	True	False

3.	A sherbet or a sorbet may contain milk or egg yolk for added creaminess.
	True	False

4.	Still-frozen desserts have a shorter shelf life than do churned products.
	True	False

5.	A coulis is a fruit purée made from either fresh or individually quick-frozen (IQF) fruits.
	True	False

6.	Quiche is an example of a baked custard.
	True	False

PART 5 MEAL SERVICE AND PRESENTATION

Chapter 33

Breakfast and Brunch

This chapter discusses the wide array of breakfast and brunch food options. The first meal of the day is the most important—not only for the consumer, but also for the chef preparing this nutritious start-up for the day.

At the end of this chapter the student should be able to:

1. Prepare eggs using a variety of cooking methods.
2. Prepare pancakes and other griddlecakes.
3. Identify a variety of breakfast meats.
4. Prepare a cereal.
5. Offer your customers a variety of breakfast foods.

Key Terms

Brunch	Pan-fried eggs	Sausages
Shirred eggs	Basted eggs	Pancakes
Quiche	Soft-boiled eggs	Waffles
Scrambled eggs	Hard-boiled eggs	Crepes
Omelettes	Bacon	Blintzes
Frittatas	Ham	French toast

Test Your Knowledge

The practice sets provided below have been designed to test your comprehension of the information found in this chapter. It is recommended that you read the chapter completely before attempting these questions.

A. Terminology

Fill in the blank spaces with the correct term.

1. _____ This egg dish is prepared in individual ramekins lined with ingredients such as bread, ham, creamed spinach or artichokes, and topped with cheese.

2. _____ A breakfast cereal made with a toasted blend of whole grains, nuts, and dried fruits.

3. _____ A breakfast dish consisting of an egg custard baked in a crust.

4. _____ Day-old bread dipped in a batter of eggs, sugar, milk or cream, and flavourings and then sautéed in butter.

5. _____ An egg dish that begins as scrambled egg and is then folded around a warm filling.

6. _____ French for "cooked in a ramekin."

7. _____ Commonly referred to as sunny-side up.

8. _____ Seasoned and sautéed while stirring.

9. _____ Usually cooked for 12–15 minutes.

10. _____ Usually cooked for 3–5 minutes.

Fill in the blank spaces with the correct definitions.

11. Crepes _____

12. Frittatas _____

13. Waffles _____

14. Basted eggs _____

15. Pancakes _____

B. Short Answer

Provide a short response that correctly answers each of the questions below.

1. Describe the basic procedures for making shirred eggs.

_____

_____

_____

_____

_____

2. Describe the basic procedures for making scrambled eggs.

_____

_____

_____

_____

_____

3. Describe the basic procedures for making soft-boiled eggs. Include cooking time.

_____

_____

_____

_____

_____

4. Describe the basic procedures for making hard-boiled eggs. Include cooking time.

_____

_____

_____

_____

_____

5. Describe the basic procedures for making pancakes.

_____

_____

_____

_____

_____

6. Describe the basic procedures for making French toast.

    _____

    _____

    _____

    _____

    _____

7. The egg is the most versatile breakfast item. Give four (4) menu examples of egg dishes that may be prepared for breakfast or brunch.

    a. _____

    b. _____

    c. _____

    d. _____

8. List the essential ingredients and describe the four-step procedure for making Quiche Lorraine.

    Ingredients: _____

    a. _____

    b. _____

    c. _____

    d. _____

9. What is a cheese blintz and how does it differ from a crepe?

    _____

    _____

    _____

    _____

10. List the essential ingredients and describe the five-step procedure for making shrimp and avocado omelette.

    Ingredients: _____

    a. _____

    b. _____

    c. _____

    d. _____

    e. _____

11. Explain the difference between a frittata and a regular omelette.

    _____

    _____

12. How can the green ring around the yolk be prevented?

    _____

    _____

C. Multiple Choice

For each question below, choose the one response that correctly answers the question.

1. Which of the following statements does *not* apply to French toast?
    a. French toast begins with day-old bread.
    b. French toast is often topped with sugar, fresh fruit, or syrup.
    c. French toast is toasted bread dipped in batter.
    d. French toast should be served very hot.

2. A frittata is:
    a. a French omelette
    b. an Italian omelette
    c. an open-face omelette
    d. a fried omelette

3. A blintz can be described as:
   a. a crepe cooked on one side
   b. a pancake stuffed with cheese
   c. a thin omelette
   d. a sweet waffle

4. A crepe is:
   a. the same as a pancake
   b. the same as a blintz
   c. a thin unleavened pancake
   d. a sweet batter

5. Shirred eggs are:
   a. baked
   b. sautéed
   c. fried
   d. boiled

6. A quiche is:
   a. the same as a frittata
   b. a custard baked in a pastry shell
   c. a type of pudding
   d. thickened with flour

7. Which of the following statements is *not* true?
   a. Items such as cheese are often added to scrambled eggs.
   b. Omelettes use two or three eggs per portion.
   c. Vinegar is often added to the poaching water.
   d. Scrambled eggs should be stirred only after cooking.

8. Basted eggs are:
   a. baked, basted with fat
   b. cooked on the griddle
   c. cooked in a pan, basted with cream
   d. covered and baked

9. Over-easy eggs will cook in approximately:
   a. 3 minutes on the first side and 30 seconds on the other
   b. 2 minutes on each side
   c. 3 minutes on each side
   d. 3 minutes on the first side and 2 minutes on the other

D. Matching

Match each "Country" in List A with the appropriate letter "Traditional Breakfast Foods" in List B.

List A: Countries

_____1. Japan

_____2. China

_____3. France

_____4. Southern Italy

_____5. Australia

_____3. Egypt

_____7. India

_____8. Costa Rica

_____9. Spain

_____10. Greece

_____11. Eastern Europe

_____12. Argentina

List B: Traditional Breakfast Foods

a. Coffee or tea; cold cuts; a variety of cheeses and breads

b. Tea; khichiri, a Hindi dish of rice, lentils and spices; apam, a thin rice pancake with spiced meat and vegetables; vada pavs, deep-fried mashed potatoes wrapped in flatbread and seasoned with chutney or chilli powder

c. Café au lait; baguette, butter and jam

d. Tea; steak and eggs; toast

e. Coffee or aqua dulce, warm water flavoured with concentrated sugar cane juice; gallo pinto, rice and beans with cilantro and onions

f. Coffee or hot chocolate; facturas, sweet pastries with dulce de leche, a paste made with milk and sugar

g. Milk, coffee; rolls and jam; chocolate y churros, hot chocolate with cinnamon-sugar coated doughnuts

h. Tea; congee, rice porridge, topped with meat, seafood and/or vegetables; you tiao, a type of fried cruller that is dipped in soy milk

i. Greek coffee or instant coffee with milk; sesame bread; yogurt with honey and/or fruit

j. Coffee granita served in brioche bread

k. Tea; asa-gohan, morning rice, with side dishes of pickles, dried seaweed, tofu, fish; miso soup

l. ful medames, slow-cooked beans seasoned with olive oil, lemon and garlic

E. True or False

For each question below, circle True or False to indicate the correct answer.

1. Most nutritionists agree that breakfast should provide a good percentage of calories and nutrients for the day.
    True   False

2. Pan-fried eggs are also known as "sunny-side up."
    True   False

3. The older the egg, the better it is for pan-frying.
    True   False

4.   Boiled eggs should actually be simmered.
     True   False

5.   A breakfast menu should not offer steak or pork chops.
     True   False

6.   Canadian bacon should be well cooked to give a crispy finish.
     True   False

7.   French toast is also known as "lost bread" in France.
     True   False

8.   When preparing vegetable omelettes, it is best to use uncooked vegetables.
     True   False

Chapter 34

Appetizers and Sandwiches

Appetizers and sandwiches create an ideal opportunity for the chef to showcase presentation and innovation skills. These small portions of food stimulate the appetite and tempt the taste buds.

At the end of this chapter the student should be able to:

1.   Prepare and serve a variety of cold and hot hors d'oeuvre.
2.   Prepare a variety of appetizers.
3.   Choose hors d'oeuvre and appetizers that are appropriate for the meal or event.
4.   Select high-quality sandwich ingredients.
5.   Identify different types and styles of sandwiches.
6.   Prepare sandwiches to order.

Key Terms

Hors d'oeuvre	Pressed caviar	Won tons
Appetizers	American sturgeon caviar	Basic hot closed sandwich
Canapés	Golden whitefish caviar	Grilled sandwich
Canapé base	Lumpfish caviar	Deep-fat fried sandwich
Canapé spread	Salmon caviar	Hot open-faced sandwich
Canapé garnishes	Malassol	Cold closed sandwich
Barquette	Crudités	Basic cold sandwich
Tartlet	Chafing dish	Multi-decker cold sandwich
Profiterole	Sushi	
Beluga caviar	Sashimi	Tea sandwich
Osetra caviar	Brochettes	Cold open-faced sandwich
Sevruga caviar	Rumaki	Smørbrød

Test Your Knowledge

The practice sets provided below have been designed to test your comprehension of the information found in this chapter. It is recommended that you read the chapter completely before attempting these questions.

A. Terminology

Fill in the blank spaces with the correct term.

1.   _____ Considered to be the best caviar, the eggs are medium-sized, golden to brown in colour and quite oily.

2.   _____ The term used to describe raw or cooked shellfish rolled or served in seasoned rice.

3. _____ This is the most expensive type of caviar, coming from the largest species of sturgeon.

4. _____ A dish with a heating unit used to keep foods warm at table-side or during buffet service.

5. _____ The body of a sandwich, providing most of its flavour.

6. _____ Perhaps the most popular sandwich spread, adding moisture and richness.

7. _____ Small skewers holding a combination of meat, poultry, game, fish, shellfish, or vegetables, baked, grilled, or broiled and often served with a dipping sauce.

8. _____ An array of raw or slightly cooked vegetables served with a dip.

9. _____ Small open-faced sandwiches constructed from a base, a spread, and one or more garnishes.

10. _____ Rice rolled in seaweed.

11. _____ Rice with raw fish.

12. _____ Asian noodle dough.

13. _____ Wasabi.

14. _____ Nori.

Fill in the blank spaces with the correct definition.

15. Hot open-faced sandwich _____

16. Hors d'oeuvre _____

17. Lumpfish caviar _____

18. Tea sandwich _____

19. Barquettes _____

20. Multi-decker cold sandwich _____

21. Rumaki _____

22. Golden whitefish caviar _____

B. Fill in the Blank

Fill in the blanks provided with the response that correctly completes the statement.

1. The most common canapé base is _____, but slices of firm _____ can also be used.

2. The base for canapé spreads is usually _____ or _____. They may also be bound _____ such as _____ or _____.

3. The best caviar is labelled _____, which means _____.

4. Sandwiches are constructed from _____, a _____, and one or more _____.

5. Cold dips generally use _____ and _____ or _____ as a base. The consistency of dips can be adjusted by adding _____, _____, or _____.

6. Hot dips often use _____, _____, or _____ as a base. The traditional Italian _____ is an example of a hot oil-based dip.

7. To prevent skewers from burning, _____ before assembly.

8. Won ton skins are _____ and can be stuffed with _____.

C. Short Answer

Provide a short response that correctly answers each of the questions below.

1. List the four (4) guidelines for preparing hors d'oeuvre.

    a. _____

    b. _____

    c. _____

    d. _____

2. List six (6) canapé spreads and an appropriate garnish for each.

    a. _____

    b. _____

    c. _____

d. _____

e. _____

f. _____

3.   Write the four (4) basic procedures for preparing cold multi-decker sandwiches.

a. _____

b. _____

c. _____

d. _____

4.   Briefly describe the six (6) guidelines for preparing appetizers.

a. _____

b. _____

c. _____

d. _____

e. _____

f. _____

5.   List four (4) classes of imported sturgeon caviar.

a. _____

b. _____

c. _____

d. _____

6.   List four (4) common North American caviars.

a. _____

b. _____

c. _____

d. _____

7. Describe the five (5) steps in cooking rice for sushi.

   a. _____

   b. _____

   c. _____

   d. _____

   e. _____

8. Describe butler service.

   _____

   _____

   _____

   _____

9. Describe buffet service; suggest some guidelines to follow.

   _____

   _____

   _____

   _____

10. Describe the three (3) basic guidelines to follow when preparing sandwiches; briefly explain each one.

   a. _____

   b. _____

   c. _____

D. Multiple Choice

For each question below, choose the one response that correctly answers the question.

1. Caviar is best stored at:
    a. 1°C (34°F)
    b. −1°C (30°F)
    c. 2°C (35°F)
    d. 0°C (32°F)

2. Connoisseurs prefer to serve caviar in which of the following?
    a. glass
    b. china
    c. metal
    d. plastic

3. Which of the following fish is *not* used for sushi?
    a. ahi
    b. flounder
    c. bluefin shark
    d. salmon

4. Which one of the following is *not* a hot appetizer?
    a. date and chorizo rumaki
    b. smoked salmon canapé
    c. chèvre tarts
    d. pouches of shrimp wrapped in filo dough

5. Which of the following has quite small eggs and is harvested from small sturgeon?
    a. Whitefish
    b. Sevruga
    c. Beluga
    d. Osetra

6. According to some connoisseurs, the best caviar is:
    a. Whitefish
    b. Sevruga
    c. Beluga
    d. Osetra

7. The term "malassol" refers to:
   a. Packed in light brine
   b. Low salt
   c. Large eggs
   d. Pressed caviar

8. Crudités refers to:
   a. Raw vegetables
   b. Cooked vegetables served cold
   c. Pickled vegetables
   d. Hors d'oeuvre in general

9. Sashimi is served:
   a. raw without rice
   b. cooked in rolls
   c. raw on top of rice
   d. rolled in nori

E. True or False

For each question below, circle either True or False to indicate the correct answer.

1. An appetizer is usually served before lunch.
   True   False

2. Sandwiches are generally prepared ahead of time.
   True   False

3. The most popular style of open-faced sandwich is the well-known Norwegian sandwich called smørbrød.
   True   False

4. Caviar should be served in a stainless steel bowl, which keeps it cooler than glass or plastic.
   True   False

5. Preferably, fish for sushi should be no more than one day out of the water.
   True   False

6. Barquettes are ideal for a large party because they can be prepared in advance.
   True   False

Chapter 35

Beverages

As food and the art of preparing it evolves, so does the beverage industry. Concerns about the integrity of our water supplies have prompted consumers to demand bottled water while the increased popularity and availability of various gourmet teas and coffees has literally created a subculture. Knowing how to choose the right tea leaf or coffee bean and understanding the proper brewing techniques is critical to satisfy this fast growing market. Wine and food pairing is also a fascinating subject that has garnered much interest among cooks, chefs and diners alike. While the pairing of wine and food, or beer and food, is somewhat subjective, there are a growing number of restaurants offering pairings. It is critical for a cook or chef to learn the basic rules that provide a firm foundation for proper wine and beer selection. It all translates into endless opportunities to experience traditional and not-so-traditional beverages while experimenting with contemporary cuisine philosophies and discovering new sensations.

After studying this chapter the student will be able to:

1. Identify a variety of beverages consumed in food service establishments.
2. Identify terminology associated with coffee production.
3. Recognize a quality brew of coffee or tea.
4. Identify terminology associated with teas and cocoa.
5. Differentiate between the wine, beer and liquor producing methods.
6. Recognize grape varietals used in wine production.
7. Understand how wine and food may be paired.

Key Terms

Demineralized water	Espresso con panna	Red wine	Brandy de Jerez
Carbonated water	Machiatto	White wine	Pomace brandy
Distilled water	Steamed milk	Rosé wine	Fruit brandy
Juice	Cappuccino	Fermentation	Calvados
Nectar	Foamed milk	VQA	Kirshwasser
Cider	Caffè latte	Port	Framboise
City roast	Café au lait	Sherry	Poire
Brazilian roast	Café crème	Madeira	Slivovitz
Viennese roast	Caffè mocha	Marsala	Distillation
French roast	Caffè freddo	Vermouth	Gin
Espresso roast	Flavoured coffees	Aromas	Rum
Decoction	Black tea	Flavours	Tequila
Infusion	Green tea	Dessert wine	Vodka
Espresso	Gunpowder	Grape brandy	Whisky
Cappuccino	Oolong tea	Cognac	Neutral spirits
Espresso corretto	Tisanes	Armagnac	
Espresso ristretto	Vintner	Metaxa	

Test Your Knowledge

The practice sets provided below have been designed to test your comprehension of the information found in this chapter. It is recommended that you read the chapter completely before attempting these questions.

A. Terminology

Fill in the blank spaces with the correct term.

1. _____ Water that has had all the minerals and impurities removed through distillation.

2. _____ Water that has had all the minerals and impurities removed by passing it over a bed of ion-exchange resins.

3. _____ Water that has absorbed carbon dioxide resulting in an effervescent mouth-feel.

4. _____ The diluted, sweetened juices of peaches, apricots, guavas, black currants, and other fruits, which are often too thick or tart to drink straight.

5. _____ The extraction of flavours from a food at a temperature below boiling.

6. _____ Found on top of espressos; it is created by the pressure.

7. _____ Made with 1/3 strong coffee or espresso and 2/3 hot milk.

8. _____ A small cup of strong black coffee or espresso.

9. _____ Espresso "marked" with a tiny portion of steamed milk.

10. _____ 1/3 espresso and 2/3 steamed milk, flavoured with chocolate syrup; usually toped with whipped cream and chocolate shavings.

11. _____ The most unusual and expensive coffee in he world.

12. _____ Herbal infusions that do not contain any "real" tea leaves.

13. _____ An alcoholic beverage made from the fermented juice of grapes.

14. _____ A wine made using a process call "estufagem." The wine is heated at temperatures of 40°C (105°F) for three to six months.

15. _____ A fortified wine named for a town in western Sicily associated with its production.

16. _____ A flavoured wine fortified with brandy; available in red, white, sweet or dry.

17. _____ Distilled from grains, flavoured with juniper berries.

18. _____ Distilled from sugar cane, available in white, amber and dark.

19. _____ Made from the fermented sap of agave.

20. _____ Most of it is made from wheat but traditionally made from potatoes. Often flavoured.

21. _____ Distilled from various grains that have been pounded and cooked into a mash, then allowed to ferment before distillation.

Fill in the blank spaces with the correct definition.

22. Cider _____

23. Juice _____

24. Decoction _____

25. Cappuccino _____

26. Caffè con panna _____

27. Espresso corretto _____

28. Espresso ristretto _____

29. Liquor _____

30. Liqueur _____

31. Vinification _____

B. Fill in the Blanks

Fill in the blank provided with the response that correctly completes the statement.

1. _____ and _____ are two ways of extracting juice.

2. As a rule, the _____, the more _____ the coffee should prepared.

3. Drip coffee is most commonly made from a machine that operates on the principles of _____ and a _____ .

4. A single serving of espresso uses _____ g (_____ oz) of coffee for _____ mL (_____ oz) of purified water.

5. Provide four (4) characteristics by which coffee is judged.

   a. _____ refers to the feeling of heaviness or thickness that coffee provides on the palate.

   b. _____ will often indicate the taste of coffee.

   c. _____ refers to the tartness of the coffee, lending a snap, life or thinness.

   d. _____ is the most ambiguous as well as the most important characteristic, having to do with taste.

6. _____ is a commercial coffee bean from which the finest coffees are produced.

7. _____ is a bean that does not produce as flavourful a coffee, but is becoming more significant commercially since the trees are heartier and more fertile than their predecessors.

8. For drip coffee, the best results are usually achieved by using _____g (___oz) of ground coffee per _____ L (____ quart) of water.

9. There are _____ general types of tea: _____, _____ and _____

10. Broken black tea leaves are graded as either _____ or _____.

11. Tea can be described according to thee characteristics: _____, _____ and _____.

12. Dutched cocoa has been treated with _____, which makes the cocoa _____ in colour, less _____ and _____ in flavour.

13. Wines may be sparkling, also known as _____, or non-effervescent _____ or _____ with additional alcohol.

14 Beer is made from _____, _____ and _____ _____, fermented yeast _____.

15. VQA stands for _____ _____ _____.

16. VQA regulations require that _____ % of the wine come from a particular grape before the varietals can be named on the label.

17. Virtually all wines produced in the world come from a single grape species known as _____ _____.

18. Port wines are generally divided into three categories: _____, _____ and _____.

19. Sherry is a fortified wine made by an extremely complicated process called _____.

20. In wine language, aromas are also referred to as _____ or _____.

21 White wines are _____ in tannins; choose a dry, light, and preferably _____ wine with a _____ _____ character to pair with vegetarian dishes.

22. Don't let the flavour of the _____ overwhelm the flavour of the _____ and don't let the flavour of the _____ overwhelm the flavour of the _____.

23. In beer production, the ground barley malt is _____ in hot water, producing a brown liquid called the _____.

24. Hops in beer provide _____.

25. Beers may be divided in two categories: _____ and _____.

C. Short Answer

Provide a short answer that correctly answers each of the questions below.

1. List and briefly explain five (5) of the standard descriptions used with various types of coffee roasting.

   a. _____

   b. _____

   c. _____

   d. _____

   e. _____

2. Explain how one would choose the proper fineness of coffee grind.

   _____

   _____

   _____

3. Explain the principles of making espresso.

   _____

   _____

   _____

4. Explain the proper procedures for holding freshly brewed coffee. Include recommended time and temperatures.

_____

_____

_____

5. Explain the proper procedures for brewing tea. Be specific and include recommended time and temperatures when appropriate.

_____

_____

_____

_____

6. Briefly explain the procedures for fabricating beer using the four basic and traditional ingredients.

_____

_____

_____

_____

7. Although there are many styles, explain the basic difference between ales and lagers.

_____

_____

_____

_____

8. Briefly explain the distillation process.

_____

_____

_____

_____

9.   Explain the difference between Scotch and Irish whisky (whiskey).

_____

_____

_____

_____

D. Multiple Choice Questions

1.   When making coffee, slowly pouring hot water over ground coffee held in a disposable cloth or paper filter is referred to as:
      a. filtering
      b. steeping
      c. extracting
      d. dripping

2.   When making coffee, mixing hot water with the ground item to be infused is referred to as:
      a. extracting
      b. steeping
      c. filtering
      d. dripping

3.   Pouring hot water over ground coffee and allowing the coffee to run through a strainer is a(n) _____ type of infusion.
      a. dripping
      b. extracting
      c. filtering
      d. steeping

4.   Once brewed coffee may be held for a short time at temperatures of:
      a. 75 to 78°C (167 to 172°F)
      b. 80 to 83°C (176 to 181°F)
      c. 85 to 88°C (185 to 190°F)
      d. 90 to 93°C (194 to 199°F)

5.   Black tea can be described as:
      a. amber brown and strongly flavoured
      b. yellow in colour with a sweet flavour
      c. not fermented, with a bitter flavour
      d. partially fermented

6. Green tea can be described as:
   a. amber brown and strongly flavoured
   b. yellow in colour with a sweet flavour
   c. not fermented, with a bitter flavour
   d. partially fermented

7. Oolong tea can be described as:
   a. amber brown and strongly flavoured
   b. yellow in colour with a sweet flavour
   c. not fermented, with a bitter flavour
   d. partially fermented

8. Souchong tea is made with:
   a. small leaves
   b. medium leaves
   c. large leaves
   d. random leaves

9. Orange pekoe tea is made with:
   a. small leaves
   b. medium leaves
   c. large leaves
   d. random leaves

10. Pekoe tea is made with:
    a. small leaves
    b. medium leaves
    c. large leaves
    d. random leaves

11. When tasting wine, words such as *fruit*, *flower*, *herb*, and *spice* refer to the wine's:
    a. flavour
    b. aroma
    c. body
    d. style

12. When tasting wine, words such as *syrupy*, *crisp*, *tart*, and dry refer to the wine's:
    a. flavour
    b. aroma
    c. body
    d. style

13. When tasting wine, words such as *light*, *medium*, and *full* refer to the wine's:
    a. flavour
    b. aroma
    c. body
    d. style

14. Which of the following types of red wine is most likely not to be a good match with grilled vegetables?
    a. Intense with lots of tannins
    b. Full-bodied
    c. Barrel aged
    d. Light-bodied

15. Beer is best stored at:
    a. 2 to 4°C (36 to 40°F)
    b. 6 to 8°C (43 to 46°F)
    c. 10 to 13°C (50 to 55°F)
    d. 15 to 18°C (59 to 64°F)

16. Ales are ideally served at:
    a. 8°C (46°F)
    b. 10° (50°F)
    c. 12°C (54°F)
    d. 15°C (59°F)

17. Lagers are ideally served at:
    a. 8°C (46°F)
    b. 10° (50°F)
    c. 12°C (54°F)
    d. 15°C (59°F)

E. Matching

I. Tea Types

Match each "Tea Variety" in List A with the appropriate letter "Tea Type" in List B. There may be more than one type matching with each variety.

List A: Tea Varieties

_____1. Black tea

_____2. Green tea

_____3. Oolong tea

List B: Tea Types

a. Assam

b. Gunpowder

c. Earl Grey

d. English Breakfast

e. Formosa

f. White tea

g. Matcha (liquid Jade)

h. Darjeeling

i. Sencha

II. Grapes into Wines

Match each of the "Grape Varietals" in List A with the appropriate letter "Wine" in List B.

List A: Grape Varietals

_____1. Pinot Noir

_____2. Chardonnay

_____3. Syrah

_____4. Cabernet Sauvignon

_____5. Sauvignon Blanc

_____6. Merlot

_____7. Zinfandel

_____8. Chenin Blanc

List B: Wine

a. Bordeaux and Red Graves

b. Saint Emilion and for blending with Cabernet Sauvignon

c. Vouvray

d. Red and White Zinfandel

e. Red Burgundy and Champagne.

f. Côte Rôtie and Hermitage

g. White Burgundy, Chablis, Champagne

h. Sauternes, Fumé Blanc White Graves & Sancerre

III. Sherry

Match each "Sherry Type" in List A with the appropriate letter "Characteristics" in List B.

List A: Sherry Type

_____1. Manzanillo

_____2. Fino

_____3. Amontillado

_____4. Oloroso

_____5. Amoroso

_____6. Cream Sherry

List B: Characteristics

a. Sweet flavour, medium-brown colour

b. Very dry with a pale golden-brown colour

c. Somewhat dry, rich flavour, full-body and medium brown colour

d. The sweetest with a dark brown colour

e. The driest

f. Rich, slightly dry, nutty flavour, light brown amber colour

IV. Red Wine Characteristics

Match each of the "Wine Varietals" in List A with the appropriate letter "Body" in List B.

List A: Wine Varietals

_____1. Syrah

_____2. Pinot Noir

_____3. Merlot

_____4. Cabernet Sauvignon

_____5. Zinfandel (red)

_____6. Sangiovese

_____7. Nebiolo

_____8. Grenache

List B: Body

a. Light to medium

b. Medium

c. Medium to full

310

V. Food and Red Wine Pairings

Match each of the "Wine Varietals" in List A with the appropriate letter "Dish" in List B.

List A: Wine Varietals

_____1. Syrah

_____2. Pinot Noir

_____3. Merlot

_____4. Cabernet Sauvignon

_____5. Zinfandel (red)

_____6. Sangiovese

List B: Dish Type/Characteristics

a. Peppery, tangy, spicy foods, game

b. Fatty dishes, game birds

c. Highly spiced dishes, grilled meat, chocolate

d. Lamb, game, beef, strong cheeses

e. Dishes with garlic, black pepper, chili con carne

f. Veal, hearty chicken dishes, tomato-based dishes

VI. Food and White Wine Pairings

Match each of the "Wine Varietals" in List A with the appropriate letter "Dish" in List B.

List A: Wine Varietals

_____1. Chardonnay

_____2. Chenin Blanc

_____3. Pinot Blanc

_____4. Pinot Grigio

_____5. Riesling

_____6. Sauvignon Blanc

List B: Dish Type/Characteristics

a. Vegetables, pastas, chicken, fish

b. Spicy foods, Asian foods, most cheeses, highly seasoned chicken

c. Light summer foods, sweet or delicate shellfish or fish

d. Spicy foods, tomato based dishes, rich and fatty fish, especially salmon, most cheeses

e. Shellfish, especially lobster; veal; chicken; foods flavoured with herbs or served with rich creamy sauces

f. Duck, goose

VII. Brandies

Match each of the "Brandies" in List A with the appropriate letter "Description" in List B.

List A: Brandies	List B: Description
_____1. Cognac	a. Pear brandy from Alsace
	b. Apple brandy from Normandy France
_____2. Armagnac	c. Spanish brandy aged in the solera system
	d. Raspberry brandy from Alsace
_____3. Metaxa	e. Cherry brandy from Bavaria
_____4. Brandy de Jerez	f. One of the best-known brandies; made in France; distilled twice
_____5. Pomace Brandy	g. Well-known brandy from Southwest France
	h. Plum brandy from Eastern Europe
_____6. Calvados	i. Made from the pressed grape pulp remaining from the pressing of the grape when making wine
_____7. Kirschwasser	j. Greek brandy with a strong resin taste
_____8. Framboise	
_____9. Poire	
_____10. Slivovitz	

F. True or False

For each question below, circle either True or False to indicate the correct answer.

1. The juice of concord grapes, cherries, raspberries and strawberries, for example, can produce unappetizing colours when mixed.
   True   False

2. A juice extractor is best used for less juicy fruits and vegetables.
   True   False

3. Adding baking soda to blended juices may help in correcting colours.
   True   False

4. Only two species of coffee bean are routinely used.
   True   False

5. For long-term storage, coffee keeps well in the refrigerator.
   True   False

6. Whole coffee beans will stay fresh for a few weeks at room temperature, whereas ground coffee will only stay fresh three or four days.
   True   False

7. In reference to making coffee, the term *steeping* means mixing hot water with the ground coffee.
   True   False

8. Espresso coffee should be brewed within 22 to 28 seconds.
   True   False

9. Café latte is made by mixing 1/4 espresso with 3/4 steamed milk without foam.
   True   False

10. Tea comes from many different species of plants.

11. The main difference among the three types of tea is the manner in which the leaves are treated after picking.
    True   False

12. Orange pekoe tea is black tea that has a light orange flavour.
    True   False

13. Green tea is yellow-green in colour and partially fermented to release its characteristics.
    True   False

14. Teas such as Darjeeling, Ceylon, and Assam are named for their place of origin.
    True   False

15. Milk when added to tea reduces its astringency.
    True   False

16. Dutched cocoa is not recommended for beverages.
    True   False

17. White wine is always made with white grapes and red wine with red grapes.
    True   False

18. Sparkling wines are still wines that undergo a complete second fermentation.
    True   False

19. Pilsner is a popular style of Lager.
    True   False

20. Stout is a type of Lager.
    True   False

21. Ales are made with yeast that rises to the top during the fermentation process.
    True   False

22. The maximum alcohol content of beer is 6%.
    True   False

Chapter 36

Plate Presentation

People eat as much with their eyes as they do with their mouths. Therefore, the art of planning and executing an effective plate presentation is paramount. This is an element of planning that should be taken seriously and allowed plenty of time for planning in order to ensure success.

At the end of this chapter the student should be able to:

1.   Understand the basic principles of plate presentation.
2.   Use a variety of techniques to add visual appeal to plated foods.

Key Terms

Sizes	Shapes
Colours	Arrangements
Patterns	Plate dusting
Textures	

Test Your Knowledge

The practice sets provided below have been designed to test your comprehension of the information found in this chapter. It is recommended that you read the chapter completely before attempting these questions.

A. Terminology

Fill in each blank with the correct term or definition.

1.   Service _____

2.   _____ The process of offering the selected foods to diners in a fashion that is visually pleasing.

3.   _____ A completed plate's structure of colours, textures, shapes, and arrangements.

4.   _____ A cookie-like dough piped very thin and baked for use in making decorations and garnishes.

B. Fill in the Blanks

Fill in the blanks provided with the response that correctly answers each statement.

1.   Proper cooking procedures can enhance the _____, _____, and _____ of many cooked foods.

2.   Once the colour or pattern is chosen for a plate, the next important element to consider is _____, keeping in mind the amount of food being presented.

3.   The _____ is often the highest point on the plate.

4.   Plate drawing is most typically done with _____ sauces.

C. Short Answer

1.   Presentation techniques are divided into two broad categories; list them:

a. _____

b. _____

2.   Explain how proper cutting techniques affect the presentation.

_____

_____

_____

_____

_____

3.   Explain how the size and shape of plates affect the presentation.

_____

_____

_____

_____

_____

4.   Explain how the colour and patterns of plates affect the presentation.

_____

_____

_____

_____

_____

5.   Explain how the colour of foods affects the presentation.

_____

_____

_____

_____

6.   Explain how the texture of foods affects the presentation.

_____

_____

_____

_____

7.   Explain how the shapes of foods affect the presentation.

_____

_____

_____

_____

8.   List the basic guidelines for arranging foods on a plate

_____

_____

_____

_____

9.   Explain the procedures for plate dusting

_____

_____

_____

_____

10. List two (2) ways in which a hippen-masse garnish will affect the presentation.

a. _____

b. _____

11. Describe how sauces are used for decorating plates; provide examples.

_____

_____

_____

_____

D. True or False

For each question below, circle either True or False to indicate the correct answer.

1. Cooked rice is a good example of food that moulds well for an attractive presentation.
   True   False

2. The garnish should always be the focal point of the plate.
   True   False

3. Generally speaking, foods with similar textures look boring together.
   True   False

4. Dusting a plate can be done after the plating of the food is complete.
   True   False

5. A piping bag would be a good choice of equipment for performing sauce drawings.
   True   False

6. The primary consideration with sauce drawing is that the colours of the sauces used contrast with each other.
   True   False

CHAPTER 1

A. Terminology

1. Grande cuisine
2. Classic cuisine
3. Marie-Antoine Carême
4. Fernand Point
5. Cooking
6. Gastronomy
7. Boulanger
8. Rôtisseur
9. Regional cuisine
10. Fusion cuisine
11. Slow Food
12. Ethnic cuisine
13. One who shows excessive appreciation for fine food and drink.
14. A chef who simplified and refined *Grande Cuisine* and applied such changes to his work in European hotels as well as his writings, which include, among others, *Le Guide Culinaire*.
15. A system of staffing the kitchen so that each worker is assigned to a set of specific tasks.
16. The pioneer of regional cuisine in Canada
17. A style of cooking that de-emphasized many classic cuisine principles and highlighted simpler, lighter cuisine.
18. The characteristic cuisine of a nation.
19. A system of cooking efficiently and economically, with knowledge and appreciation for ingredients and procedures.

B. Fill in the Blank

1. Carlo Petrini
2. Front of the house
3. Back of the house
4. Russian service
5. Mise en place
6. Poissonier
7. Garde Manger
8. Saucier
9. Tournant
10. Confiseur
11. Decorateur

C. Short Answer

1.
   a. Simultaneous cooking of many items, especially those needing constant and delicate attention.
   b. Cooks could more comfortably and safely approach the heat source and control its temperatures.
   c. Cooks could efficiently prepare and hold a multitude of smaller amounts of items requiring different cooking methods or ingredients for later use or service.

2.
   a. Canning
   b. Freezing
   c. Freeze-drying
   d. Vacuum-packing

3.
   a. Age
   b. Type of household
   c. Income
   d. Education
   e. Geography

4.
   a. Personal appearance
   b. Behaviour in and around the kitchen
   c. Good grooming practices
   d. In uniform while working
   e. The wearing of the toque

5. Nouvelle Cuisine reflects a trend towards lighter, more naturally flavoured and more simply prepared foods. Fernand Point was a master practitioner of this movement, which was brought to even greater heights by his trainees, Paul Bocuse, Jean et Pierre Troisgros, Alain Chapel, François Bise and Louis Outhier. Following their path were Michel Guérard and Roger Vergé in the early 1970s.

6. A switch from organic to chemical fertilizers and the introduction of pesticides and drought or pest-resistant strains have resulted in increased yields of crops. Traditional hybridization techniques and, more recently, genetic engineering have produced new or improved grains and, for better or for worse, fruits and vegetables that have a longer shelf life and are more amenable to mass production handling, storage, and transportation methods. Animal husbandry and agriculture have led to a larger and better supply of meat, poultry and fish.

7. The Slow Food movement started in 1986 in Rome, Italy

8. To protect cultural regional food and drink and encourage the use of local ingredients.

These changes have created new consumer groups with their own designs and needs. Consumers are defined by age, type of household, income, education or geography and food service operators tailor menus, prices and décor accordingly.

D. Multiple Choice

1. c
2. c
3. b
4. d
5. d
6. c
7. c
8. c
9. d
10. b

E. Matching

I. Defining Professionalism

1. Dedication
2. Skill
3. Training
4. Judgment
5. Taste
6. Pride

II. Brigade Members

1.	k	6.	h
2.	c	7.	j
3.	g	8.	f
4.	i	9.	d
5.	e	10.	a

F. True or False

1. False (p. 11). Today most food service operations utilize a simplified version of Escoffier's kitchen brigade.
2. False (p. 8). Advances in the transportation industry began to positively influence the food service industry during the early 1800s.
3. True (p. 13).
4. False (p. 9). Most issues in the food service industry that are brought to the forefront for discussion are brought about by the demands of the customer. Such concerns may eventually encourage government interaction to ensure public well-being.
5. False (p. 10). Restaurants offering buffet service generally charge by the meal; if they charge by the dish, they are known as cafeterias.
6. False (p. 14). A chef who prepares effective mise en place is one who is organized and ready to prepare all styles of cuisine. Proper mise en place is a habit that should be emphasized in all preparations.
7. True (p. 5).
8. True (p. 11).
9. False (pp. 8–9). Many of the preserving techniques used prior to the 19th century destroyed or distorted the appearance and flavour of the foods. Therefore, when new preserving techniques were developed in the early 19th century, many of them were adopted due to their minimal effect on appearance and flavour.
10. True (p. 10).

CHAPTER 2

A. Terminology

1. Intoxication
2. Cross-contamination
3. Clean
4. pH
5. Bacteria
6. Infection
7. Temperature Danger Zone
8. Viruses
9. Direct contamination
10. Sanitize
11. 15–30 minutes
12. Chemical hazard
13. Salmonella
14. Binary Fission
15. 15 mL (1 tbsp)
16. 30 seconds
17. 45°C (113°F)
18. A rigorous food safety system of self-inspection that focuses on the flow of food through the food service facility.
19. A disease-causing, living microorganism.
20. Glass chips, metal shavings, bits of wood, or other foreign matter in food that may cause danger to the consumer.
21. Endangering the safety of food by exposing it to disease-causing microorganisms such as bacteria, moulds, yeasts, viruses, or fungi.
22. To destroy all living microorganisms.
23. A large group of plants living in the soil, air, and water, which range in type from single-celled organisms to giant mushrooms.

24. Bacteria that spoil food without rendering it unfit for human consumption.

25. A by-product of some bacteria life process that cannot be smelled, seen or tasted.

26. Tiny, multi-celled organisms that depend on nutrients from a living host to complete their life cycle.

27. Canadian Food Inspection Agency

B. Fill in the Blank

Food-Borne Diseases Review

1. *Hepatitis A*

   O: Virus

   S: Enters food supply through shellfish harvested from polluted waters. Humans, often without knowledge of infection, also carry it.

   P: Confirm source of shellfish, good personal hygiene, avoid cross-contamination.

2. *Botulism*

   O: Clostridium Botulinum

   F: Toxin, cells, spores

   S: Cooked foods held for an extended time at warm temperature with limited oxygen, rice, potatoes, smoked fish, canned vegetables.

   P: Keep internal temperature of cooked foods above 60°C (140°F) or below 4°C (40°F); reheat leftovers thoroughly; discard swollen cans.

3. *Norwalk Virus*

   O: Virus

   S: Spread almost entirely by poor personal hygiene of food service employees. It is found in human feces, contaminated water, or vegetables fertilized with manure.

   P: The virus can be destroyed by high cooking temperatures but not by sanitizing solutions or freezing.

4. *Strep*

   O: Streptococcus

   F: Cells

   S: Infected food workers

   P: Do not allow employees to work if ill; protect foods from customers' coughs and sneezes.

5. *Perfringens or CP*

   O: Clostridium Perfringens

   F: Cells and toxin

   S: Reheated meats, sauces, stews, casseroles

   P: Keep cooked foods at an internal temperature of 60°C (140°F) or higher; reheat leftovers to internal temperature of 74°C (165°F) or higher.

6. *Salmonella*

   O: Salmonellosis

   F: Cells

   S: Poultry, eggs, milk, meats, fecal contamination

   P: Thoroughly cook all meat, poultry, fish and eggs; avoid cross-contamination with raw foods, maintain good personal hygiene.

7. *Trichinosis*

   O: Parasitic worms

   S: Eating undercooked game or pork infected with trichina larvae.

   P: Cook foods to a minimum internal temperature of 58°C (137°F) for 10 seconds.

8. *E. Coli or 0157*

   O: Escherichia coli 0157:H7

   F: Cells and toxins

   S: Any food, especially raw milk, raw vegetables, raw or rare beef; humans

   P: Thoroughly cook or reheat items.

9. *Staphylococcus*

   O: Staphylococcus Aureus

   F: Toxin

   S: Starchy foods, cold meats, bakery items, custards, milk products, humans with infected wounds or sores.

   P: Wash hands and utensils before use; exclude unhealthy food handlers; avoid having foods at room temperature.

10. *Anisakiasis*

    O: Parasitic roundworms

    S: The organs of fish, especially bottom feeders or those taken from contaminated waters. Raw or undercooked fish are often implicated.

    P: Fish should be thoroughly cleaned immediately after being caught so that the parasites do not have the opportunity to spread. Thoroughly cook to a minimum internal temperature of 60°C (140°F).

11. *Listeriosis*

    O: Listeria Monocytogenes

    F: Cells

    S: Milk products, humans

    P: Avoid raw milk and cheese made from unpasteurized milk.

C. Short Answer

1. a. staphylococcus aureus

    b. clostridium perfringens

c. Escherichia coli 0157:H7

d. Clostridium botulinum

2. a. food

b. temperature

c. moisture

d. proper PH

e. proper atmosphere (with or without oxygen)

f. time

3. a. gradually under refrigeration

b. under cold running water if items are wrapped in plastic

c. in microwave, but only if the food is to be prepared and served immediately

4. a. ensure personal cleanliness

b. clean dishes and equipment

c. proper pest control

5. a. wash hands frequently

b. keep fingernails short

c. keep any cuts or wounds antiseptically bandaged

d. bathe daily, or more if required

c. keep hair clean and restrained

d. wear clean and neat work clothes

e. do not eat, drink, smoke or chew gum in food preparation areas

D. Multiple Choice

1.	a	5.	c	9.	b	13.	a	17.	d
2.	a	6.	a	10.	d	14.	d	18.	b
3.	b	7.	b	11.	d	15.	a	19.	d
4.	d	8.	c	12.	c	16.	c	20.	b

E. True or False

1. False (p. 21). Toxins cannot be smelled, seen, or tasted.

2. True (p. 23).

3. False (p. 31). A licensed pest control operator should be contacted immediately. Such professionals will go beyond simply locating the source of infestation, and will also prescribe a plan of action to prevent ongoing occurrences in the future.

4. True (p. 28).

5. True (p. 23).

6. True (p. 29).

7. False (p. 28).

8. False (p. 25).

9. False (p. 24).

10. False (p. 29).

11. True (p. 31).

12. False (p. 30).

13. True (p. (pp. 31–32).

14. True (p. 28)

15. False (p.36)

16. True (p. 36)

17. True (p. 36)

18. False (p. 36)

CHAPTER 3

A. Terminology

1. Vitamins

2. Macronutrients

3. Fats

4. Proteins

5. Minerals

6. Dietary fibre

7. Saturated fats

8. Monounsaturated fats

9. Polyunsaturated fats

10. Coenzymes

11. Phytochemicals

12. The unit of energy measured by the amount of heat required to raise 1000 grams of water 1°C.

13. Nutrients that must be provided by food because the body does not produce them in sufficient quantities.

14. The replacement of one ingredient with another, which is done for nutritional purposes and is done for those individuals who, for dietary reasons, cannot eat a particular ingredient.

15. A group of compounds composed of oxygen, hydrogen, and carbon that supply the body with energy and can be classified as either simple or complex.

16. All of the chemical reactions and physical processes that continually occur in living cells and organisms.

17. A process by which liquid fats are made more solid (saturated).

18. The building blocks of proteins.

19. Recommended Nutrient Intake

20. Vitamins and minerals

21. Milk sugar

22. Malt sugar

23.   Plant pigments that dissolve readily in water; found in red, purple and white vegetables, such as blueberries, red cabbage onions and tea.

B. Fill in the Blank

Parts of a Product Label (and respective significance)

a.   Portion size: Similar products now list similar portion sizes, making nutritional comparison easier. The serving size declaration must be given in grams or millilitres and should also include a common or household measure.

b.   Fat content: If this food contained a very small amount of fat, it would be labelled "fat free," because the amount would be nutritionally insignificant; for example, only 0.5 grams per serving and per reference amount.

c.   Nutrients content: Macronutrients are listed in grams and micronutrients are given in percentage of RNI. RNI are for adult males and can be misleading for children as well as pregnant or lactating women.

d.   Nutrients content: Macronutrients are listed in grams and micronutrients are given in percentage of RNI. RNI are for adult males and can be misleading for children as well as pregnant or lactating women.

e.   Language: Most mandatory information must be shown in both English & French.

C. Short Answer

1.   a.   Use proper purchasing and storage techniques in order to preserve nutrients.

       b.   Offer a variety of foods from each food group of Canada's Food Guide so that customers have a choice.

       c.   Offer entrées that emphasize plant instead of animal foods.

       d.   Offer dishes that are considerate of special dietary needs such as low fat or low salt.

       e.   Use cooking procedures that preserve rather than destroy nutrients (see p. 54 for more).

2.   canola, olive, soybean, cottonseed, sunflower, corn, and safflower oils

3.   tropical oils, all animal fats, and dairy products

4.   For a professional perspective, see p. 55, "The Customers Who Count."

5.   Prepare vegetables as close to service time as possible. Choose cooking methods that will minimize the leaching of water-soluble vitamins. Example: steaming, microwaving or

baking. Minimize exposure to air and light by practising proper storage procedures.

6.   Terms such as "a good source of," "low in," "sugar free" and "low calorie" have specific definitions and must be used accurately. In general, these terms are related to recommended daily intakes for the particular ingredient. For example a "fat-free" item cannot contain more than 0.5 g per serving and in a "reference amount" defined by regulation, as the amount a person would typically consume at one time. The language of health claims is also tightly regulated as certain terms may suggest that a particular ingredient may prevent disease. For example, a food may be described as wholesome but should not be described as healthy.

7.   Carbohydrates are found in three forms: simple, complex and fibre. Most carbohydrates come from plants and are associated with vitamins, minerals and amino acids, thereby forming the bases of balanced nutrition. Carbohydrates supply energy, provide vitamins and minerals and regulate digestion.

8.   The replacement of one ingredient for the more nutritious characteristics of another that may offer different taste, texture, or appearance but will not compromise, although it may slightly change, the original taste of the dish. Although it does not taste the same, it should still taste good.

9.   a.   Reduce the amount of the ingredient(s)

       b.   Replace the ingredient(s) with a substitute that will do the least to change the flavour and appearance of the dish

       c.   Eliminate the ingredient(s)

10.   a.   Peanuts

       b.   Tree nuts

       c.   Sesame seeds

       d.   Milk

       e.   Eggs

       f.   Fish and shellfish

       g.   Soy

       h.   Wheat

       i.   Sulphites

D. Multiple Choice

1.   a

2.   c

3.   d

4.   c

5.   b

6.   d

7.   a

8. b
9. c
10. a
11. c
12. a

E. Matching

Nutrition Review

1. a   4. b   7. j   10. h
2. d   5. c   8. i   11. g
3. d   6. k   9. n

CHAPTER 4

A. Terminology

1. Cycle menu
2. Hybrid menu
3. Conversion factor
4. Par stock
5. Table d'hôte
6. Prime cost
7. Metric
8. FIFO
9. Standardized recipe
10. Market menu
11. Total recipe cost
12. US system
13. A menu from which every item is priced and ordered separately.
14. The ratio of cost of food served to food sales dollars.
15. The main course.
16. A periodic check of all food items in the kitchen, storerooms, and refrigerators.
17. A set of written instructions for preparation of the menu item.
18. The total cost of ingredients that go into the preparation of the menu item.
19. The cost of the item as received from the supplier, broken down into individual units.
20. The amount of product lost during preparation.
21. The amount of food available for consumption after trimming and cooking.
22. A measuring system that uses pounds and ounces for weight, and pints and fluid ounces for volume.
23. The number of individual items in a recipe and in portion control.
24. A prefix signifying 1000 times larger.
25. A prefix signifying 100 times larger.
26. A prefix signifying 1000 times smaller.
27. A prefix signifying 100 times smaller.
28. A prefix signifying 10 times smaller.

B. Fill in the Blank

I. Units of Measure

1. 16 oz
2. 28.35 g
3. 454 g
4. 1 000 g
5. .035 oz
6. 35 oz = 2.187 lb / 2 lb
7. 16 tbsp = 8 fl. oz
8. 1 qt = 32 fl. oz
9. 1/2 gal = 4 pt
10. 16 tbsp = 8 fl. oz

II. Recipe Conversion

Purée of Split Pea Soup

	New Yield I	New Yield II
	3.24 L	9.6L
	18 Portions	*40 Portions*
	180 ml (6 oz)	*240 ml (8 oz)*
	each	*each*
Split peas	648 g (1 lb 7 oz)	1920 g (4lb 4 oz)
Salt pork	81 g (2.5 oz)	240 g (8.5 oz)
Mirepoix	405 g (13 oz)	1200 g (2 lb 10.5 oz)
White stock	2.43 L (2 qt 6oz)	7.2 L (6 qt 13 oz)
Garlic cloves	8.1 g (2)	24 g (5)
Ham hocks	567 g (1 lb 4 oz)	1680 g (3 lb 11 oz)
Sachet:		
Bay leaves	*1.62*	*4.8*
Dried Thyme	*0.20 g (1/4tsp)*	*0.6 g*
Peppercorns	*0.5 g*	*0.41 g*
Sat & pepper	*TT*	*TT*
Croutons	as needed for garnish	

III. Unit Costs

1. $1.70
2. $0.16
3. $1.70
4. $0.58
5. $0.25

IV. Recipe Costs

1. $43.75   4. $637.50
2. $0.85   5. $6.45
3. 12   6. 40

F. Fill in the Blank

V. Yield Factor and Percentage

Total Yield Weight	Yield Factor	Percentage
1. 3600 g (8 lbs)	0.8	80%
2. 192 g (6.75 oz)	0.8	80%
3. 756 g (27 oz)	0.84	84%
4. 5265 g (11 lbs 10 oz)	0.78	78%
5. 7088 g (15 lbs 10 oz)	0.63	63%
6. 15 750 g (34 lbs 12 oz)	0.7	70%

VI. Applying Yield Factors

	A.P. Unit Cost	Yield Factor	E.P. Unit Cost
1.	$1.33	0.8	$1.06
2.	$64.75	0.8	$51.8
3.	$3.62	0.84	$3.04
4.	$2.12	0.78	1.65
5.	$1.93	0.63	1.22
6.	$0.82	0.70	0.57

VII. Food Cost

1. 36%
2. $4.17
3. a. $11.61   b. $29.00
4. $1.00

VIII. Cost of Goods Sold

1. a. $25,347.00
   b. 28.13%
   c. $24,329.70

C. Short Answer

1. The metric system is divided in units of 10, making it very easy to increase or decrease quantities. The imperial system uses different units for weight and for volume. As well, units are divided in odd numbers such as 16 ounces to a pound which makes calculations more complicated.

2. No, all things being equal, cooking time will not change when recipe size changes. For example, a muffin requires the same amount of baking time, whether you prepare 1 dozen or 4 dozen.

3. Value of inventory at the beginning of the accounting period PLUS food purchased during that period, minus the inventory at the end of the period and minus staff meals, promotions, write-offs and returns.

D. Multiple Choice

1. a
2. b
3. d
4. a
5. c
6. c
7. d
8. a
9. a
10. d
11. a
12 c

CHAPTER 5

A. Terminology

1. Knife
2. Thermometer
3. Oven
4. Carbon steel
5. Bolster
6. Similar to a paring knife but with a curved blade.
7. Another name for sharpening tool.
8. A metal most commonly used in commercial utensils, light-weight, best heat conductor after copper.
9. An instant source of heat for cooking, either an open flame or a cast-iron solid plate.
10. A type of oven that can function as a steamer, a convection oven or a combination of the two.
11. A work area that is dedicated to one specific task, for example, sandwich preparation.
12. An area where several different tasks are grouped together.
13. The French chef who created "Lamb Chops Reform."

B. Fill in the Blank

I. General Questions

1. Canadian Standards Association
2. Utility
3. 1. tip   4. tang   7. cutting edge
   2. spine   5. rivets
   3. bolster   6. heel
4. Induction, cast iron, magnetic stainless steel
5. Griddle
6. Buffalo chopper
7. Wooden
8. Scimitar

I. Equipment Identification

1. French or chef's knife—all-purpose chopping
2. Serrated slicer—slicing cooked meat
3. Boning knife—separating meat from bone
4. Paring knife—cutting curved surfaces, namely vegetables
5. Whisk—mixing sauces
6. Grill spatula—lifting/turning items on grill
7. Chef's fork—carving meats
8. Palette knife or cake spatula—spreading frosting
9. Ladle—serving soups
10. Portion scoop—ice-cream service
11. Stockpot—making large quantities of soup/stock
12. Sautoir—frying
13. Wok—stir-frying
14. Sauteuse—frying
15. Hotel pan—warming food
16. Liquid measuring cup—measuring liquids or solids
17. Conical strainer or Chinoise—straining stocks, soups, and sauces
18. Food mill—puréeing and straining food at the same time
19. Drum sieve—sieving dry foods
20. Spider—removing items from liquids

C. Short Answer

1. a. Is it necessary for production?
    b. Will it do the job in the space available?
    c. Is it the most economical for the establishment?
    d. Is it easy to clean and repair?
2. a. Carbon steel
    b. Stainless steel
    c. High-carbon stainless steel
3. Balance scales use a two-tray and free weights counterbalance system. Balance scales do not rely on spring systems, which makes them more precise and able to handle more weight.
4. Fill a glass with shaved ice, then add water. Place the thermometer in the iced water and wait until the temperature stabilizes. Adjust the calibration enough until the temperature reads 0°C (32°F).
5. Candy/fat thermometers are designed to measure temperatures up to 200°C (400°F) using mercury in a column of glass.

D. Multiple Choice

1. b
2. c
3. a
4. d
5. c
6. c
7. a
8. d
9. b
10. c

E. Matching

1. i
2. h
3. a
4. e
5. g
6. d
7. c
8. f
9. j
10. b

F. True or False

1. False (p. 89). Stem-type thermometers should be calibrated when dropped.
2. False (p.101). Ventilation heads should be cleaned by professionals.
3. True (p. 91).
4. True (p. 101).
5. True (p. 86).
6. False (p. 99). Because a steam kettle heats the kettle's sides, it heats food more quickly than does a pot sitting on a stove.
7. True (p. 84).
8. True (p. 98).
9. False (p. 97).
10. False (p. 97).

CHAPTER 6

A. Terminology

1. Whetstone
2. Steel
3. Brunoise
4. Chiffonade
5. Oblique
6. Rounds/rondelles
7. Batonnet
8. 20 degrees
9. gaufrette
10. butterfly
11. underhand grip

12. The act of straightening the edge of the blade after sharpening.

13. A stick-shaped piece of vegetable (1/16 inch × 1/16 inch × 1 to 2 inches) (1–2 mm × 1–2 mm × 2.5 to 4 cm).

14. A small cube that can be cut from the allumette (1/8 inch × 1/8 inch) (3 mm × 3 mm).

15. Cutting away the edges of a piece of vegetable to leave a long football shape.

16. A cube-shaped piece of vegetable measuring 1/4 inch × 1/4 inch (6 mm × 6 mm).

17. Another term applied to finely chopped food.

18. A flat cut of vegetable that is used for garnishing soups.

19. A cube-shaped cut measuring 1/2 inch × ½ inch (12 mm × 12 mm).

20. A cut similar to rondelles, except it is cut at an angle.

21. A cutting technique that does not require each piece to be identical in size.

B. Fill in the Blank

1. two; knife tip; wrist
2. tip; rocking
3. away; steel; glass; marble
4. heel; coarsest; finest
5. root
6. does not, hone
7. heel, 20 degrees
8. Parisiennes

C. Short Answer

1. No, the heat and harsh chemicals can damage the edge and the handle. The blade can also be damaged if it knocks against cookware. In addition, the knife could injure an unsuspecting worker. Always wash and dry your knives by hand immediately after use.

2. a. Use the correct knife for the task at hand.
   b. Always cut away from yourself or your fingers.
   c. Always use a cutting board.
   d. Always keep knives sharp.
   e. Carry a knife with the point down, parallel to and close to your leg as you walk.
   f. Do not attempt to catch a falling knife.
   g. Never leave a knife in a sink of water.

h. Never place items (e.g., towels, boxes, food cutting boards etc.) on top of your knives.

i. Wash knives by hand, dishwashers may cause damage to the blade or the handle.

j. To wipe a blade properly, place the knife in a folded towel with the cutting edge pointing away from you. Pull the knife through the towel with your palm on the top of the towel.

3. Hold the handle with three fingers while gripping the blade between the thumb and index finger.

4. To ensure even cooking and enhance appearance of the finished product.

D. Matching

Cuts of Vegetables

1. 1–2 mm × 1–2 mm × 2.5 to 4 cm (1/16 inch × 1/16 inch × 1 to 2 inches)
2. 6 mm × 6 mm × 5 to 6 cm (1/4 inch × 1/4 inch × 2 to 2-1/2inches)
3. 3 mm × 12 mm × 12 mm (1/8 inch × 1/2 inch × 1/2 inch)
4. 1–2 mm × 1–2 mm × 1–2 mm (1/16 inch × 1/16 inch × 1/16 inch dice)
5. 3 mm × 3 mm (1/8 inch × 1/8 inch dice)
6. 6 mm × 6 mm (1/4 inch × 1/4 inch dice)
7. 3 mm × 3 mm × 5–6 cm (1/8 inch × 1/8 inch × to 2-1/2 inches)

Similarities: 1. Brunoise comes from julienne. 2. Small dice comes from allumette.

D. True or False

1. False (p. 110).
2. False (p. 111). A steel does not sharpen a knife. Instead, it is used to hone or straighten the blade immediately after and between sharpening.
3. True (p. 120).
4. False (p. 111). A whetstone can be moistened with either water or mineral oil, but not both.
5. False (p. 117).
6. True (p. 117).
7. True (p. 110).
8. True (p. 111).
9. False (p. 111).
10. False (p. 111).

CHAPTER 7

A. Terminology

1. Flavour
2. Taste
3. Mouth-feel
4. Aromas

5. Palate
6. Umami
7. Decoction
8. Aromatic
9. Spice blend
10. Bouquet garni
11. Condiment
12. Infusion
13. Nut
14. Oil
15. Sweet Cicely
16. Italian parsley
17. Bay
18. Fine herbs
19. Nonpareils
20. Used to add flavours, an oignon piqué is prepared by peeling an onion, trimming the root end, and attaching one or two dried bay leaves to the onion using whole cloves as pins.
21. The large group of aromatic plants whose leaves, stems, or flowers are used to add flavours to other foods.
22. Strongly flavoured or aromatic portions of plants used as flavourings.
23. Foods that are used in almost all stations of the kitchen with much regularity.
24. A thin, sour liquid used for thousands of years as a preservative, cooking ingredient, condiment, and cleaning solution.
25. An item that adds a new taste to a food and alters its natural flavours. The category of flavourings may include herbs, spices, vinegars, and condiments.
26. An item added to enhance the natural flavours of a food without dramatically changing its taste. Salt and pepper would be good examples of a seasoning.

B. Fill in the Blank
1. Umami
2. Taste buds
3. Olfactory neurons
4. Piperine
5. Capsaicin
6. Wine, malt and cider

C. Short Answer
1. a. Sweet.
   b. Sour.
   c. Salty.
   d. Bitter.
   e. Umami.
2. a. Sweet.
   b. Sour.
   c. Salty.
   d. Bitter.
   e. Umami.
3. a. Sweet.
   b. Sour.
   c. Salty.
   d. Bitter.
   e. Umami.
4. a. Flavourings should not hide the taste or aroma of the primary ingredients.
   b. Flavourings should be combined in balance, so as not to overwhelm the palate.
   c. Flavourings should not be used to disguise poor quality or poorly prepared products.
5. a. Preserves foods
   b. It heightens food flavours.
   c. It provides the distinctive taste of saltiness.
6. It refers to the temperature at which a given fat begins to break down and smoke. Deep-fat frying and sautéing require the use of temperatures that necessitate fats with a high smoke point.
7. Rancidity is a chemical change caused by exposure to air, light or heat. It results in objectionable flavours and odours.

D. Multiple Choice
1. c
2. d
3. a
4. b
5. c
6. a
7. d
8. b
9. b

E. Matching
1. d
2. h
3. g
4. a
5. f
6. c
7. b
8. i

Herb		Spice	
1.	Cilantro	6.	Paprika
2.	Oregano	7.	Coriander

327

3. Lavender

4. Thyme

5. Lemon grass

8. Ground mustard

9. Capers

10. Black pepper

F. True or False

1. False (p. 143). Use less dried herbs than you would fresh herbs in a recipe. The loss of moisture in the dried herbs supposedly strengthens and concentrates the flavours.

2. True (p. 144).

3. True (p. 150).

4. True (p. 149).

5. False (p. 146). A shortening is a fat, usually made from vegetable oils, that is solid at room temperature.

CHAPTER 8

A. Terminology

1. Yolk

2. Chalazae cords

3. Homogenization

4. Pasteurization

5. Buttermilk

6. Lowfat

7. Omega-3 eggs

8. A, D, E and K, B complex

9. Cholesterol

10. Salt, cream of tartar

11. 500, 30, buttermilk

12. light, whipping

13. Indian version of clarified butter (from buffalo milk)

14. A substance made from drained curds processed by cutting, kneading and cooking

15. Cultured whipping cream

16. A non-processing technique, certification is a method of controlling the quality of milk by controlling the condition of the animals from which the milk is obtained.

17. From the French word for melted, it can refer to Swiss cheese, melted with white wine and seasonings in a special earthenware pot over a flame, for dipping bread cubes into.

18. The clear portion of the egg often referred to as the white. It contains more than half of the protein and riboflavin and the white itself accounts for nearly 2/3 of the egg.

19. Whole butter that has had the water and milk solids removed.

20. Sometimes referred to as European butter, cultured butter contains 82% to 86% milk fat.

Cultured butter is used to produce a rich nutty flavour. It is not presently available in Canada.

B. Fill in the Blank

Parts of an Egg

a. shell

b. yolk

c. white

d. chalazae

C. Short Answer

1.

Primary part	Grade A	Grade B	Grade C
Albumen	Firm	Watery	Thin & watery
Yolk	Round, well centred	Slightly flattened	Loose
Shell	Clean, no cracks Normal shape	No cracks, but rough texture	May be cracked

2. a. Use fresh egg white and warm them to room temperature.

   b. Use a clean bowl and a clean whisk.

   c. Whip the whites on medium speed until very foamy, then add salt or cream of tart

   d. Continue whipping until soft peaks form, do not overwhip. If required, add sugar or hot syrup (if preparing meringues) as directed. Whip until a stiff peak forms.

3. Vegetable oil (and/or animal fat), water, flavourings, colourings, emulsifiers, preservatives and vitamins.

4. Eggs out of the shell available as whole eggs, yolks or whites. They are available frozen, refrigerated or dried. Precooked, proportioned and blended eggs are also available.

5. There are 2 types of substitutes: complete substitute made from soy and milk protein and a partial substitute that contains real albumen but the yolk has been replaced with vegetables and milk products.

D. Multiple Choice

1. d
2. a
3. b
4. c
5. b

6. d
7. b
8. d
9. c
10. a

11. d
12. b
13. a
14. b

15. d
16. c
17. b
18. a

14.	False (p. 157). Eggs at room temperature will form a better foam.

CHAPTER 9

A. Terminology

1.	A moist-heat cooking method that uses convection to transfer heat from the cooking liquid to the food. Food is submerged in a liquid held at temperatures between 71°C (160°F) and 82°C (180°F).

2.	The process of surrounding a food with dry, heated air in a closed environment. The term baking usually refers to cooking such products as fish, fruits, vegetables, starches, breads, or pastry items.

3.	The proper term used for the cooking of starches, it usually occurs gradually over a temperature range of 66°C–100°C (150–212°F).

4.	Energy is transferred by waves of heat or light striking the food product. Two kinds of radiant heat are used in the kitchen: infrared and microwave.

5.	The movement of heat from one item to another through direct contact.

6.	To very briefly and partially cook a food in boiling water or hot fat.

7.	A combination cooking method, stewing is most often associated with smaller cuts of food that are first cooked by browning or blanching and then finished in a liquid or a sauce. The liquid used in the second step of the cooking process completely covers the pieces of food and at a low, long simmer, the stew develops flavour, thickens, and becomes tender.

8.	A dry-heat cooking method in which heat is transferred by conduction from the pan to the food, using a moderate amount of fat. Heat is also transferred to the food by the hot fat by convection.

9.	This type of cooking relies on radiation generated by a special oven to penetrate the food. It is generally faster than traditional cooking methods.

10.	This uses a radiant, dry-heat source located below the cooking surface and may be electric, gas, wood, or charcoal.

11.	A moist-heat cooking method that uses convection to transfer heat to the food being cooked. The food must be placed in a basket or in a rack so the steam can circulate around it and cook, and a lid-like apparatus must also contain the steam in order to be able to cook with it.

E. Matching

I. Cheeses

1.	e	5.	f	9.	i
2.	g	6.	a	10.	d
3.	b	7.	c		
4.	j	8.	h		

II. Creams

1.	f
2.	h
3.	g
4.	e
5.	a
6.	d
7.	b
8.	c

F. True or False

1.	False (p. 150). Shell colour has no effect on the quality (grade), flavour, or nutrition.

2.	True (p. 151).

3.	True (p. 152).

4.	False (p. 152). Eggs should be stored at temperatures below 4°C (40°F) and at a relative humidity of 70–80%.

5.	True (p. 154).

6.	False (p. 153). The egg whites should be brought to room temperature to maximize the volume when whipping.

7.	True (pp. 157–159).

8.	False (p. 157). Yogurt is only as healthful, or low in fat, as the milk it is made from.

9.	False (pp. 158–159). Margarine is not a dairy product and is included in this chapter only because it is so commonly used as a substitute for butter. It is actually made from animal or vegetable fats or a combination thereof. Flavourings, colourings, emulsifiers, preservatives, and vitamins are added before it is hydrogenated.

10.	False (pp. 165–166). Processed cheese food contains less natural cheese and more moisture than regular processed cheese. Often vegetable oil and milk solids are added to make the cheese food soft and spreadable.

11.	True (p. 160).

12.	False (p. 152). Egg substitutes have a different flavour from real eggs and cannot be used in recipes where the eggs are required for thickening.

12. The length of time it takes the fat to return to the desired cooking temperature after food is submerged in it.

13. The preferred method for frying battered foods that would otherwise sink to the bottom of food baskets and stick during the cooking process.

14. The temperature at which the fat/oil visibly begins to smoke and chemically begins to break down.

15. A deep-fat frying method that uses a basket to hold foods that don't tend to stick together.

16. A chemical process that turns liquid oil into a solid.

17. Roasting

18. Sautéing

19. Coagulation

20. Convection

12. Simmering

22. Deep-fat frying

23. Boiling

24. Braising

25. Broiling

26. Induction

27. Caramelization

28. Infrared cooking

29. Maillard reactions

30. Double basket method

31. breaded, battered

32. vegetable oils, soybean, sunflower and canola

33. Sous-vide

B. Fill in the Blank

	Method	Medium	Equipment
1.	Stewing	fat then liquid	stove (and oven), tilt skillet
2.	Deep-fat frying	fat	deep fryer
3.	Broiling	air	broiler, salamander, rotisserie
4.	Poaching	water/other liquid	stove, oven, steam-jacketed kettle, tilt skillet
5.	Grilling	air	grill
6.	Simmering	water/other liquid	stove, steam-jacketed kettle, tilt skillet
7.	Baking	air	oven
8.	Roasting	air	oven
9.	Steaming	steam	stove, convection steamer
10.	Braising	fat then liquid	stove (and oven), tilt skillet

C. Short Answer

1. a. Braising: Large pieces of food
      Stewing: Smaller pieces of food
   b. Braising: Brown, then simmer/steam
      Stewing: Brown or blanch, then simmer/steam
   c. Braising: Cooking liquid covers 1/3–1/2c.
      Stewing: Cooking liquid completely covers
   d. Braising: Cooking time is longer (large pieces)
      Stewing: Cooking time is shorter (small pieces)

2. a. The food product must be placed in a basket or on a rack to allow for circulation of the steam.
   b. A lid should cover the steaming unit to trap steam and allow heat to build up.

3. a. Heat a sauté pan over high heat.
   b. Add a small amount of fat and heat until just below smoking point.
   c. Add dry, seasoned chicken breast (or dredge in seasoned flour), placing in a single layer and presentation side down first.
   d. Adjust temperature as needed to control browning; flip when half cooked.
   e. Test for proper doneness, remove from pan, and serve as requested.

4. a. Bring liquid to a boil in an appropriate pan.
   b. Add food product to the cooking liquid.
   c. Adjust the temperature to a gentle simmer, 71°C to 82°C (160°F to 180°F).
   d. Test the product for desired doneness.
   e. If desired, use poaching liquid to make sauce that will be served with the final dish.
   f. Serve with appropriate sauce and accompaniments.

5. When heated, food changes in shape, texture, colour and flavour.

6. As proteins cook, they loose moisture, shrink and become firm.

7. Gelatinization is the proper term for the cooking of starches. When starch and liquid are heated, the starch granules absorb water, causing them to

swell, soften and clarify slightly. Gelatinization occurs gradually over a range of temperatures 66°C to 100° C (150°F to 212°F) depending on the type of starch used.

8.
a. air
b. fat
c. water
d. steam

9.
a. Element: Salt
Effect: Fat becomes dark
b. Element: Water
Effect: Fat smokes
c. Element: Overheating
Effect: Fat foams
d. Element: Food particles
Effect: Fat develops flavours
e. Element: Oxygen
Effect: Fat becomes rancid

10.
a. Helps to keep food moist.
b. Prevents excessive greasiness.

11.
a. The fat must be hot enough to quickly seal the surface of the food so it doesn't become excessively greasy.
b. The fat shouldn't be so hot that the food's surface burns before the interior is cooked.

12.
a. Flavour
b. Smoke point
c. Resistance to chemical breakdown

13. Large, thick items should not exceed 2.5 kg (5.5 lbs) or maximum thickness of 100 mm (4 in.). After cooking, large pieces should be cooled to 10 °C (50 °F within 2.5 hours and than chilled to 0 °C to 3 °C (32 °F to 37 °F) for storage.

14. Food items, whether large or small, must be reheated to a minimum internal temperature of 74°C (165°F) and held at that temperature for 15 minutes.

15. Using a shock or blast freezer, the core temperature must be lowered to –5 °C (23°F) within 90 minutes. It is then lowered to –18 °C (0°F) for storage.

D. Multiple Choice

1. a	7. d	13. b	19. a
2. d	8. b	14. d	20. d
3. c	9. c	15. b	21. b
4. a	10. a	16. d	22. c
5. c	11. d	17. a	
6. b	12. a	18. c	

E. Matching

I. Cooking Methods

1. e
2. c
3. b
4. a
5. d
6. h
7. g

II. Effects of Heat on Food

1. b
2. d
3. c
4. e
5. a

F. True or False

1. False (p. 181). This method is best used for foods that float.
2. True (p. 182).
3. True (p. 181).
4. False (p. 181). Foods that are fried together should be the same size and shape that allows them to float freely in the fat.
5. True (p. 562).
6. True (p. 563).
7. True (p. 185).
8. False (p. 185). Specific equipment and systems are required to ensure strict quality controls.
9. True (p. 185).
10. True (p. 185).
11. True (p. 185).
12. True (p. 185).
13. False (p. 185).
14. False (p. 185). Most common in hospitals, airlines, convention centres etc.

CHAPTER 10

A. Terminology

1. Connective tissue
2. Salsa
3. Remouillage
4. Demi-glace
5. Gelatin
6. Stock
7. Jus lié
8. Venting

9. Degrease

10. Sauce

11. Mirepoix

12. Cartilage

13. Body

14. Clarity

15. Flavour

16. Broth

17. Vegetables cooked in an acidic liquid used for poached fish or vegetables.

18. Proteins which are extracted from bones during the cooking process and form a jelly when cooked.

19. A sweet and sour condiment made from a mixture of fruits and/or vegetables.

20. The process of shocking food items in cold water after blanching.

21. The process by which normally unmixable combinations of food items such as oil and vinegar are forced to blend together, for example hollandaise and mayonnaise.

22. A mixture of egg yolk and heavy cream which adds richness and smoothness to sauce.

23. The process of removing caramelized particles from the bottom of a pan with a liquid.

24. A sauce made from puréed fruit or vegetables.

25. Literally means mounted with butter, swirling butter into the sauce to give it richness and sheen.

26. A combination of equal parts of butter and flour, used to thicken sauces at the end of the cooking process.

27. A cooked mixture of equal parts fat and flour which is used to thicken sauces.

28. To cook without browning, usually covered.

29. A stock made from fish bones and vegetables simmered in a liquid with flavourings.

30. A protein found in nearly all connective tissue; it dissolves when cooked with moisture.

B. Short Answer

I. General Questions

1. a. Start the stock in cold water.
   b. Simmer the stock gently.
   c. Skim the stock frequently.
   d. Add mirepoix, herbs and spices.
   e. Strain the stock carefully.
   f. Cool the stock quickly.
   g. Store the stock properly.
   h. Degrease the stock.

2. Hollandaise preparation: Reference p. 218.

3. a. Incorrect temperature of eggs and/or butter.
   b. Butter added too quickly.
   c. Egg yolks overcooked.
   d. Too much butter added.
   e. Sauce not whipped enough.

4. a. Use only cold water.
   b. Never cover a stock during cooking.
   c. Always cook a stock at a simmer, not a boil.
   d. Never stir a stock.

5. For meat stocks, since bones from younger animals have more cartilage, they will produce more gelatin. Also, younger animals tend to have a milder flavour, best appropriate for standard stocks.

6. a. Chlorophyll will turn grey as it cooks.
   b. Anthocyanins will make a stock turn red.
   c. Strong flavour vegetables (cabbages, cauliflower, turnips, peppers, etc.).

7. Because a broth is made with bones and/or meat, broths have more gelatin (body) and flavour.

8. Reference p. 195.

9. Reference p. 196.

10. Reference p. 202.

11. Reference p. 202.

12. Reference pp. 203–205.

13. Reference p. 207.

14. Reference p. 221.

15. Reference p. 223.

16. Reference p. 224.

17. Reference p. 227.

II. Stock-Making review

1. White stock: Reference pp. 195–196.

2. Brown stock: Reference pp. 196–198.

3. Fish stock: Reference p. 198–199.

III. Sauce Review—Basic Sauces

	Basic Sauce	Thickener	Liquid
1.	Béchamel	White roux	Milk
2.	Velouté	Blond roux	White/chicken/ veal/fish stock
3.	Espagnole	Brown roux	Beef stock
4.	Tomato	Tomato purée	White stock
5.	Hollandaise	Eggs	Butter

IV. Sauce Review—Derivative Sauces

Ingredients Added — Basic Sauce

1. Grated cheese and cream — Béchamel
2. Shallots, tarragon and chervil — Hollandaise
3. Shallots, white wine, butter and parsley — Velouté
4. Sliced mushrooms, green/black olives — Tomato
5. Allemande sauce with mushrooms, shallots — Velouté
6. Red wine, shallots, bay leaf, thyme and bone — Espagnole
7. Heavy cream, crayfish butter, paprika — Béchamel
8. Mushrooms and a liaison — Velouté
9. Onion, paprika, and suprême sauce — Velouté
10. Allemande sauce, tomato paste, and butter — Velouté
11. Poivrade sauce with bacon trimmings — Espagnole
12. Sliced mushrooms, cooked ham, and tongue — Espagnole

C. Multiple Choice

1. a
2. d
3. c
4. a
5. b
6. c
7. a
8. c
9. a
10. a
11. d
12. c

D. Matching

1. c   3. e
2. a   4. d

E. True or False

1. True (p. 205).
2. False (p. 205).
3. False (p. 207). Temperatures over 85°C (185°F) will cause the yolks to curdle.
4. True (p. 203).
5. True (p. 206).
6. True (p. 210).
7. False (p. 207). Tempering gradually raises the temperature of a cold liquid such as a liaison, by adding hot liquid.
8. True (p. 208).
9. True (p. 208).

10. False (p. 198). Fish stock should only simmer for 30 minutes.

CHAPTER 11

A. Terminology

1. Raft
2. Onion brûlé
3. Render
4. Bisque
5. Velouté
6. Paysanne
7. Clarification
8. Garnish
9. A mixture of ground meat, egg whites, mirepoix, herbs, and spices used to clarify the stock or broth.
10. A preparation of diced, peeled, and seeded tomato.
11. A seafood soup of French origin (faire chaudière).
12. A soup with similar preparation to a stock except that it is more full-bodied. Meat as well as bones forms the basis for the soup and it is garnished with meats and vegetables.
13. A broth that is clarified to remove the impurities.
14. A cream soup flavoured with onion.

B. Short Answer

I. General Questions

1. a. Never add cold milk or cream to hot soup.
   b. Add milk or cream just before service.
   c. Do not boil soup after cream has been added.

2. The common categories of soup are broths and bouillons, consommés, cream soups, purée soups, bisques, chowders, and cold soups (cooked and uncooked).

3. a. Beef broth and beef consommé both are similar; both are made with bones and /or meat, which gives them more body and a fuller flavour. Consommé uses a clarification to improve its body, clarity, flavour and colour.

   b. A cream of mushroom soup uses a roux to thicken the soup, but lentil soup uses a purée of the vegetable to thicken the soup. They may both use stock to form the base for flavour and both may use cream to finish the soup. A cream of mushroom soup is usually strained before service, whereas the lentil soup is usually not, since the purée of lentils is the thickening agent

   c. Both are cold soups; however, gazpacho uses uncooked ingredients and the cold consommé uses cooked ingredients and then cools them for service.

4. A broth is made with meat instead of just bones. Also, broths are often served as finished dishes by simply adding some garnish as opposed to stocks that are generally used to prepare other dishes.

5. A bisque is creamy soup most often flavoured with shellfish. It is classically thickened with rice as well as the pureed shellfish it is made with.

6. Cool the soup before cream or milk is added. Reheat as needed and finish with boiling cream or milk as desired.

7. Reference p. 246.

8. Reference p. 247.

II. Consommé Preparation Review I

Reference p. 241.

III. Consommé Preparation Review II

1. The consommé has been allowed to boil, or it has been stirred after the raft has been formed.

2. Stock was not degreased.

3. Poor quality stock.

4. Onion brulée omitted.

IV. Cream Soup Preparation Review

Reference p. 243.

C. Multiple Choice

1. b
2. d
3. a
4. b
5. c
6. d
7. c
8. a
9. b
10. c

D. True or False

1. True (p. 244).
2. True (p. 246).
3. True (p. 241).
4. False (p. 239). A consommé is a clarified broth.
5. False (p. 243). Cream soups are thickened with a roux or other starch.
6. False (p. 237). Additional items added to the soup are always referred to as garnishes;

therefore, the onion in French onion soup is also garnish.

7. False (p. 253). Cold soups should be served as cold as possible.

8. False (p. 242). If the consommé is insufficiently clear, a clarification can be performed.

9. False (p. 249). Cold dulls the sense of taste; therefore, more seasoning is required.

10. True (p. 248).

CHAPTER 12

A. Terminology

1. Primal cuts
2. Carve
3. Elastin
4. Marbling
5. Barding
6. Mignonette
7. Freezer burn
8. Marinating
9. Panada
10. Larding
11. Collagen
12. Milk fed
13. Emincé
14. Ragoût
15. Navarin
16. Paprikash
17. Tagine
18. Abodo
19. Brown Stew
20. Fricassée
21. Blanquette
22. A water-soluble protein resulting from the cooking of collagen.
23. A condition that causes muscles to contract and stiffen 6 to 24 hours after slaughtering.
24. A small round portion of meat cut from the rib.
25. A preservation method in which meat is put into a plastic container and all the air is removed.
26. To break down animals for consumption.
27. The basic cuts from each primal cut.
28. To trim or prepare an animal carcass for consumption.
29. To cut larger cuts down into portions.
30. Exterior fat or the layer of fat between the hide and the tissues.
31. Individual cuts from the subprimals.

32. A cut of meat which includes part of the rib.

33. The French for stock or base.

B. Fill in the Blank

1. Good quality
2. Low; long
3. Soft; very red; firm; non-red
4. Dredged in flour
5. Carryover; Retain more juices
6. Cold
7. Tough, stringy
8. 120°C to 150°C (250°F to 300°F)

C. Short Answer

I. General Questions

1. a. The animal's age determined by the degree of bone ossification.
   b. The colour of the meat.
   c. The conformation of the muscling.
   d. The fat colour.
   e. The sex of the animal.
2. a. Canada Prime
   b. AAA
   c. AA
   d. A
   e. B1
   f. B2
   g. B3
   h. B4
   i. D
   j. E
3. a. 60°C (140°F)
   b. 68°C (155°F)
   c. 77°C (170°F)
4. a. Product to be breaded
   b. Flour
   c. Egg wash
   d. Bread crumbs
   e. Pan to hold final product
5. Use one hand for dipping the food into the liquid ingredients and one hand to dip into the dry ingredients.
6. Reference p. 282.
7. Reference p. 279.
8. Reference p. 290.
9. Reference p. 275.

II Cooking Methods
Reference pp. 271–292.

D. Multiple Choice

1. d
2. a
3. b
4. c
5. b
6. c
7. b
8. d
9. c
10. d

E. Matching

1. d
2. e
3. f
4. b
5. c

F. True or False

1. False (p. 269). Fresh meats should be stored at –1°C to 2°C (30–35°F).
2. False (p. 267). Green meats are meats that are frozen before rigor mortis has had an opportunity to dissipate.
3. True. (pp. 285–286).
4. True. (pp. 265). The Canada meat inspection stamp only insures that the meat is processed in a sanitary way.
5. False (p. 267). Yield grades apply only to pork and beef.
6. True (p. 268).
7. True (p. 268).
8. True (p. 268).
9. True (p. 269).

CHAPTER 13

A. Terminology

1. Porterhouse
2. Plate; skirt
3. Square chuck
4. Ponderosa hip
5. Hip
6. Chateaubriand
7. Shank
8. Cow
9. Bull
10. Steers
11. Kobe beef

12. Cows before their first calving.

13. Male cattle castrated after maturity.

14. The cut of meat located beneath the loin eye muscle on the other side of the backbone. It is the most tender cut of all.

15. Includes the organ meats such as heart, kidney, liver, tongue, tripe, and oxtail.

16. Located directly below the loin and can be ground or used for London broil.

17. The front portion of the beef loin, it contains a single rib, the thirteenth, and yields T-bone, porterhouse, and club steaks.

18. This primal cut consists of ribs 6 through 12 and produces full-flavoured roasts and steaks.

19. Located beneath the primal chuck at the front of the carcass and is used for corned beef or pastrami.

B. Fill in the Blank

I. Primal Cuts of Beef

1. Square chuck
2. Rib
3. Short loin
4. Sirloin
5. Long loin
6. Hip
7. Point brisket and shank
8. Plate
9. Flank

II. Cuts from the Round

	Cut	Method
1.	Inside (top) round	Roast
2.	Eye round	Braise
3.	Outside (bottom) round	Braise
4.	Knuckle or tip	Roast
5.	Leg or round bone	Simmer—stocks, soups, consommé

III. Cuts of Beef and Applied Cooking Methods

	Method	Subprimal/ Fabricated	Primal
1.	Bake	Ground beef	Chuck
2.	Bake	Tenderloin	Short loin
3.	Roast	Tenderloin	Short loin
4.	Broil	T-bone steak	Short loin
5.	Sauté/grill/ broil	Strip loin	Short loin
6.	Grill/broil	Flank steak	Flank
7.	Braise	Top (inside round)	Hip
8.	Roast	Oven-ready rib roast	Rib
		Rib eye roll	
9.	Simmer	Brisket	Point brisket and shank

10. Broil/grill   Skirt steak   Plate

C. Short Answer

1. a. rib
   b. short loin
   c. sirloin
2. a. heart
   b. kidney
   c. tongue
   d. tripe
   e. oxtail
3. a. shoulder clod
   b. chuck roll
   c. chuck tender
   d. stew meat
   e. ground chuck

D. Multiple Choice

1. b
2. c
3. d
4. a
5. c
6. c
7. b
8. d
9. c
10. a
11. d
12. a
13. c
14. b
15. d
16. d
17. c

E. Matching

1. Match the primal cuts with the appropriate description.

1. c
2. d
3. a
4. b

2. Match the cuts to the primal or secondary cuts.

a. 3
b. 7
c. 4
d. 7
e. 2

f. 8

g. 1

h. 5

i. 6

j. 6

k. 4

F. True or False

1. False (p. 301). The butt tenderloin is a part of the sirloin.

2. False (p. 298). The chuck has a high proportion of connective tissue which makes it more flavourful than the tenderloin.

3. False (p. 301).

4. False (p. 300). Prime rib refers to the fact that the rib is made up of the majority of the primal cut from which it comes.

5. True (p. 300).

6. True (p. 301).

7. True (p. 300–301).

8. False (p. 300). Pastrami is made by curing and peppering the brisket.

CHAPTER 14

A. Terminology

1. Formula fed

2. Aitch bone

3. Back

4. Loin

5. Breast

6. Veal

7. Shoulder

8. The thymus gland of veal or lamb.

9. The breast and this portion of veal are considered one primal cut.

10. Two racks, each with seven rib bones and a portion of the backbone.

11. Young bulls used for the production of veal.

B. Fill in the Blank

I. Common Cuts of Veal

1.	Front/shoulder	6.	Leg
2.	Rib	7.	Breast
3.	Loin	8.	Flank
4.	Whole loin	9.	Shank
5.	Leg		

II. Cuts of Veal and Applied Cooking Methods

	Method	Subprimal/ Fabricated	Primal
1.	Braise	Hindshank	Leg
2.	Pan-fry	Bottom round	Leg
3.	Stew	Cubed veal	Shoulder
4.	Sauté	Top round	Leg
5.	Roast/sauté	Leg	Leg
6.	Sauté	Veal loin	Loin
7.	Sauté	Tenderloin	Loin
8.	Braise	Bottom round	Leg
9.	Braise	Breast	Foreshank & breast
10.	Stew	Leg	Leg
11.	Broil/grill	Ground	Shoulder
12.	Kidney pie	Kidneys	Offals

C. Short Answer

1. a. Remove the shank.

    b. Remove the butt tenderloin.

    c. Remove the pelvic bone.

    d. Remove the top round.

    e. Remove the shank meat.

    f. Remove the round bone and knuckle.

    g. Remove the sirloin.

    h. Remove the eye round.

2. a. Top round

    b. Eye round

    c. Knuckle

    d. Sirloin

    e. Bottom round

    f. Butt tenderloin

3.	Primal	Subprimal/ Fabricated	Menu Example
a.	Rib	Hotel rack	Roast veal with porcini mushrooms
b.	Rib	Rib chops	Braised veal chop with risotto
c.	Rib	Rib eye	Broiled rib eye with chipotle sauce

Any three of the following would be appropriate answers:

a.	Loin	Veal loin	Roasted veal loin with wild mushrooms
b.	Loin	Loin chops	Sautéed veal chops with mushroom sauce
c.	Loin	Boneless strip loin	Roasted veal loin, sauce poulette
d.	Loin	Veal tenderloin	Sautéed tenderloin with garlic and herbs

4. Reference p. 308.

5. The anterior portion of the carcass severed between the 11th and 12th rib. It contains the primal shoulder, foreshank, breast and rib.

6. The posterior portion of the carcass that includes the primal loin and leg.

7. The thymus gland of veal and lamb. This gland shrinks as the animal ages; therefore, it is only available from young animals.

8. Reference p. 322.

9. Reference p. 323.

10. Reference p. 324.

D. Multiple Choice

1. c
2. b
3. c
4. b
5. d
6. a

E. Matching

1. f
2. a
3. b   *d is appropriate for the breast only
4. e
5. c

F. True or False

1. True (p. 319).
2. True (p. 314).
3. False (p. 322). Sweetbreads are pressed to improve their texture.
4. False (p. 320). Émincé should be cut across the grain.
5. True (p. 319).
6. False (p. 317). The thymus glands shrink in older animals.
7. True (p. 317).
8. True (p. 317).
9. True (p. 317).
10. True (p. 323, 326).

CHAPTER 15

A. Terminology

1. A young lamb that has not been fed grass.
2. The common name for scapula.
3. Also known as the hotel rack, this primal cut is located between the primal shoulder and loin. It contains 8 ribs and portions of the backbone and is valued for its tender rib eye muscle.

4. Mutton is the meat from sheep slaughtered over the age of one year.
5. Lamb
6. Frenched
7. Saddle
8. Foresaddle
9. Hindsaddle

B. Fill in the Blank

I. Primal Cuts of Lamb

1.	Front	5.	Leg
2.	Ribs (rack)	6.	Shank
3.	Loin	7.	Breast
4.	Whole loin	8.	Flank

II. Subprimal or Fabricated Cuts

		Suprimal/ Fabricated	Method
1.	a.	Chops	Broil/grill
	b.	Diced	Stew
	c.	Ground	Broil/grill/sauté
2.		Breast	Braise
3.	a.	Chops	Grill
	b.	Lamb rack	Roasted
4.	a.	Chops/boneless roast	Grill/roast
	b.	Medallions/noisettes	Sauté
5.	a.	Lamb leg (bone-in)	Braised
	b.	Boned leg	Roast

III. Cuts of Lamb and Applied Cooking Methods

	Method	Subprimal/ Fabricated	Primal
1.	Broil/grill	Diced lamb	Leg/shoulder
2.	Stew	Diced lamb	Leg
3.	Sauté	Boneless loin	Loin
4.	Stew	Diced lamb	Shoulder
5.	Roast	Frenched lamb rack	Hotel rack

C. Short Answer

1. Reference p. 337.
2. Reference p. 338.
3. Reference p. 339.

D. Multiple Choice

1. b
2. c
3. d
4. b

E. True or False

1. False (p. 334). Lamb primals are not classified into a forequarter and hindquarter as with beef, or a foresaddle and hindsaddle as with veal.

2. False (p. 334). Spring lamb is the term used to describe young lamb that has not been fed on grass or grains.

3. True (p. 334).

4. True (p. 336).

5. True (p. 336).

6. False (p. 335). The chine bone runs through the primal lamb whole loin.

7. True (p. 336).

8. False (p. 334).

CHAPTER 16

A. Terminology

1. Located below the loin, this primal cut produces spare ribs and the belly is cured and smoked and used for bacon.

2. The meat of pigs which are butchered before they are one year old.

3. The hind leg of the hog which may be fresh, cured, or smoked.

4. The ribs taken from the loin.

5. Spareribs

6. Picnic shoulder

7. Shoulder blade

8. Back bacon

9. Back ribs

10. Suckling pig

B. Fill in the Blank

I. Primal Cuts of Pork

1. Loin
2. Leg
3. Shoulder
4. Belly

II. Subprimal or Fabricated Cuts

	Cut	Method	Cured/ Smoked	Fresh
1.	Shoulder blade	Broil/grill/sauté	X	X
	Picnic shoulder	Bake	X	X
2.	Spare ribs	Simmer—grill	X	X
	Bacon	Sauté/Grill	X	
3.	Pork back ribs	Steam—grill		X
	Pork loin chops	Broil/grill		X
	Pork tenderloin	Sauté/roast/braise / broil/grill		X
	Pork loin	Roast/braise		X
4.	Fresh leg	Roast	X	X

III. Cuts of Pork and Applied Cooking Methods
(Reference pp. 350–356)

	Method	Subprimal/ Fabricated	Primal
1.	Braising	Loin Chops	Loin
2.	Hot smoking	Boneless-centre cut	Loin
3.	Sauté	Bacon	Belly
4.	Stewing	Hock	Shoulder/picnic
5.	Baking	Backribs	Loin
6.	Roasting	Pork loin strips	Loin
7.	Roasting	Boneless loin	Loin
8.	Stir-frying	Émincé	Leg/loin/ shoulder

C. Short Answer

1. Reference p. 353.

2.
   a. Picnic shoulder—picnic ham
   b. Shoulder hock
   c. Shoulder butt—cottage ham
   d. Side ribs—spare ribs
   e. Pork belly—bacon
   f. Boneless pork loin—Canadian bacon
   g. Leg—Ham

D. Multiple Choice

1. c
2. a
3. c
4. d

E. Matching

1. d
2. f
3. a
4. b
5. c

F. True or False

1. False (p. 352). The shoulder blade is located in the forequarter.

2. True (p. 354).

3. True (p. 353).

4. False (p. 352). The foreshank is called the pork hock.

5. False (p. 354). Centre-cut pork chops are the choicest chops from the primal loin.

6. False (p. 354). Canadian bacon is made from the boneless pork loin.

7. True (p. 354).

8. True (p. 354).

9. False (p. 352).

10. False (p. 352).

11. True (p. 352).

12. False (p. 352). The blade is very meaty and tender, with a good percentage of lean to fat.

13. True (p. 353). Wild game is still a concern.

14. True (p. 354).

CHAPTER 17

A. Terminology

1. A collective name given to livers, gizzards, hearts, and necks.

2. Trussing is tying the bird into a more compact shape using butcher's twine.

3. A surgically castrated male chicken.

4. A chicken suprême or frenched breast is half of a boneless chicken breast with the first wing bone attached.

5. The official term Agriculture Canada uses instead of categories.

6. A subdivision of categories.

7. French for chicken.

8. A young duck.

9. A domesticated descendant of a game bird with a flavour similar to pheasant.

10. A point

11. Game hen

12. Foie gras

B. Fill in the Blank

1. Protein; Myoglobin

2. 77°C (170°F)

3. Roaster duckling; Dark; Fat

4. White wine or lemon, oil, salt, pepper, herbs and spices; Barbecue

C. Short Answer

1. Reference p. 387

2. Similarity: Overused muscles are tougher than underused ones.

   Difference: Red meat has marbling—poultry does not.

3. Reference p. 376.

4. Reference p. 370.

5. Chicken, duck, goose, pheasant, quail, ostrich, guinea, pigeon and turkey.

6. Reference pp. 392, 394, 396, 399.

7. a. Be sure all work surfaces and equipment are clean.

   b. Avoid getting poultry juices in contact with other food.

   c. Anything coming in contact with raw poultry should be sanitized before it comes in contact with any other food.

   d. Cooked foods should never be placed in containers that were used to hold the raw product.

   e. Kitchen towels used to handle poultry should be sanitized before being reused to prevent cross-contamination.

8. Reference p. 378.

9. Ratites are a category of flightless, bird-like animals with small wings and flat breastbones. They include ostrich, emu and rhea.

10. Ratite meat is classified as red meat, is dark cherry-red in colour with a sweet taste. It is low in fat and calories and considered one of the healthiest red meats.

11. Duck, reference p. 372.

    Pigeon, reference p. 373.

    Turkeys, reference p. 373.

12. Reference p. 380.

13. Reference p. 383.

14. Reference p. 384.

15. Reference p. 387.

16. Safety, practicality and quality

17. Reference p. 392.

18. Reference p. 392.

19. Reference p. 394.

20. Reference p. 397.

21. Reference p. 399.

D. Multiple Choice

1. c

2. b

3. a

4. a

5. c

6. a

7. b

8. c

9. d
10. c
11. c
12. b
13. a

E. Matching
1. f
2. e
3. a
4. h
5. c
6. b
7. d

F. True or False
1. False (p. 370). Poultry fat has a lower melting point than other animal fats.
2. True (p. 386).
3. True (p. 371).
4. False (p. 371). Poultry that is left too long in an acidic marinade may take on undesirable flavours.
5. False (p. 371). The cooking time for dark meat is longer.
6. False (p. 376). Poultry should be frozen at 0°F/18°C or below.
7. False (p. 371). The skin colour of poultry is related to what it is fed.
8. True (p. 375).
9. False (p. 371). Older male birds have less flavour than older female birds.
10. False (p. 374). Overcooking foie gras will cause it to melt away.
11. False (p. 373). A young pigeon is known as a squab.
12. False (p. 373). The gizzard is the bird's stomach.

CHAPTER 18
A. Terminology
1. Game
2. Hanging
3. Partridge
4. Antelope
5. Chevreuil
6. Venison
7. Bison

B. Short Answer
1. a. sausages
   b. forcemeats
   c. pâtés
2. Reference p. 420.
3. A close relative of domesticated hog, its meat is leaner and has a stronger flavour. Baby wild boar (under 6 months) is a delicacy; however, mature boar (1 to 2 years) have the best flavour.
4. Reference p. 420.
5. It is typically dark red meat with a mild aroma. Also, it is leaner than other meats, having almost no intramuscular fat or marbling.
6. It has a mild flavour and is excellent for roasting, stewing or braising. The hen is smaller than the cock.
7. Rabbit meat is mild, lean and relatively tender. Its taste and texture are similar to chicken.
8. Less delicate than pheasant, and the meat tends to be tougher.
9. Rather small and very lean; benefits from barding.
10. Turkeys, pheasants, quails, doves, woodcocks, larks.
11. Ducks, geese
12. Reference p. 417.

C. Multiple Choice
1. b
2. c
3. b
4. a
5. d
6. c
7. c
8. b
9. b
10. a
11. d
12. a
13. c
14. a
15. d
16. c

D. True or False
1. False (p. 420).
2. False (p. 420).
3. True (p. 418).
4. False (p. 420). Wild game can only be served by those who hunt and share their kill.
5. True (p. 418).

6. False (p. 416). Game is lower in fat and higher in protein and minerals than other meats.

7. False (p. 417). There is no marbling in venison flesh.

8. False (p. 416). Large game animals are available only precut into subprimals or portions.

9. True (p. 420).

10. True (p. 421).

CHAPTER 19

A. Terminology

1. En papillote
2. Mollusks
3. Aqua farming
4. Pan-dressed
5. Flat fish
6. Crustaceans
7. Steak
8. Drawn
9. Tomalley
10. Coral
11. Pen
12. Sometimes referred to as rock sea bass.
13. A type of salmon found in the far northern rivers.
14. The second most commercially important fish.
15. The side of a fish is removed intact boneless or semi-boneless, with or without the skin.
16. A slice cut, usually on an angle, from fillets of large flat or round fish.
17. The viscera, gills, fins, and scales are removed from the fish.
18. These fish have asymmetrical, compressed bodies, swim in a horizontal position, and are found in deep ocean waters around the world. Both eyes are on one side of the head, their scales are small, and their dorsal and anal fins run the length of their bodies.
19. Used for swordfish and sharks, which are cut into large boneless pieces, from which steaks are then cut.

B. Fill in the Blanks

1. fish, mollusks, crustaceans
2. truly round, oval, compressed
3. intramuscular, fat
4. sable fish
5. gray cod
6. Atlantic oyster, Pacific oyster
7. crayfish, crawfish
8. hard shell, soft shell
9. temperature
10. brushed, butter, oil
11. marine invertebrate
12. anglerfish or goosefish or rape or lotte
13. dorado
14. St. Peter's
15. surimi

C. Short Answer

1. a. They cook evenly.
   b. They cook quickly.
2. a. Translucent flesh becomes opaque.
   b. Flesh becomes firm.
   c. Flesh separates from the bones easily.
   d. Flesh begins to flake.
3. Reference p. 448.
4. a. shallow poach
   b. sauté
   c. broil
   d. bake
5. Oily:
   a. trout
   b. swordfish
   Lean:
   c. bass
   d. snapper
6. a. scallops
   b. lobster
   c. shrimp
   d. crab
7. a. baked stuffed shrimp
   b. oysters Rockefeller
   c. baked stuffed lobster
8. a. They are naturally tender.
   b. They cook relatively quickly.
9. a. eyes
   b. gills
   c. fins and scales
   d. smell
   e. texture
   f. appearance, and movement for shellfish
10. a. In the submersion method, the fish is completely covered with the poaching liquid, usually a court bouillon, fish stock or fish fumet. The poaching liquid is most often not used to make the accompanying sauce.

b. Shallow poaching combines poaching and steaming. The poaching liquid covers the items half way and the covered item is cooked on the stove top or in the oven. The poaching liquid is reduced and used as the base to produce the accompanying sauce.

11.
a. bluefin
b. yellowfin
c. bonito
d. bigeye
e. black fin

12. Reference p. 450.
13. Reference pp. 458–459.
14. Reference p. 460.
15. Reference p. 462.
16. Reference p. 464.
17. Reference p. 466.
18. Reference p. 468.
19. Reference pp. 468–469.
20. Reference p. 471.
21. Reference p. 472.
22. Reference p. 478.
23. Reference p. 482.

D. Multiple Choice

1.	b	7.	a
2.	d	8.	d
3.	c	9.	c
4.	a	10.	d
5.	d	11.	c
6.	b	12.	c

E. Matching

1. drawn		5.	steaks or darnes
2. pan-dressed		6.	butterflied fillets
3. fillets		7.	wheel or centre-cut
4. whole or round			

F. True or False

1. True (p. 445).
2. False (p. 445). The Federal Fisheries Inspection in collaboration with the Canadian Food Inspection Agency.
3. True (p. 444).
4. True (p. 466).
5. False (p. 444). Atlantic lobsters have meat both in their tails and claws and are considered superior in flavour to all other lobsters. Spiny lobsters primarily have meat in the tails.
6. False (p. 442). Atlantic hard-shell clams are also known as quahogs.
7. True (p. 463).
8. False (p. 467). En papillote is actually an example of steaming.
9. False (p. 445). In general, shellfish has less cholesterol than red meat.
10. False (p. 469). A cuisson is the liquid used when shallow poaching.
11. True (p. 437).

CHAPTER 20

A. Terminology

1. Smoking
2. Brine
3. Sausage
4. Basic forcemeat
5. Rillettes
6. Terrine
7. Confit
8. Quenelles
9. Brawns
10. Forcemeat
11. Dominant meat
12. Binders
13. Side-bacon
14. Canadian back-bacon
15. Pancetta
16. Prosciutto
17. A mixture of several spices and herbs that can be premixed and used as needed.
18. A type of forcemeat made with five parts of meat, four parts of fat and three parts of ice. It is finely ground and emulsified.
19. A traditional country-style forcemeat that is heavily seasoned with onions, garlic, pepper, juniper berries, and bay leaves. It is the simplest of the forcemeats to prepare.
20. A mixture of salt and sodium nitrite.
21. Made from forcemeats of poultry, game, or suckling pig and wrapped in the skin of the bird or animal and poached in an appropriate stock.
22. Pâtés baked in pastry.
23. A savoury jelly produced by increasing the gelatin content of a strong stock and then clarifying the stock like a consommé.
24. Traditionally a fine savoury meat filling wrapped in pastry, baked, and served hot or cold.

25. A light, airy, and delicately flavoured forcemeat. It is usually made with fish or shellfish, but also pork, veal, feathered game, or poultry. Often egg whites and cream are added to lighten the texture.

26. Similar to a galantine, it is made by removing the bones of a poultry leg, filling the cavity with an appropriate forcemeat, and poaching or braising the leg with vegetables, serving it hot.

27. Something other than fat that is added to a forcemeat to enhance smoothness, and aid in emulsification.

B. Short Answer

1. a. basic forcemeat
    b. country-style forcemeat
    c. mousseline forcemeat

2. Add small quantities of crushed ice, bit by bit, to the machine while it is grinding.

3.

galantine	ballotine
a. uses whole chickens, ducks, etc.	uses poultry legs
b. all bones are removed	all bones are removed
c. cavity of bird is filled with forcemeat	cavity of leg is filled with forcemeat
d. it is wrapped in skin, plastic, cheesecloth	cooked without wrapping
e. it is poached	it is roasted, poached or braised
f. always served cold	usually served hot

4. a. keep a precise ratio of fat to other ingredients
    b. maintain temperatures below 4°C (40°F) during preparation
    c. mix ingredients properly

5. a. to glaze, preventing drying out and oxidation of food
    b. to cut into decorative garnish
    c. to add flavour and shine
    d. to bind mousses and salads
    e. to fill cooked pâtés en croûte

6. a. Chill all ingredients and equipment.
    b. Cut meat into appropriate size for processing.
    c. Grind the meat in a cold food processor until smooth (do not over-process).
    d. Add eggs and pulse until blended.

e. Add seasonings and cream in a stream while machine is running, stop and scrape down the sides of the bowl as needed.

f. Pass the forcemeat through a drum sieve to remove any sinew.

7. A pâté is a fine savoury meat filling wrapped in pastry, baked and served hot or cold. A terrine may use the same type of meat filling, although it is often less refined, and it is baked in a water bath in an earthenware mould. Terrines are generally served cold.

8. Foie gras terrine is made with fattened geese or duck liver (foie gras) and not a forcemeat like other terrines. Foie gras is very delicate and sensitive to heat—it must be cooked carefully at low temperature to prevent melting.

9. Reference p. 503.

10. Reference p. 508.

11. Reference p. 510.

12. Reference p. 515.

13. Reference p. 515.

14. Reference p. 519.

15. Reference p. 519.

C. Multiple Choice

1. a	5. d	9. a	13. b
2. c	6. b	10. c	14. b
3. c	7. d	11. b	15. a
4. a	8. a	12. d	16. c

D. Matching

1. f	4. d	7. g
2. i	5. b	8. c
3. e	6. a	9. j

E. True or False

1. False (p. 505). Mousseline forcemeats can only be made out of protein items such as meats, poultry, fish, or shellfish.

2. False (p. 511). The best type of mould to use is a collapsible, hinged, thin metal pan.

3. True (p. 517).

4. True (p. 520).

5. True (p. 513).

6. True (p. 507).

7. False (p. 520). A fresh ham is made from the pig's hind leg.

8. True (p. 505).

9. True (p. 520).

10. False (pp. 518–519). Brining is wet while curing is dry.

CHAPTER 21

A. Terminology

1. Defines the motif and sets the tone of the event.
2. The complete list of food selections to be offered.
3. A metal dish with a heat source located beneath, used to keep foods hot.
4. A centrepiece consisting of a large piece of the principal food offered.
5. Used on a buffet as a base for platters, trays or displays.
6. Kosher
7. Halal
8. Flow
9. Negative space
10. Butler service
11. Smorgasbord

B. Short Answer

1. a. Offer dishes featuring different principal ingredients.
   b. Offer foods cooked by different cooking methods.
   c. Offer foods with different colours.
   d. Offer foods with different textures.
2. Buffet presentation: reference pp. 549–552.
3. a. Use a double-sided buffet.
   b. Use a single-sided buffet, divide into two, three or more zones, each of which offers identical foods.
   c. Divide the menu among various stations, scattered throughout the room, each station devoted to a different type of food.
4. a. Choose foods that hold well.
   b. Cook small amounts of delicate foods.
   c. Ladle a small amount of the sauce on the bottom of the pan before adding slice meats.
   d. Keep chafing dish closed whenever possible.
5. Reference p. 532.
6. Reference p. 533.
7. Reference p. 535.
8. Reference p. 536.
9. Reference p. 538.
10. a. Do not add new foods to old food
    b. Do not use a chafing dish to heat food

c. Be careful of steam when changing pans
d. Provide clean utensils for each dish & change them often
e. provide an ample supply of clean plates

11. a. Serve relatively small quantities (exchange frequently).
    b. Keep food on ice.

C. Multiple Choice

1. c
2. b
3. d
4. c
5. c

D. Matching

1. c
2. d
3. a
4. b

E. True or False

1. True (p. 554).
2. False (p. 555).
3. False (p. 544).
4. True (p. 544).
5. True (p. 553).
6. False (p. 554).
7. False (p. 552).
8. True (p. 554).
9. False (p. 528).
10. True (pp. 556–557).
11. True (p. 542).
12. True (pp. 554–555).

CHAPTER 22

A. Terminology

1. Refreshing or shocking
2. Cellulose
3. Parboiling
4. Chayote
5. Nopales
6. Jicama
7. Vegetable
8. Fiddlehead
9. Haricot vert
10. Chlorophyll
11. Carotenoid
12. Anthoxantins

13. Anthocyanins
14. Peeled, seeded, and diced tomatoes.
15. Briefly or partially cooking a food in boiling water or hot fat.
16. Exposing food to gamma rays in order to sterilize, prevent sprouting, and slow ripening.
17. The cabbage family.
18. The family of plant to which peppers belong.

B. Short Answer

1.

	Fresh	Dried
a.	Anaheim	red mild or California
b.	jalapeño (smoked)	chipotle
c.	pimiento	paprika
d.	poblano	ancho

2.

	Colour	Texture
a.	drab olive green	Firm
b.	no change	Firm
c.	white	Firm
d.	red (brighter)	Firm

3.

	Colour	Texture
a.	drab olive green	Firm
b.	no change	Firm
c.	white	Firm
d.	red (brighter)	Firm

4. Roast the pepper over an open flame until completely charred. Place it in a bowl and cover it. After a few minutes, remove all the burnt skin and rinse well.

5. Cut the jalapeno in half lengthwise; remove the rib and seeds with your thumb while wearing a glove. Most of the heat of the pepper is in the seeds and core. Removing it makes the pepper milder and more pleasant.

6. Reference p. 554.
7. Reference p. 555.
8. Reference p. 558.
9. Reference p. 566.
10. Reference p. 567.
11 Reference p. 581.
12. Reference p. 582.
13. Reference p. 584.
14. Reference p. 585.
15. Reference pp. 591–592.
16. Reference p. 596.
17. Reference p. 595.

C. Multiple Choice

1. b	6. c	11. c	16. c
2. c	7. d	12. a	17. b
3. b	8. b	13. c	18. d
4. c	9. b	14. d	19. a
5. d	10. a	15. d	

D. Matching

1. e	5. a
2. b	6. c
3. f	7. g
4. h	8. d

E. True or False

1. False (p. 590). Puréed vegetables are usually prepared by baking, boiling, steaming, or microwaving.
2. False (p. 560). Winter squash is not commonly braised or stewed.
3. True (p. 574).
4. True (pp. 554–557).
5. True (p. 566).
6. True (p. 572).
7. False (p. 573). They are usually stored at 4°C–16°C (40–60°F).
8. True (p. 576).
9. False (p. 576). Red and white vegetables such as red cabbage, beets, and cauliflower contain flavonoids.
10. False (p. 577). Testing the texture, looking for an al dente consistency, is generally the best determination of doneness.

CHAPTER 23

A. Terminology

1. Grains
2. Sfoglia
3. Extrusion
4. Pearling
5. New potatoes
6. Mealy potatoes
7. Risotto
8. Cracking
9. Pilaf
10. Al dente
11. Russet
12. Solanine
13. Macaire
14. Marquis
15. Dauphine
16. Château

17. Croquette
18. Parisienne
19. A milling process in which grains are reduced to a powder.
20. A finely ground flour made from hominy used for making breads, tortillas, tamales, etc.
21. Those varieties that have a low starch content and thin skin.
22. Any dried pasta made with wheat flour and water.
23. A hard wheat milled into semolina and used for making pasta.
24. A milling process in which the hull is removed from the grains.
25. A small mound of dough cooked by steaming or simmering in a flavourful liquid.
26. Sliced potatoes mixed with cream and seasonings, topped with gruyère cheese and baked.

B. Short Answer

1.

Potato	Starch	Moisture	Sugar
Russet	high	low	low
White Rose	high	low	low
Red	low	high	high
Purple	high	low	low
Bintje	low	high	high
Yukon Gold	low	high	high

2. a. mealy
   b. waxy

3. Cut the potatoes in desired shape, cook in 150ºC (300ºF) oil until tender and finish cooking in 175ºC (350ºF) oil until crisp and golden brown.

4. Boil peeled starchy potatoes until tender, drain and keep warm to allow excess moisture to evaporate. Puree the potatoes; add some butter and season to taste.

5. Reference p. 606.
6. Reference p. 607.
7. Reference p. 609.
8. Reference p. 608.
9.

Rice	Water:Rice	Time
Arborio	1:2.5-3	15–20 min.
Basmati	1:1.75	15 min.
Brown (long grain)	1:2.5	45–50 min.
Converted	1:2	20–25 min.
White (long, regular)	1:2	15 min.
Wild	1:3	35–60 min. (depending on grade)

10. Reference p. 618.
11. Reference p. 619.
12. Reference p. 635.
13. Reference p. 635.
14. Reference p. 637.
15. Cornmeal is made by drying and grinding a special type of corn known as dent. It may be yellow, white or blue.
16. a. long grain
    b. medium grain
    c. short grain
17. To allow the pasta ample space to move freely and so that the starches that are released don't cause the pasta to become gummy and sticky.
18. a. Wrapping the potato in foil causes it to steam instead of bake and the skin will be soggy.
    b. Microwaving also causes steaming to occur and causes the skin to be soggy.
19. a. Italian risotto
    b. Spanish paella
    c. Japanese sushi
20. This gives the dough a rich, yellow colour, and the dough is more resilient to the machinery during high-scale production. It also produces pasta that has a lightly pitted surface, causing the pasta to absorb sauces well.
21. a. Ribbon
    b. Tubes
    c. Shapes
22. a. Simmering
    b. Pilaf
    c. Risotto
23. a. The water softens the noodle strands.
    b. The bundles begin to separate.
    c. The noodles cook more evenly.

C. Multiple Choice

1. a
2. c
3. d
4. d
5. c
6. b
7. b
8. b
9. b
10. b
11. c
12. c
13. d
14. b
15. a
16. a
17. c

D. Matching

1. f
2. a
3. b
4. e
5. c

1. True (p. 618).
2. True (p. 612).
3. True (p. 611).
4. False (p. 620). Semolina flour, although it makes the dough more yellow, makes a dough tougher and more difficult to work with.
5. True (p. 622).
6. False (p. 603). A yam is botanically different from both sweet and common potatoes. Although it is less sweet than a sweet potato, they can be used interchangeably.
7. False (p. 605). Potatoes should be stored at 7–10°C (45–50°F).
8. False (p. 604). Waxy potatoes are best for these applications.
9. True (p. 623).
10. True (p. 623).
11. False (p. 615). Quinoa contains all of the essential amino acids and important vitamins and minerals.
12. True (p. 620).

CHAPTER 24

A. Terminology

1. Soy-milk
2. Tofu
3. Tempeh
4. Textured soy protein
5. Seitan
6. Edamame
7. Soft, firm, extra firm
8. Soybeans, soy-milk, coagulated
9. A term used until the 19th century to describe people who chose to eat only plant foods.
10. A person who eats no meat, fish, poultry or any products derived from animals, such as milk, cheese, eggs, honey and gelatin.
11. A person on a raw food diet
12. A person who adheres to a simple meal plan of brown rice miso soup and seaweed.
13. A tofu with custard-like texture and a silky-smooth appearance.
14. A thick paste made by salting and fermenting soybeans and rice or barley.
15. Foods made from soy, wheat, grains and other plant material, designed to mimic the appearance and texture of popular animal based products.

16. Made from coagulated soy-milk. The curd is pressed and weighed to remove the liquid.

B. Short Answer

1. B-12
2. Iron
3. a. Religious beliefs
   b. Philosophical beliefs
   c. Environmental concerns
   d. Health concerns
4. *Diet for a Small Planet* explored vegetarianism from an environmental perspective, showing concern that the problem of world hunger is caused in great part by the wasteful use of agricultural resources on supporting animals raised for meat. She justifies her claim by noting that in 1971, 80% of the grain grown in the U.S. was fed to livestock.
5. a. Nuts
   b. Canola oil
   c. Flax and other seeds
   d. Soy products
6. a. Animal rights (meaning the ethical treatment of animals)
   b. Strong proponent of vegetarianism
7. A chef cannot just assume that a guest who claim to be a vegetarian only eats vegetables or grains since there are so many different variations on the diet. S/he really needs to ask specific questions directly of the guest to delineate the parameters for a meal s/he will prepare to meet the vegetarian guest's diet.
8. a. Greens
   b. Cruciferous vegetables
   c. Soy products
   d. Take supplements
9. White miso is wild and mildly sweet, containing a high percentage of rice. Red or dark miso contains a larger percentage of soybeans, is aged longer and has a stronger, saltier flavour.
10. Reference p. 650.
11. Reference p. 652.
12. a. whole grains
    b. fruits and vegetables
    c. legumes and beans
13. a. egg whites, soy-milk and dairy
    b. nuts and seeds
    c. plant oils
14. eggs and sweets
15. Reference pp. 653–654.

1.	a, c	9.	d
2.	b	10.	c
3.	c	11.	c
4.	a	12.	b
5.	d	13.	b
6.	a	14.	a, c
7.	a,b,d	15.	a
8.	b		

D. True or False

1. True
2. False (p. 648). About 4% of Canadians eat a vegetarian diet.
3. True (p. 644).
4. False (p. 649).
5. False (p. 645). Eggs are only consumed by ovo- or lacto-ovo vegetarians.
6. False (p. 645). Fruitarians do not consume grains.
7. True (p. 650).
8. False (p. 650). According to the United Soybean Board, soy protein is the only plant protein that is equivalent to animal protein and it is a rich source of phytochemicals as well.
9. False (p. 650). Once opened, the soy-milk must remain refrigerated but only has a shelf life of 5–7 days.
10. True (pp. 644–645).
11. False (p. 652). Cooking does temper tempeh's flavour, but it should be cooked due to the type of live culture it contains.
12. False (pp. 650–651).
13. True (p. 645).
14. False (p. 650).
15. False (p. 651).
16. True (p. 651).
17. True (p. 650).

CHAPTER 25

A. Terminology

1. A more elegant version of the green salad that uses the green as the base and artistically arranges the other ingredients on top. It usually has four components.
2. An informal green salad that tosses all ingredients; greens, dressing, and garnish, in a bowl before plating.
3. A temporary emulsion of oil and vinegar with the addition of seasonings.
4. Another name for Romaine lettuce.

5. Also known as Belgian endive.
6. Also known as broad leaf endive.
7. Also known as rocket.
8. Also known as lamb's lettuce.
9. Emulsion
10. Bound salad
11. Mesclun
12. Mayonnaise
13. Micro-greens

B. Fill in the Blank

1. whole eggs, modified starches or vegetable gums
2. lecithin, egg yolk
3. thinner
4. tossed and composed
5. celery, apples, walnuts and mayonnaise
6. à la grecque
7. base, body, garnish, dressing

C. Short Answer

1. a. pansies
   b. nasturtiums
   c. calendulas
2. Fold the leaf in half and hold it with one hand while exposing the rib. Pull off the stem and midrib.
3. Fill the sink with water and place the greens in the water. Gently stir the water and greens and remove the greens. Repeat the procedure until no grit can be seen on the bottom of the sink. Do not soak the greens and dry them properly when removed. Wet greens do not keep well.
4. a. Cheese and other high-fat dairy products
   b. Most meats (especially if high in fat)
   c. Most emulsified dressings
5. a. The gas causes the greens to wilt.
   b. Accelerates spoilage
6. a. Buttermilk   d. Spices
   b. Vinegar   e. Vegetables
   c. Herbs
7. a. base   c. garnish
   b. body   d. dressing
8. a. liqueur
   b. fruit purée
   c. yogurt
   d. sweetener, such as honey
9. Combine the yolks with the dry ingredients and whip until frothy. Begin adding the oil a little at a time, allowing it to emulsify. Continue adding oil and maintain the consistency by thinning the

mayonnaise with vinegar as needed. Adjust seasonings and acidity before storing.

10. Reference p. 666
11. Reference p. 676
12. Reference p. 668

D. Multiple Choice

1.	b	6.	d	11.	a
2.	b	7.	a	12.	d
3.	c	8.	c	13.	b
4.	c	9.	d	14.	c
5.	d	10.	b	15.	c

E. Matching

1. a, c
2. b
3. d

F. True or False

1. True (pp. 662).
2. False (p. 663). Mesclun is a mixture of several kinds of baby lettuce, herbs and flowers.
3. True (p. 663).
4. True (p. 665).
5. False (p. 664). Although radicchio resembles a cabbage, it is a chicory.
6. True (p. 666).
7. False (p. 666). Lettuce is usually packed in cases of 24 heads.
8. True (p. 668).
9. False (p. 669). The standard ratio is 3 parts of oil to 1 part of vinegar, although that can vary.
10 False (p. 671). Some dressings use modified starches or vegetable gums as an emulsifier.
11. True (p. 671).
12 True (p. 671).
13 True (p. 671).
14. True (p. 675).
15. False (p. 675). Blue cheese dressing should be reserved for hardy greens.

CHAPTER 26

A. Terminology

1. Marmalade
2. Jelly
3. Papain
4. Jam
5. Ripe
6. Preserve
7. Hybrid
8. Citrus
9. Tangerine
10. Currants
11. Cranberries
12. Blueberries
13. Grapefruit
14. Seville
15. Cape gooseberries
16. Fig
17. Star-fruit
18. Citrus segments, also known as fillets.
19. Another name for persimmons.
20. A carbohydrate obtained from certain fruits; used to thicken jams and jellies.
21. The thin, coloured part of a citrus peel.
22. A colourless, odourless hydrocarbon gas naturally emitted from fruits and fruit-vegetables that encourages ripening.
23. Immersing cut fruits in an acidic solution to retard enzymatic browning.

B. Fill in the Blank

1. poaching
2. apples
3. gourd
4. grapes
5. batter
6. cucurbitaceae
7. grapes, vitis vinifera
8. thin skin, fuzz, thin, smooth
9. hands, berry
10. Chinese gooseberries
11. pawpaws
12. enzyme, papain, tenderize
13. hybrid
14. variety
15. pomegranate
16. rhubarb

C. Short Answer

1. Cut off the entire peel (including the pith). With the knife, cut along the side of each membrane to lift the fillets.
2. Golden Delicious, Granny Smith, Jonathan, McIntosh, Red Delicious, Pippin (Newton), Rome, Winesap
3. Anjou (Beurre d'Anjou), Bartlett (Williams), Bosc, Comice, Seckel
4.   a. bananas   c. apples
      b. tomatoes   d. melons

5. A greyish cast or colour on the fruit

6. **Vitamin C**   **Vitamin A**   **Potassium**

a. citrus   b. apricots   c. bananas

    melons   mangoes   raisins

    strawberries   kiwis   figs

7. Process the fruit into:
   - a. sauces
   - c. jellies
   - b. jams
   - d. preserves
8.
   - a. irradiation
   - d. acidulation
   - b. canning
   - e. drying
   - c. freezing
9.
   - a. apples
   - c. pears
   - b. bananas
   - d. peaches
10.
    - a. apples
    - d. bananas
    - b. cherries
    - e. pineapples
    - c. pears
11.
    - a. berries
    - e. melons
    - b. citrus
    - f. pomes
    - c. exotics
    - g. stone fruit
    - d. grapes
    - h. tropical
12. Reference p. 716.
13. Reference p. 721.
14. Reference p. 722.
15. Reference p. 716.
16. Reference p. 725.
17. Reference p. 726.
18. Reference p. 725.

D. Multiple Choice

1. d
2. a
3. b
4. a
5. d
6. c
7. b
8. a
9. b
10. d

E. True or False

1. True (p. 720).
2. False (p. 719). Sulfur dioxide is added to prevent browning and extend the shelf life.
3. False (p. 719). Freezing is generally one of the worst methods for preserving the natural appearance since all fruits are 75–95% water which seeps out of the fruit when it defrosts.

4. False (p. 716). Canada No. 1.
5. True (p. 717).
6. True (p. 718).
7. False (p. 714). Papayas are also referred to as paw paws.
8. True (p. 712).
9. True (p. 710).

CHAPTER 27

A. Terminology

1. Beating vigorously to incorporate air.
2. An alcoholic beverage made by distilling grains, vegetables, or other foods, may include rum, whiskey, and vodka.
3. Sugar that is liquefied by combining it with water so it then can be incorporated into certain prepared items in this liquid form.
4. The fat found in chocolate mass, which usually averages about 53%.
5. Mixing two or more ingredients until evenly distributed.
6. One form of a baked good that has a low water content compared to a batter. The other ingredients are embedded in gluten that is developed by beating, blending, cutting, or kneading.
7. An alcoholic beverage made from the fermented juice of grapes.
8. The most common form of refined sugar in the kitchen that is obtained from sugar cane or beets.
9. The migration of cocoa butter crystals to the surface of chocolate during storage due to temperature change. Bloom appears in the form of grayish-white spots, will disappear when chocolate is melted, and does not affect the flavour or function of chocolate.
10. Very gently incorporating ingredients, such as dry ingredients with whipped eggs.
11. A mixture containing more fat, sugar, and liquids than a dough, with minimum gluten development. It is usually prepared by blending, creaming, stirring, or whipping and is thin enough to pour.
12. The brown powder resulting from removing virtually all of the cocoa butter from the chocolate liquor.
13. Ingredients, such as cream of tartar, vinegar, and glucose, that interferes with the formation of sugar crystals.
14. Flavouring oils mixed into water with the aid of emulsifiers.
15. Also known as staling, it is a general loss in the moisture of a baked good which includes a change

in the location and distribution of water molecules within the product.

16. Sanding sugar
17. Regular granulated sugar
18. Brown sugar
19. Hydrometer
20. Couverture
21. fat-bloom or bloom
22. peanuts
23. Cutting
24. Gluten
25. Gelatin
26. Sifting
27. Brandy
28. Liqueur
29. Extracts
30. Beating
31. Stirring
32. Kneading
33. Chocolate liquor
34. Creaming
35. Carbon dioxide
36. Steam
37. Glutenin
38. Filbert

B. Fill in the Blank

1. Vital Wheat Gluten
2. soft, hard
3. blended, high protein
4. sucrose
5. molasses
6. turbinado, raw
7. superfine, castor
8. Icing, confectioner's sugar, 10X, 6X and 4X
9. hygroscopic, attract
10. 2 parts, 1 part
11. 1 part, 1.5 part
12. 2 parts, 2 parts
13. vanillin
14. fat, cocoa butter
15. a. 7.5–10%
    b. 10–13%
    c. 12–15%
16. baking, 53%
17. pistoles, calets

18. pecans
19. pistachios

C. Short Answer

1. Any flour develops better qualities if allowed to rest for several weeks after milling. Freshly milled flour produces sticky dough and products with less volume than those made with aged flour. While aging, flour turns white through a natural oxidation process referred to as bleaching.

2. Also known as high-ratio shortenings, they are used in the commercial production of cakes and frostings where the formula contains a large amount of sugar. Substituting with any other shortening will result in poor texture.

3. a   Appearance, even colour, glossy, no discoloration.
   b   Smell, no off odours or staleness.
   c   Break should snap clean without crumbling.
   d   Texture should melt quickly and evenly on the tongue.

4. a   Chocolate should never exceed 49°C (120°F) or it will lose flavour.
   b   Water or steam should never touch the chocolate as it will cause it to seize.

5. Reference p. 751.

D. Multiple Choice

1. d   6. a   11. b
2. b   7. d   12. a
3. c   8. d   13. d
4. b   9. a
5. d   10. d

E. Matching

I. Mixing Methods

1. d   6. e
2. i   7. a
3. f   8. j
4. b   9. g
5. c

II. Alcoholic Beverages.

1. c   4. f
2. e   5. b
3. a

F. True or False

1. False (p. 740). Self-rising flour is all-purpose flour with salt and baking powder added to it.

2. False (p. 739). Glutenin and gliadin are the proteins which, when introduced to moisture and manipulated, form gluten.

3. True (p. 750).

4. True (p. 750).

5. True (p. 750).

6. True (p. 751).

7. True (p. 739).

8. False (p. 738). Flour derived from this portion of the endosperm is finer than other flours.

9. True (p. 740).

10. False (p. 741). Unopened flour should be stored in the manner described, except it is also very important to store it away from strong odours, as it will absorb them easily.

11. True (p. 741).

12. True (p. 746). In addition to these qualities, unsalted butter tends to be preferred because it is generally fresher than salted butter.

13. True (p. 772).

14. True (p. 770).

15. False (p. 742). 10X is the finest.

16. True (p. 742).

17. False (p. 750).

18. False (p. 751).

CHAPTER 28

A. Terminology

1. Chemical leavening agents

2. Muffin method

3. Biscuit method

4. Streusel

5. Baking soda

6. Bannock

7. Makeup

8. Crumb

9. Overmixing causes toughness and may cause holes to form inside the baked product.

10. Sodium bicarbonate and one or more acids, generally cream of tartar and/or sodium aluminum sulfate. It also contains a starch to prevent lumping and balance chemical reactions.

11. Much like the mixing method, it produces products with a fine, cake-like texture. It usually contains a higher fat content which tenderizes the batter and lessens the danger of overmixing.

12. Made with the biscuit method, this biscuit of English origin usually contains eggs and butter.

13. An acid, a component of baking powder.

14. Another name for baking soda.

15. Tartaric acid, also a component of baking powder.

B. Fill in the Blank

1. gases, acids, bases

2. buttermilk, sour-cream, lemon juice, honey, molasses, fresh fruit

3. ammonia carbonate, leavening agent

4. biscuit, muffin, creaming

5. flaky pie dough

6. carbon, dioxide, moisture

7. carbon, dioxide, moisture, heat

C. Short Answer

1. a. Solid (chilled)

   b. Liquid (oil or melted butter)

   c. Soften (room temperature)

2. Baking soda can only release carbon dioxide to the extent that there is also an acid present in the formula. If the soda/acid reaction alone is insufficient to leaven the product, baking powder is needed for additional leavening.

3. Batters/doughs that may sit for some time before baking often use double-acting baking powder, which has a second leavening action that is activated only with the application of heat.

4. The higher fat content in the creaming method shortens the strands of gluten and therefore makes the final product more tender.

5. Softening the fat makes it easier to cream it with the sugar and therefore creates better aeration.

6. Reference pp. 765–766.

7. A scone is seen by many as a rich biscuit that also has butter and eggs in it. It is speculated that biscuits, at least the North American form of the word, contain a less expensive type of fat, such as lard, and will omit the eggs.

8. Mix the dry ingredients, mix the wet ingredients, mix the dry with the wet until just combined; do not overmix.

9. Combine dry ingredients, cut in the fat, add liquids and knead lightly to form a soft dough.

10. Cream the fat and sugar, add eggs and mix well, stir in the dry ingredients alternating with wet ingredients.

11. Reference p. 764.

12. Reference p. 766.

D. Matching

1. c, f

2. a

3. g, e

4. e

5. b

6. h, d, a

1. False (p. 765). All-purpose flour or a mixture of hard and soft flour is used in all biscuit methods.

2. True (p. 767).

3. True (p. 762).

4. False (p. 762). Baking powder already contains both an acid and a base and therefore only moisture is needed to induce the release of gases.

5. False (p. 762). All quick breads use chemical leavening agents; because they don't need to ferment like yeast-leavened doughs, they are considered "quick."

6. True (p. 763).

7. False (p. 763). Fats used in the muffin method should be in the liquid form.

8. False (p. 767). There is less danger of overmixing with the creaming method.

9. True (p. 762).

10. False (p. 762). Batters and doughs made with single-acting baking powder should be baked as soon as they are assembled and mixed together.

CHAPTER 29

A. Terminology

1. A method of mixing yeast dough in two stages. In the first stage, the yeast, liquid, and approximately one half of the flour are combined to make a thick batter known as the sponge, which is allowed to rise until bubbly and double in size. The second stage involves mixing in the rest of the flour as well as the salt, fat, and sugar. The dough is kneaded and allowed to rise again.

2. The rise given to shaped yeast products just prior to baking.

3. It is what occurs when yeast products are first put in the oven, the gases expand, and the product experiences a sudden rise.

4. A living organism, it is a one-celled fungus.

5. This organic process occurs when yeast feeds on carbohydrates, converting the sugars into carbon dioxide and alcohol.

6. Slashing

7. Wash

8. Sourdough

9. Kneading

10. Straight dough method

11. Rolled-in dough

B. Fill in the Blank

1. fresh yeast, starch, 70%

2. quick-rise, dry, 52°C to 54°C, (125°F to 130°F)

3. straight dough, sponge

4. sugar, alcohol and carbon dioxide

5. doubled, springs back

6. elasticity, stringy, slimy

7. 0.33, 0.54

8. 2°C (34°F), 59°C (138°F)

C. Short Answer

1.   a. The yeast, liquid, and approximately one half of the flour are combined to make a thick batter known as a sponge, which is allowed to rise until bubbly and doubled in size.

    b. Then the salt, fat, sugar, and remaining flour are added. The dough is then kneaded and allowed to rise again. This creates a different flavour and a lighter texture than breads made with the straight dough method.

2. The organism is considered dormant because virtually all of the moisture has been removed, which helps to increase the shelf life, among other things.

3.   a. product size

    b. the thermostat's accuracy

    c. crust colour

    d. tapping loaf on the bottom and listening for hollow sound

4.   a. croissants

    b. Danish pastries

    c. non-yeast-leavened pastry

5. Halve the specified weight of compressed yeast when substituting dry yeast in a formula.

6. Combine all ingredients and mix.

7.   a. Scale ingredients

    b. Mix and knead dough

    c. Ferment dough

    d. Punch down dough

    e. Portion dough

    f. Round portions

    g. Shape portions

    h. Proof products

    i. Bake products

j. Cool and store finished products

8. a. shine and colour

   b. shine and colour with a soft crust

   c. shine and a firm crust

   d. crisp crust

   e. texture and contrast

   f. colour with a soft crust

9. a. The butter is incorporated through a folding process after the dough is fermented and punched.

   b. Rolled-in doughs are portioned some what differently than yeast dough.

   c. The portions are shaped without rounding.

10. a. Shape the butter and chill it.

    b. Roll out the dough evenly, then top with the chilled butter and enclose it completely.

    c. Roll out the dough into a rectangle; maintain right angles.

    d. Fold the dough in thirds, chill for 20 to 30 minutes. This completes the first turn.

    e. Repeat the rolling and folding a second and third time and allow to rest several hours.

11. Bread is judged by its external and internal appearance, flavour, aroma and keeping properties (reference p. 788).

D. Multiple Choice

1.	c	6.	a
2.	d	7.	d
3.	c	8.	a
4.	b	9.	c
5.	b	10.	a

E. Matching

1.	e	6.	u, b, n
2.	c, i, m	7.	c, i, m
3.	m, f	8.	t.
4.	d, r, o	9.	h, q, p
5.	g	10.	a, k, s

F. True or False

1. True (p. 780). More specifically, though, it occurs just after fermentation.

2. True (p. 779).

3. True (p. 783).

4. False (p. 782). Under-proofing results in poor volume and texture.

5. True (p. 783).

6. True (p. 777).

7. True (p. 778).

8. True (p. 778).

9. True (p. 782).

10. True (p. 782).

11. True (p. 777).

12. False (p. 777).

CHAPTER 30

A. Terminology

1. Chiffon

2. Detrempe

3. Bouchées

4. Vol-au-vents

5. Cream puffs

6. Profiteroles

7. Croquembouche

8. Pie

9. Tart

10. Pâte brisée

11. Pâte sucrée

12. Torte

13. A dough cooked before baking, it has batter-like smoothness with a firm texture.

14. Another term for puff pastry, it is a rich, buttery dough that bakes into hundreds of light, crispy layers.

15. To bake a pie shell before it is filled, lining it with parchment paper and rice or beans during baking.

16. Pricking small holes in an unbaked dough or crust to allow steam to escape and to prevent the dough from rising when baked.

17. Baked fingers of pâte à choux filled with pastry cream; the top is then coated with chocolate glaze or fondant.

18. Rings of baked pâte à choux cut in half horizontally and filled with pastry cream and/or flavoured whipped cream. The top is dusted with powdered sugar or drizzled with chocolate glaze.

19. Squares or strips of pâte à choux deep-fat fried and dusted with powdered sugar.

20. A Spanish and Mexican pastry in which sticks of pâte à choux flavoured with cinnamon are deep-fat fried and rolled in sugar while still hot.

21. A Dutch pastry in which a loop or strip of twisted pâte à choux is deep-fat fried.

22. A foam made of beaten egg whites and sugar.

23. Small, flat cookies usually eaten alone and rarely used as a component in other desserts.

B. Fill in the Blank

1. gelatin, stirred custard, whipped egg whites, pre-baked, chilled
2. overmixing, overworked dough, not enough fat
3. modified
4. not enough fat or over-mixing
5. insufficient starch or starch insufficiently cooked
6. blitz
7. feuilletés
8. soft, twice
9. soft peaks
10. hot sugar syrup, 115°C, 238°F, whipped
11. baking soda, baking powder, air or steam
12. logs, rectangles
13. pressed or layered
14.

Texture	Fat	Sugar	Liquid
Crispness	high	high	low
Softness	low	low	high
Chewiness	high	high	high
Spread	high	high	high

C. Short Answer

1. a. chiffon
   b. cooked juice
   c. cream
2. a. cream
   b. chiffon
   c. cooked juice
   d. cheesecake
3. a. baked fruit
   b. custard
4. a. lattice coverings
   b. pie top crusts
   c. pre-baked shells later to be filled with cooked fillings
5. It is richer, non-flaky, and sturdier than flaky or mealy dough due to the addition of egg yolks and the blending of the fat.
6. When the crust has a potential of becoming soggy, as in the making of custard and cooked fruit pies.
7. One can have better control because you can feel the fat being incorporated and therefore prevent over-mixing.

8. It is cooked before baking.
9. The ratio of sugar to egg whites.
10. a. vol-au-vents   b. Napoleons
    c. feuilletés   d. bouchées
11. Sweet pastes are pastries generally high in sugar and fat; they are the basis of many cookies and can be flavoured as needed.
12. Cream the butter and sugar, add the eggs and mix until smooth. Add the flour, do not overmix. The dough should be firm, smooth and not sticky.
13. a. chocolate cookies
    b. graham crackers
    c. gingersnaps
    d. vanilla wafers
    e. macaroons
14. Bring the milk and part of the sugar to a boil. Meanwhile, whisk the egg yolk with the remaining sugar and the cornstarch (or flour). Temper the egg mixture, combine with the remaining milk and return to the heat. Bring to a simmer while stirring; simmer for 30 seconds to one minute.
15. Reference p. 804.
16. Reference p. 808.
17. Reference p. 811.
18. Reference p. 812.
19. Reference pp. 816–817.
20. Reference p. 820.
21. Reference p. 822.

D. Multiple Choice

1. d   5. d   8. d
2. b   6. c   9. a
3. b   7. a   10. d
4. c

E. Matching

I. Trouble Shooting Pies

1. c, e, m   5. k, a
2. d, g, n   6. j, i
3. f, b   7. l, h
4. m, c

II. Trouble Shooting Meringues

1. e, m, i, a, l, b,   3. d, j
2. g, k, c   4. h, f

F. True or False

1. True (p. 822).
2. False (p. 811). Strawberries, pineapples, and blueberries would be more appropriate.

3. True (p. 809).
4. True (p. 813).
5. False (p. 808). A typical ratio for crumb crusts consists of one part melted butter to two parts sugar to four parts crumbs.
6. True (p. 803).
7. False (p. 803). Pâte sucrée should be used specifically over flaky and mealy doughs because it is less flaky and due to the addition of the egg yolks is still tender, but is stronger to withstand the removal of the tart pan during service.
8. True (pp. 822–823).
9. False (p. 814). 2 months maximum
10. False (p. 814). Eggs will separate making the product runny.
11. True (p. 808).

CHAPTER 31
A. Terminology
1. Royal icing
2. Butter cakes
3. Buttercream
4. Stencil
5. Icing
6. Chiffon cakes
7. Spongecakes
8. Glucose
9. A cooked mixture of water and sugar that is applied warm to the cake.
10. A blend of melted chocolate and cream that is used as a frosting.
11. A creaming method cake that is made up of a pound of each ingredient: flour, butter, eggs, and sugar.
12. A creaming method cake that requires emulsified shortenings and liquids that are added in two stages.
13. Applying decoration to the sides of the cake.
14. A whipped egg cake made by whipping whole eggs and sugar, adding the dry ingredients, and folding in melted butter or oil.
15. A fat-free whipped egg cake, which uses a large amount of egg whites for leavening.

B. Fill in the Blank
1. decreased, underwhipped, increased, 4 degrees
2. a. high fat or creamed fat
   b. egg foam or whipped eggs
3. 165°C (325°F) and 190°C (375°F)

4. decorator's icing
5. flour, shortening, oil
6. leavening
7. structure
8. moisture
9. lecithin, smooth, volume
10. poundcakes, layer cakes, coffee cakes and brownies
11. génoise, sponge cake, angel food cake and chiffon cakes
12. whole eggs, whipped, sugar, egg yolk, egg white
13. gum paste
14. marzipan
15. side masking

C. Short Answer
I. General
1. leavening, structure, moisture, emulsifying properties, shortening, colour, flavour
2. Reference p. 857

II. Basic Cake Mixes Review
Reference pp. 870–878.

III. Frostings Revised
Reference pp. 884–890.

D. Multiple Choice
1. b
2. d
3. c
4. c
5. d
6. a
7. a
8. b

E. Matching
I. Cake Ingredients
1. f
2. a
3. e
4. c
5. d
6. g

II. Cake Mixing Categories
1. B   6. A
2. B   7. A
3. A   8. B
4. B   9. A
5. A   10. A

F. True or False

1. False (p. 882). All cakes should be left away from drafts which may cause them to collapse. Cakes should not be refrigerated as rapid cooling will cause cracking.
2. True (p. 882).
3. True (p. 881).
4. True (p. 880).
5. False (p. 876).
6. True (p. 879).
7. False (p. 879). The results from package mixes are consistent and acceptable to most customers.
8. False (p. 870). High-ratio cakes require emulsified shortenings to absorb the large amounts of sugar and liquid in the formula.
9. True (p. 867)
10. False (p. 867)
11. False (p. 873) (Gum paste)
12. False (p. 873) (Pastillage)

CHAPTER 32

A. Terminology

1. Sundae
2. Temper
3. Sorbet
4. Steep
5. Baked Alaska
6. Sabayon
7. Overrun
8. Soufflé
9. Bombe
10. Crème Chantilly
11. Ice cream served with a fruit topping.
12. An egg custard made with egg yolks, sugar, and milk and thickened with starch.
13. An ice cream that has little incorporated air.
14. A sauce made from a mixture of egg yolks, sugar, and milk or half and half, cooked over low heat, which may be served either hot or cold.
15. Ice cream served in a long slender glass with alternate layers of topping or sauce.
16. A mousse is softer than a Bavarian or chiffon, is generally too soft to mould and can be served alone or used as a filling in cakes.
17. A frozen mousse-like dessert, usually chocolate.
18. A round mould lined with spongecake or ladyfingers, filled with a Bavarian cream, and chilled.
19. A three-layer loaf or cake of ice cream, each layer a different flavour.
20. A Bavarian cream is prepared by first thickening custard sauce with gelatin and then folding in whipped cream.
21. A chiffon is most often used as a pie filling and is similar to a Bavarian except that whipped egg whites (instead of whipped cream) are folded into the thickened base of custard or a fruit mixture thickened with cornstarch.

B. Fill in the Blank

1. zabaglione
2. mousseline, Italian meringue
3. Bavarians, chiffons, mousses, crème Chantilly
4. a. egg whites will whip to a better volume
    b. the two mixtures are more easily incorporated

C. Short Answer

1. Reference p. 891
2. Reference p. 891
3. Reference p. 893
4. Reference p. 896
5. Reference p. 898
6. Reference p. 899
7. Reference p. 902
8. Reference p. 905
9. Reference pp. 906–907
10. a. vanilla custard sauce
    b. pastry cream
    c. crème brulée
    d. sabayon
11. a. crème caramel
    b. cheesecake
    c. bread pudding
    d. rice pudding
12. a. Bavarian creams
    b. chiffons
    c. mousses
    d. Chantilly cream

D. Multiple Choice

1. d
2. d
3. a
4. c
5. a

6.   b
7.   d
8.   d
9.   b
10.   a

E. True or False

1.   False (p. 911).
2.   True (p. 915). A frozen soufflé is a creamy custard mixture thickened with gelatin, lightened with whipped egg whites or whipped cream, and placed in a soufflé dish wrapped with a tall paper collar.
3.   True (p. 923).
4.   True (p. 924).
5.   True (p. 925).
6.   True (p. 914).

CHAPTER 33

A. Terminology

1.   Shirred eggs
2.   Granola
3.   Quiche
4.   French toast
5.   Omelettes
6.   en cocotte
7.   Pan fried
8.   Scrambled
9.   Boiled
10.   Soft boiled
11.   Thin, delicate, unleavened pancakes cooked in a small, very hot sauté pan.
12.   An open-faced omelette of Spanish-Italian origin, which is cooked in a small pan and may be finished in the oven or under a salamander.
13.   A leavened batter that is cooked on a waffle iron and forms square, griddle-like, crisp shapes.
14.   This egg dish is a variation of sunny-side-up eggs. The eggs are cooked in a pan over low heat with butter spooned over them as they cook.
15.   A leavened batter cooked on a very hot griddle with very little fat, usually served with flavoured butter, fruit compote, or syrup.

B. Short Answer

1.   Reference p. 924.
2.   Reference p. 926.
3.   Reference p. 931

4.   Reference p. 931
5.   Reference p. 933
6.   Reference p. 935
7.   Any four of shirred eggs, quiches, omelettes, scrambled eggs, frittata, hard- or soft-boiled eggs, pan-fried eggs, or poached eggs.
8.   Reference p. 925. Bacon, onion, gruyere
9.   Reference p. 934. A cheese blintz is a crepe that is cooked on only one side and is filled with cheese, browned in butter, and served with sour cream, fruit compote, or preserves.
10.   Reference p. 927.
11.   Regular omelettes are most often rolled in a cigar shape while frittatas are essentially open-faced omelettes that are cooked in a small pan for individual portions or in large pans, then cut into wedges.
12.   Cook the eggs for the right amount of time and cool them rapidly when cooked.

C. Multiple Choice

1.   c
2.   c
3.   a
4.   c
5.   a
6.   b
7.   d
8.   b
9.   d

D. Matching

1. k   7. b
2. h   8. e
3. c   9. g
4. j   10. i
5. d   11. a
6. l   12. f

E. True or False

1.   True (p. 956).
2.   False (p. 949). Sunny-side-up is only one type of pan-fried egg; the others are over-easy, over-medium, and over-hard.
3.   True (p. 949).
4.   True (p. 949).
5.   False (p. 951). A hearty breakfast menu may include a steak or pork chop.
6.   False (p. 951). Canadian bacon is very lean and requires very little cooking.
7.   True (p. 954).

8. False (p. 947). Fillings for omelettes should be cooked before being added to the omelette; otherwise the egg will be cooked while the filling is still raw.

CHAPTER 34

A. Terminology

1. Osetra
2. Sushi
3. Beluga
4. Chafing dish
5. Filling
6. Mayonnaise
7. Brochettes
8. Crudités
9. Canapés
10. Norimaki zushi
11. Nigiri zushi
12. Won ton skins
13. A strong aromatic root purchased in a green powder or green paste.
14. A dried seaweed purchased in same size sheets.
15. Bread is placed on a serving plate, covered with hot meat or other filling and topped with gravy, sauce, or cheese.
16. The French term which translates to "outside work."
17. Readily available caviar that is reasonably priced, this caviar is dyed black, red, or gold.
18. Small, fancy construction made with light, soft, trimmed breads and delicate filling and spreads, cut into small shapes.
19. A tiny boat-shaped shell made from savoury dough such as pâte or brisée.
20. Made with three or more pieces of bread, one or more spreads, and two or more fillings—all layered.
21. Bacon wrapped around chicken livers, olives, pickled watermelon rind, water chestnuts, pineapple, or scallops.
22. The small and very crisp eggs of whitefish native to the northern Great Lakes.

B. Fill in the Blank

1. a thin slice of toasted bread cut into an interesting shape, vegetables
2. flavoured butter, cream cheese, salads, egg, chicken
3. Malassol, little salt
4. bread, filling, spread
5. mayonnaise, sour cream, cream cheese, milk, buttermilk, cream or sour cream
6. béchamel, cream sauce, cheese sauce, bagna cau
7. soak them in water
8. Asian noodle dough used to make egg rolls; pork, chicken, shellfish, and/or vegetables

C. Short Answer

1. Reference p. 946.
2. Reference p. 947.
3. Reference p. 964.
4. Reference p. 960.
5. a. Beluga
   b. Osetra
   c. Sevruga
   d. Pressed
6. a. American sturgeon caviar
   b. Golden whitefish
   c. Lumpfish
   d. Salmon
7. Reference pp. 974–975.
8. Reference p. 958.
9. Reference p. 958.
10. Reference pp. 965–966.

D. Multiple Choice

1. d
2. b
3. c
4. b
5. b
6. d
7. b
8. a
9. a

E. True or False

1. False (p. 946). Appetizers are usually the first course before the evening meal.
2. False (p. 960). Sandwiches are generally prepared to order.
3. True (p. 965).
4. False (p. 950). Caviar reacts with metal, producing off-flavours.
5. True (p. 952). Fish used for sushi should preferably be no more than one day old.
6. False (p. 954). Barquettes should be filled at the last minute; otherwise they become soggy.

CHAPTER 35

A. Terminology

1. Distilled water
2. Dimineralized water
3. Carbonated water

4. Nectar
5. Infusion
6. Cream
7. Café-au-lait or caffè latte or café crème
8. Demitasse
9. Espresso machiatto
10. Caffè Mocha
11. Kopi Luak
12. Tisanes
13. Wine
14. Madeira
15. Marsala
16. Vermouth
17. Gin
18. Rum
19. Tequila
20. Vodka
21. Whisky
22. Mildly fermented apple juice
23. The liquid extracted from any fruit or vegetable.
24. Boiling a food until its flavour is removed.
25. 1/3 espresso, 1/3 steamed milk, 1/3 foamed milk.
26. Espresso with a dollop of whipped cream.
27. A shot of espresso "corrected" with the addition of liquor.
28. Espresso made with 1/2 the water normally used for a regular espresso.
29. An alcoholic beverage made by distilling grains, fruits vegetables and other foods.
30. A strong, sweet, syrupy alcoholic beverage made by mixing or redistilling neutral spirits with fruits, flowers, herbs, spices, etc.
31. The process of transforming grapes into still wine.

B. Fill in the Blank

1. pressure, blending
2. finer, quickly
3. gravity, filter
4. 7 to 8 g (1/4oz)
5. body, smell, acidity, flavour
6. arabica
7. robusta
8. 55g (2oz), 1L (1qt)
9. black, green, Oolong
10. orange Pekoe, Broken Pekoe
11. astringency (or briskness), body, aroma
12. alkali, darker, bitter and richer
13. effervescent, still and fortified
14. water, hops, barley, yeast
15. Vintner Quality Alliance
16. 85%
17. vitis vinifera
18. tawny, vintage, ruby
19. soleras
20. bouquet (or nose)
21. low, un-oaked, fruit-driven, aromatic
22. food, wine, wine, food
23. mashed (or soaked), wort
24. bitterness
25. ales, lagers

C. Short Answer

1. a. City roast
   b. Brazilian
   c. Vienese
   d. French roast
   e. Espresso roast
2. The fineness of the grind of coffee depends entirely on the type of coffee maker being used. The proper grind is simply whatever allows optimum extraction in the time it takes the coffee brewer to complete its brewing cycle.
3. Espresso is made with a pump-driven machine that forces hot water through compressed, finely ground coffee.
4. Reference p. 994.
5. Reference p. 999.
6. Reference p. 1012.
7. Reference p. 1012.
8. Reference p. 1014.
9. Reference p. 1015.

D. Multiple Choice

1. a	7. d	13. c
2. b	8. a	14. d
3. a	9. a	15. c
4. c	10. b	16. b
5. a	11. b	17. d
6. c	12. a	

E. Matching

I. Teas

1. a, d, h
2. b, f, g
3. e

II. Grapes into Wines

1. 1e   5. h

2.   g   6.   b
3.   f   7.   d
4.   a   8.   c

III. Sherry

1.   e   4.   c
2.   b   5.   a
3.   f   6.   d

IV Red Wine Characteristics

1.   b   5.   c
2.   a   6.   a
3.   b   7.   b
4.   c   8.   c

V. Food & Red Wine Pairing

1.   c   4.   e
2.   f   5.   b
3.   a   6.   d

VI. Food & White Wine Pairing

1.   e   4.   a
2.   c   5.   b
3.   f   6.   d

VII. Brandies

1.   f   6.   b
2.   g   7.   e
3.   j   8.   d
4.   c   9.   a
5.   i   10. h

F. True or False

1. True (p. 995).
2. True (p. 991).
3. False (p. 991). Acid should be added.
4. True (p. 992).
5. False (p. 993). For long storage, coffee is best frozen.
6. True (p. 993).
7. False (p. 993).
8. True (p. 994).
9. False (p. 996).
10. False (p. 997).
11. False (p. 997).
12. True (p. 998).
13. True (p. 998).
14. True (p. 1000).
15. False (p. 1001).
16. False (p. 1002).
17. True (p. 1004).
18. True (p. 1012).
19. False (p. 1012).
20. True (p. 1012).

CHAPTER 36

A. Terminology

1. The process of delivering the selected foods to diners in the proper fashion.
3. Presentation
4. Composition
5. Hippen masse

B. Fill in the Blank

1. Texture, shape, colour
2. Size
3. Focal point
4. Cold

C. Short Answer

1. a. Those applied to specific foods

   b. Those applied to the plate as a whole

2. Proper cutting of foods will promote even cooking and dramatically improve its general eye appeal and sense of precision as well as professionalism. Proper carving of meats may also contribute to the perceived tenderness of the food.

3. Reference p. 1023.
4. Reference p. 1023.
5. Reference p. 1024.
6. Reference p. 1024.
7. Reference p. 1024.
8. Reference p. 1025.
9. Reference p. 1025.
10. Reference p. 1026.
11. Reference p. 1027.

D. True or False

1. True (p. 1022).
2. False (p. 1025). The food should always be the focal point of any plate.
3. True (p. 1024).
4. False (p. 1025). Dusting of a plate should be done before the food is plated.
5. False (p. 1027). A squirt bottle would be a good choice of equipment for preparing sauce drawings.
6. True (p. 1027). An equally important concept is that the sauces need to be thick enough to hold a pattern and all sauces used in the drawing need to be the same viscosity.